Successful Marketing to the
50+ Consumer

*How to Capture One of the Biggest
and Fastest-Growing Markets
in America*

Jeff Ostroff

Foreword by Ken Dychtwald, Ph.D.

PRENTICE HALL
Englewood Cliffs, New Jersey 07632

Prentice-Hall International (UK) Limited, *London*
Prentice-Hall of Australia Pty. Limited, *Sydney*
Prentice-Hall Canada, Inc., *Toronto*
Prentice-Hall Hispanoamericana, S.A., *Mexico*
Prentice-Hall of India Private Limited, *New Delhi*
Prentice-Hall of Japan, Inc., *Tokyo*
Simon & Schuster Asia Pte. Ltd., *Singapore*
Editora Prentice-Hall do Brasil, Ltda., *Rio de Janeiro*

© 1989 by

PRENTICE-HALL, Inc.

Englewood Cliffs, NJ

10 9 8 7 6 5 4 3 2 1

Library of Congress Cataloging-in-Publication Data

Ostroff, Jeff
  Successful marketing to the 50+ consumer / by Jeff Ostroff.
    p.   cm.
  Bibliography: p.
  Includes index.
  ISBN 0-13-860271-9
    1. Marketing—United States.   2. Advertising—United States.
  3. Aged as consumers—United States.   I. Title.   II. Title:
  Successful marketing to the fifty-plus consumer.
  HF5415.1.O87   1989
  658.8′00880564—dc19   89-31324
                                                                          CIP

ISBN 0-13-860271-9

PRENTICE HALL
BUSINESS & PROFESSIONAL DIVISION
A division of Simon & Schuster
Englewood Cliffs, New Jersey 07632

Printed in the United States of America

Dedication

To my loving parents, Isreal and Sherry, my "almost" parents, Helen, Michael, and Anna, and . . . most of all, my dear wife, Maryann, without whose love, patience, understanding, support, and "hands-on" assistance, this book would never have been possible.

Acknowledgments

This book would never have been possible were it not for the contribution of many personal friends and business associates. While it is not possible for me to thank everyone who helped me with this book, I'd like to take the time now to recognize those whose roles were particularly significant.

Several people inspired me to write this book and gave me guidance on how it could be done. They include Michael Le Boeuf, Debra Jones, Herman Holtz, Peter Boland, and Earl Nightingale. Another source of inspiration was Dr. Ken Dychtwald, who was also kind enough to write the foreword.

I want to thank a number of people who encouraged me to endure the vicissitudes of the book-writing process by helping me to recognize that, in the end, everything would turn out fine. They include Barbara Palumbo, Jim McGee, Chuck Martini, Rod McKelvie, Gary Ford, Dr. Matti Gershenfeld, Dorothy Watson, Tim Bristow, Laura Ruekberg, Richard Fox, and Ted Reed, my general manager at The Data Group Inc./PrimeLife Marketing.

A few individuals took the time to review sections from my manuscript and give me constructive suggestions on how to make them better. They include Dr. Arlene Weissman, Dr. James Lumpkin, Peter Hanson, Allyn Kramer, Dana Winslow, A. J. Newman, and Art Weinstein. Another invaluable resource in this effort was Cathy Johnson, who edited my work for Prentice-Hall.

This book would never have been completed were it not for the assistance provided by Bibi Ibrahim and Barbara Grelock. Bibi handled some of my project-related work while I was absorbed in writing my manuscript, and Barbara transcribed the many telephone interviews I conducted in gathering information for the book.

As for interviews, many people graciously shared their mature market knowledge and information with me so that I could put together a meaningful and practical business publication. They include Steve Krivian, Louisa Budd, Steve Goldstein, Bard Lindeman, Gerry Hotchkiss, Paula Meyerhoffer, Duncan Beardsley, Frank Forbes, Jeff Atkinson, Kit Carlson, Chris Jennings, Gary Christopherson, Don Fowles, Chuck Nelson, Cynthia Taeuber, Ellie Baugher, Dave Lewis, Beth Hodges, Susan Grad, Yvonne Dodd, Paula

Baratta, Jean Van Ryzin, Patti Hoath, Katie Sloan, Phil Jos, Kay Lacy, Kirk Kaneer, and Don Sloo.

Finally, but of utmost importance, I'd like to thank my editor at Prentice-Hall, Bette Schwartzberg. Without her belief in me and my area of expertise, these pages surely would never have been written.

Foreword

With each passing day, the profile of our nation grows just a little older, just a little grayer. More than 60 million Americans are now at least a half-century old. And every day, some 6,000 others join them. To truly appreciate how amazing those numbers are, consider the fact that at the turn of this century *life expectancy* itself wasn't even 50!

Indeed, the aging of America—a phenomenon the likes of which has never been experienced in this country's history—is now upon us. In the years to come, propelled by the force of 76-million baby boomers, this demographic shift will surely change the entire fabric of our society: political, economic, social, cultural, and spiritual. Moreover, this transformation is not decades away. It has, in fact, already begun to surface. And, with the first of the baby boomers about to enter the "over-50 club" in less than seven years, the dramatic impact which aging will have on our nation is literally right around the corner.

For more than fifteen years, I've tried to help leaders in government, industry, business, and the social services anticipate and respond to the inevitable "age wave" our country is about to witness. From this experience, I am convinced that virtually *no one*—merchandisers, employers, politicians, policy makers, social scientists, medical researchers, health care practitioners, or family members—*can* and *should* wait for the baby boomers to turn gray before paying attention to the over-50 population. In fact, only by understanding today's mature adults can we begin to successfully plan for tomorrow's vast number of older Americans. Through this effort, we can help assure that our nation remains a thriving, respected world leader in the twenty-first century.

For marketers, an understanding of today's older consumer is essential to both short and long-term prosperity. Not only are these consumers many and diverse, but their needs and wants are enormous. With a large and growing percentage of America's purchasing power resting in their hands, mature adults are showing an increasing willingness to spend considerable sums of money for goods and services which benefit themselves or their families. The mature market offers businesses a myriad of intergenerational marketing opportunities which will only magnify as our society continues to age.

Jeff Ostroff has been both a visionary and a pioneer in seeing and addressing the challenges and opportunities afforded by an aging America. Over the past few years, I and the staff of Age Wave, Inc. have had the pleasure of collaborating with Jeff on a variety of challenging projects. He has developed through his writing, frequent lectures, and acclaimed consulting ventures, a national reputation as a leading authority on the maturing American marketplace. In this comprehensive and practical book, Jeff has gathered the best of his knowledge and insight. In addition, he helps you profit from the research and experiences of others who have, in one way or another, demonstrated *how* companies can successfully serve the age 50+ customer today and in the years ahead.

There is no shortcut to understanding how to successfully reach and serve the mature market. I have no doubt, however, that with this book, you and your organization will find that undertaking a whole lot easier. More importantly, armed with the wide scope of information, data, tips, ideas, strategies, examples, resources, trends, and forecasts this book offers, you'll be far more likely to prosper in an aging America.

Ken Dychtwald, Ph.D.
President, Age Wave, Inc.
October 1988

Preface

I've written *Successful Marketing to the 50+ Consumer* to assist the many individuals and organizations who have (or will soon) come to recognize the purchasing power, size, growth, and strategic influence of the mature market. Not surprisingly, the number of companies who believe the over-50 group is vitally important to their business' success is growing rapidly. The fact is, it's becoming increasingly more difficult to overlook a market of 64 million people, most of whom are active consumers with money to spend.

Unquestionably, the mature market represents a tremendous opportunity for the business community. Yet, because of its complexity, many marketers are wary of this potential pot of gold. Ironically, this may, in part, be due to the nature of the information that has been available to help businesses understand older consumers. While articles, studies, reports, and books about the mature market do exist, virtually all of these works have been produced independently. This presents several problems for the marketer. For example, it

- makes it nearly impossible to draw a complete picture of the mature market or to see any consistent patterns from which to shape one's marketing strategies.
- practically compels organizations to make critical marketing decisions based on fragmented pieces of information about the mature market; as a result, business opportunities and strategies are limited, and the chance to achieve lasting success is measurably impaired.
- makes the acquisition of relevant materials about the mature market a difficult, costly, and time-consuming process.

What I believe makes *Successful Marketing to the 50+ Consumer* different from existing publications is that it is a *comprehensive, how-to* book about marketing to older consumers. But more importantly, this book focuses on what actually *works* when serving the mature market! As you'll see, it provides information about organizations that have already learned how to successfully attract and serve the older customer.

Madison Avenue's recent attention to the mature market is not a passing fancy. For that reason, I've made a concerted effort to write a book that is *enduring* as well as practical. Indeed, the strategies, ideas, tips, examples, data, and resources provided in the book are dedicated to serving businesses for many years to come. This includes the years just before and after the beginning of the twenty-first century, a time when the baby boomers will join the mature market, and the marketplace's interest in the 50 + consumer will be intense.

As a note of clarification, I'd like to point out that, throughout this book, there are several terms used to describe those over 50. For simplicity's sake, I have chosen the words "mature" or "mature market" to refer to people over 50 in general. The words "prime lifers" or "prime life" generation pertain to those between the ages of 50 and 64. And, the words "senior" and "seniors" primarily are used to describe those over 65.

Please bear in mind that these words have been chosen *only to make your reading easier*, and not because I believe they are either the best terms to describe older consumers, or ones that those over 50 prefer. Moreover, as I note in the book, businesses should be very careful about using *any* label to depict or communicate with the mature market.

One final thought: In today's highly competitive environment, businesses can no longer afford to take years to introduce their new product offerings to the consumer. At the same time, they cannot afford to impulsively plunge headfirst into the marketplace. This is especially true with respect to the mature market.

It is my hope that *Successful Marketing to the 50 + Consumer* will be a solution to this apparent "Catch 22"; that through its assistance, your organization will flourish in the years ahead.

Jeff Ostroff
May 1989

Introduction

Mature consumers are not an easy target for marketers to reach, but in to-day's highly competitive environment, businesses can no longer afford not to target older adults. Those over 50 represent 64 million consumers—one out of every three adults. And they account for more than one-third of all consumer dollars spent!

This book will help you develop and implement successful strategic marketing programs tailored for the mature market. You'll learn how to recognize—and capitalize on—key trends affecting mature consumers. You'll find practical tips, checklists, and examples on how to communicate your marketing message effectively for your specific business activities.

Here are just a few of the many topics covered in this book:

- How to avoid eight critical misconceptions about mature adults in your marketing
- Six major trends and their impact on the mature market
- Why a low-priced marketing strategy to those over 50 may fall short of your expectations
- Ten needs and concerns of the mature market and how you can fill them
- Techniques on identifying the needs and concerns of the older consumers you wish to target
- Tips on recruiting a team of older adults to assist you
- Key groups and influential people who can help you reach the 50+ population
- Marketing approaches for tapping into the mature adult network
- How to segment the mature market and respond to its diversity
- The benefits of using a soft-sell approach to attract older customers
- The importance of the older parent-adult child relationship to your marketing effort
- How to capitalize on the older parent-adult child bond
- Six fundamental principles of successful mature market advertising and promotion

- Guidelines on using the most effective communication channels to reach older consumers
- Seven outstanding business opportunities in serving tomorrow's mature consumers (including the aging baby boomers)
- How to anticipate the needs of the twenty-first century's mature market

In addition, a comprehensive reference section in Appendix A details the purchasing behavior of older consumers as well as their demographic, health, and socioeconomic characteristics. Appendix B is packed with a listing of more than 250 mature market resources, including public and private organizations, data suppliers, periodicals, books, and special reports.

How This Book Is Organized

This book is conveniently divided into four parts. In Part I, you'll learn the essentials to long-term success in the mature market. Chapter 1 focuses on eight deadly misconceptions about the 50+ group—and how to avoid them in your marketing effort. Chapter 2 identifies six key trends that will affect how you market to mature consumers now and in the years to come.

Part II, with its eight chapters (3–10), represents the heart of *Successful Marketing to the 50+ Consumer*. Each chapter highlights one of eight key strategies necessary to successfully capture the mature market. And you'll learn the success stories of nine organizations that have applied one or more of these strategies.

Part III shows you how to communicate more effectively with the over-50 consumer. Chapter 11 offers six critical principles of successful mature market advertising and promotion. Chapter 12 has a wealth of information about the 50+ group's media behavior and preferences. You'll also be advised of the best communication channels for your specific marketing activities.

Part IV takes a look at the future of the mature market. You'll discover what some of the twenty-first century's most lucrative mature market opportunities may be—including those which involve serving aging *baby boomers* and an aging *world*. You'll also be given five practical tools to help you predict—and prepare for—business opportunities in tomorrow's grayer marketplace.

Finally, the appendixes offer an indispensable reference section about the mature market. They will be a treasured ally which helps you prosper in an aging America.

In all, you'll find this book to be a comprehensive resource that offers the practical and timely information you need on how to successfully market to today's—and tomorrow's—mature consumers.

Contents

Chapter 2

Recognizing and Capitalizing on Key Trends, 20

Chapter 6

Key 4: Involve the Older Consumer in Your Mature Market Programs, 103

Chapter 7
Key 5: Establish Relationships with Key Groups and Influencers, 122

1

Targeting the Mature Market: Essentials for Long-term Success

Chapter **1**

Dispelling the "Eight Deadly Misconceptions" About Mature Adults

Successful companies are those who understand their customers. Not surprisingly, to prosper in an aging America, your organization must have an accurate, well-grounded understanding of the older customer. This may strike you as a logical and a simple undertaking; unfortunately, it is not so easy.

This chapter examines the most common misconceptions held about mature adults—what I call the "Eight Deadly Misconceptions." Many people would never admit to holding them. Nevertheless, these myths often lie at the subconscious, emotional levels that dictate our actions.

There are two key factors responsible for the eight misconceptions: *mass communications* and *limited personal exposure*. Not until recently have the media begun to portray a more realistic, balanced picture of gray America. Unfortunately, the distortions presented over the years have been imprinted in the minds of many, particularly those most influenced by television . . . the "baby boom" generation.

The baby boomers are the ones most likely to form impressions based upon limited contact with the older population. As one ad agency executive said, "We're dealing with clients whose staffs are in their twenties and thirties. Most of these people simply don't feel comfortable in developing marketing strategies for a customer from another generation with whom they have little day-to-day contact." Ad agency account executives and creative personnel have been known to experience similar level of discomfort and unfamiliarity.

As you read about the eight misconceptions, please keep this in mind: *Even if you personally do not subscribe to them, others in your company may.* This includes not only employees in marketing, sales, or customer service functions, but anyone else who may come into direct contact with one

of your current or potential older customers (such as clerical staff, maintenance personnel, stock clerks, and so forth).

Remember: In holding one or more of these perceptions, any of these
individuals may impede your company's ability to successfully attract and
serve the mature market.

Misconception 1: Mature Adults Are All the Same

Like other groups having a few common characteristics, older persons are
often lumped into the same category. They are perceived as a bloc of individuals sharing the same lifestyles, interests, values, idiosyncrasies, and capabilities. For the marketer, this concept has its advantages, since it certainly
makes it easier to develop a marketing strategy for the older customer. Unfortunately, the notion of a monolithic mature market is pure myth!

Most people who subscribe to this misconception tend to apply it to
those over 60. Thus, while differences among persons ages 50 through 59
may be recognized, those applicable to the 60+ group are not. Why? Perhaps
because most persons over 60 are not in the work force.

Most people start to drop out of the work force as they reach their sixties. Once this happens, many of their fellow employees lose contact with
them. They also lose the major common interest they shared . . . employment. The combination of these two losses seems to create a "we versus
they" perception of the older person. A byproduct of the perception that
older people are a different breed is the all-too-easy assumption that they all
must be alike. But are those members of the retiree crowd really all the same?

Why Older Adults Have Less in Common
Than Younger People

The notion that older persons are all the same, or that they become more
alike with age, simply isn't true. In reality, they become less and less alike.
Studies in gerontological research have shown that lifestyle patterns tend to
persist as one ages.

Noted social gerontologist, Bernice Neugarten, has likened people's
lives to the spreading of a fan. The longer they live, the greater the differences between them. To underscore this fact, Ms. Neugarten has said that a
group of 18-year-olds is more alike than a group of 60-year-olds.[1] When you
consider factors like economic status, geographic location, ethnic background, career experiences, and educational attainment, it becomes easy to
see why.

Despite such evidence, there are marketers whose comments and actions give credence to the "sameness" concept. *Example*: An executive from

a large hospital chain was discussing marketing strategies for older consumers. He believed that it would be extremely difficult for the chain to attract older patients because "these people never want to change their physician." While many older persons do have strong ties to a specific physician, there are still quite a few others who lack such a relationship. Some of these individuals could very well be interested in developing an affiliation with a specific health care provider.

Danger: By lumping all older consumers into one group, you will unnecessarily limit your company's mature market potential.

Four Questions That Can Help You Avoid Falling Victim to the "Sameness" Trap

How can you tell if your company may be falling victim to the "older persons are all the same" trap? Here are four questions you need to ask yourself:

1. Is your overall marketing strategy based on the concept of a one-dimensional, monolithic mature market?
2. Have you identified segments within the mature market, especially those that are *not* age-specific?
3. Have you educated your staff about the differences to be found among members of the mature population?
4. Have you sufficiently test marketed a product or service before deciding it is unsuitable for any segment of the mature market?

Misconception 2: Mature Adults Think of Themselves as Being "Old"

While working with one of my clients, I had the opportunity to speak with Sandy, a member of the staff. Sandy mentioned that she wanted to crochet a shawl for her 93-year-old grandmother. When Sandy told this to her grandmother, the elderly woman immediately asked Sandy to abandon the idea. Why? "Because," Sandy's grandmother told her, "shawls are for *old* people."

Getting Old: A Matter of Interpretation

The fact is, Sandy's grandmother typifies the perceptions which many older Americans have about themselves. *They simply don't think of themselves as old.* This characteristic was perhaps best noted by the great American statesman, Bernard Baruch, who once said, "Old age is always 15 years older than you are."[2] When you think about it, haven't you raised the definition of what "old" is as you've aged?

Research shows that Baruch's quip has quite a bit of substance to it. A recent survey conducted by Cadwell Davis Partners, a New York advertising agency, found that "getting old" begins well after the age of 70. Among those over 60, 40 percent defined "getting old" as something that happens to people over age 75.[3]

Tip: Most older persons are much more willing to believe and accept that getting old happens to the "other guy," not themselves.

Sydney J. Harris, the late Chicago-based syndicated columnist, once aptly described the pysche of the older adult as it responds to aging. Harris, himself over 50, said:

> Nearly everyone finds it hard to believe he or she has reached a certain milestone in life, be it 50, 60, or 70; and no one (excepts perhaps the critically ill) feels internally that he is really that old. The cliche that 'time flies' becomes truer every decade, and that much harder to accept.
>
> What young people fail to recognize until they themselves reach ripeness is that older people continue to regard themselves as young 'inside' at any age, until death overtakes them. No matter how they may look, or sound, or even act, a core deep inside themselves clings to the feeling that they remain perpetually young.[4]

The recent appearance of Senior Olympic games, "senior" proms, and even senior beauty pageants, supports the validity of Mr. Harris's comments.

Warning: By failing to recognize the internal youthfulness felt by most older persons, your business will seriously undermine its mature market success.

Suggestions for Avoiding the "Think They're Old" Trap

How can your company's marketing strategy steer clear of this misguided notion about the older consumer? Here are a few suggestions:

- Remember that the *attitudes* and *lifestyles* of mature adults are a greater indication of their age than are their birth dates.

- Make certain your staff understands how the older consumer perceives himself in terms of his age.

- Make every effort you can to portray the older person in a positive but realistic light.

- Avoid absolute terms like "old" and "young" when referring to your customers and prospects. Use comparative terms like "younger" and "older" instead.

- Keep in mind the immortal words of legendary pitcher, Satchel Paige, who said, "How old would you be if you didn't know how old you was?"[5]

Misconception 3: Older Adults Aren't an Important Consumer Segment

Recently, an urban FM radio station with widespread appeal among those over 50 decided to abandon its instrumental-only, beautiful music format in favor of a more vocal-oriented, easy listening sound. The shift was made to attract more younger listeners to the station.

In appraising this shift, the program director of another FM station had this to say:

> It's a great move. . . . Those people over 55 do not put as much into the credit bins, the houses, the cars, the banks, the stores. They often live on fixed incomes and, as a result, that audience is not [interesting] to advertising people.

Yes, many radio advertisers have not been particularly interested in reaching stations popular with mature adults. One major reason for this is that, like the program director, these advertisers—or their ad agencies— often underestimate, or are unaware of, the mature market's consumer clout.

A Vital Consumer Market

The 50+ population is a major force in the marketplace. Collectively, this group

- possesses nearly *half* of all discretionary income held by American consumers[7]
- accounts for more than *one-third* of the dollars spent by American consumers

Older adults are responsible for a sizable percentage of the monies spent to purchase many products and services. For example, according to the Bureau of Labor Statistics' 1985 Consumer Expenditure Survey, households headed by those 55 and over account for *30% or more* of all dollars spent for such things as

- home repairs and remodeling
- life, home, and auto insurance
- vacation homes
- ranges and refrigerators
- air, train, and bus fares
- floor coverings
- new cars
- grocery store purchases

- out-of-town lodging
- silverware, dinnerware, and china
- jewelry[8]

Note: Even among the oldest consumers—those 75 and over—a significant amount is spent on such things as food and beverages, home maintenance and repairs, refrigerators, airline travel and cruises.

Example: Lee Cassidy, president of the Mature Market Institute, recently pointed out that his 78-year-old mother spent more for new furniture and carpeting in 1987 than her three children combined![9]

When considering the over-50 group, many marketers also forget something else: Consumer needs and wants do not suddenly cease to exist once a person enters the later years of life. In reality, most older adults continue to have some of the same needs and desires they had when they were younger. Furthermore, changes in lifestyle, health, income, or family status may generate *new* or *different* consumer purchases.

Example: Grandparenthood stimulates the older consumer to buy numerous products and services for the family.

Five Suggestions to Help You Understand and Appreciate the Mature Consumer's Significance in the Marketplace

Make sure your company doesn't make the mistake of ignoring or undervaluing the mature consumer. Here are five suggestions to help you sidestep this misconception:

1. Review and analyze data from surveys that report on the mature market's consumer purchases (such as the Bureau of Labor Statistics' annual Consumer Expenditure Survey). This will give you a truer picture of the group's needs, wants, and purchase behavior.

2. Remember that those over 50 often have little or no expenses for children or for home mortgages. They also have had years to accumulate a personal nest egg.

3. Keep in mind that health-care related purchases account for a *small* percentage of most older consumers' expenses. This is especially true for those younger than age 75.

4. Recognize that most older adults continue to be active participants in the marketplace during their retirement years. Like younger persons, these consumers have needs and wants which can only be met through the purchase of specific goods and services.

5. Remember that within the mature market you'll find a diversity of consumers . . . some much more ready, willing, and able to purchase your products and services than others.

Misconception 4: Mature Adults Won't Try Something New

In her late eighties, Lucille Thompson worked toward passing the test. At the age of 89, she did it: Lucille Thompson earned her black belt in Tae Kwon Do, a form of Korean karate. Nicknamed "Killer" by her fellow students, Lucille is thought to be the oldest woman ever to achieve such a rating.

Doing Something Different

As spectacular an achievement as Lucille Thompson's was, it is only one example of what many older Americans choose to do in their later years: try new things. In fact, in a readership survey conducted by *Modern Maturity*, AARP's magazine, *most respondents said they would be willing to experiment simply for the sake of variety or novelty.*[10] This phenomenon is often seen with travel.

Example: Betty Hoffman is chairman of Evergreen Travel Service in Lynnwood, Washington. For more than 25 years, she's been running tours for older adults. According to Hoffman, "There's almost nothing seniors won't try if we tell them it's safe." Yet, if you look at where Hoffman's groups have gone, "safe" includes elephant rides in India and whitewater rafting trips.[11] Another group, Society Expeditions, which specializes in travel to exotic places like the North Pole and Tibet, reports that two-thirds of its customers are over 50!

The mature person's desire to try new things, however, extends well beyond the realm of travel. Many persons over 50 are active participants in today's "high-tech" society. They purchase videocassette recorders and microwave ovens, use automated teller machines and credit cards, or work with computers. Consumers over 50 also display a willingness to experiment when shopping at retail stores and supermarkets.

Example: According to Goldring & Company's "Geromarket" study of age 50+ consumers, within the twelve-month period preceding the survey

- 45.3 percent of those polled had tried a new brand of ready-to-eat cereal
- 34.1 percent had tried a new brand of ice cream
- 30 percent had tried a new brand of canned soup
- 30.5 percent had tried a new brand of carbonated soft drink
- 22.2 percent had tried a new brand of frozen fruit juice

Looking at food products in total, more than 75% of those surveyed had tried a new brand within the past year![12]

Overcoming the Myth

To prevent your business from being sabotaged by the notion that those over 50 are too old to change their consumer behavior, keep this in mind:

Your ability to influence a mature adult to try a product or service for the first time will improve if you

- Focus on how the product or service will more effectively meet his/her needs, concerns or desires
- Disseminate as much "user-friendly" information as possible about the item or service
- Do everything possible to lessen the real or perceived risks associated with the product or service

To determine if your company's marketing strategy reflects the fact that many older consumers *will*—and *do*—try new things, you should also ask yourself these specific questions:

1. In the absence of solid research findings, have you ruled out marketing one of your existing products or services to those over 50 because you believe "they'd never try it" or "never switch brands"?

2. When older consumers have not responded well to a new, high-tech, or adventuresome product/service you've offered, did you (a) fully investigate the reasons why and (b) attempt, where feasible, to make any necessary modifications in your marketing plan?

3. Have you strongly linked *your* product or service to benefits which an older consumer may expect to gain from trying it?

4. Have you done whatever is reasonably possible to minimize the real or perceived risks which the mature consumer may believe your product or service carries?

Misconception 5: Older Persons Have Impaired Mental Faculties

William D. Hersey is the author of the book, *How to Cash in on Your Hidden Memory Power* (Englewood Cliffs, N.J.: Prentice-Hall, Inc., 1963). He began conducting memory training courses at the age of 60. Today, in his seventies, Mr. Hersey travels around the country speaking on memory improvement.

Hersey is a living refutation of one of the most commonly held misconceptions about aging and the older population: *that most of those in their golden years will experience a steady decline in their mental capabilities . . . a decline that ultimately will lead them to senility.*

The Three Musketeers: Aging, Gray Hair, and Senility?

Unfortunately, many people associate the later years of life with memory failure and senility. At one time or another, you too probably have been teased about getting "old and senile" because you forgot or misplaced something. This label has been inappropriately tagged on countless numbers of older adults when they may actually have been hard of hearing, overtranquilized, experiencing the side effects of medication, or suffering from an undiagnosed case of clinical depression.

According to Robin Marantz Henig, author of *The Myth of Senility*, even among those over 65, only about 5 percent are victims of serious mental impairment. Furthermore, only 10 percent of the older population display even mild to moderate loss of memory.[13] In reality, most people retain their memory functions throughout their lives. And, according to Robin L. West, author of *Memory Fitness Over 40* (Gainesville, Florida: Triad Publishing Company, 1985), there are techniques for minimizing even the small losses that may occur naturally.

Tip: Recognize that the majority of older Americans will not experience a measurable decline in their mental faculties.

Indeed, an individual's intellectual skills can remain sharp through mid-life and beyond. *Example*: On the verbal scale of the Wechsler Adult Intelligence Test—the most widely used intelligence test in the United States, and perhaps, the world—there is, from age 17 until age 80, a change of barely one standard deviation. Furthermore, when the following areas are tested—arithmetic, vocabulary, comprehension, general knowledge about the world, and the ability to make judgments about the outcomes of various situations—the scores remain stable throughout life.[14]

Intellectual Abilities: Use Them or Lose Them

Let there be no confusion. As people grow older, some may experience real and measurable declines in specific intellectual abilities. For some, these declines may be rapid and caused by depression or diseases that affect the brain such as atherosclerosis or Alzheimer's disease. Most healthy individuals, however, will experience gradual reductions in selected abilities such as concentrating, remembering telephone numbers, or recalling something previously learned.

What can be concluded is that partial declines in certain intellectual abilities may be due more to disuse than disease. In other words, *as with physical exercise, the mind works under the principle of "use it or lose it."* And, when it comes to using their minds, many older people do. Below are some examples from past and present of those whose names you'll immediately recognize.

- At 100, Grandma Moses was still painting.
- At 94, Bertrand Russell led international peace drives.
- At 93, George Bernard Shaw wrote the play, "Farfetched Fables."
- At 77, Ronald Reagan was the 40th President of the United States.
- At 81, Vladimir Horowitz performed in concerts and recitals.
- At 83, Helen Hayes wrote the book, *Our Best Years*.

Keep in Mind: Thousands of lesser-known older persons exhibit strong intellectual capabilities every day.

Marketing Effectiveness Checklist

To help ensure that your organization's marketing effectiveness is not hampered by the aging = gray hair = senility mindset, here is a checklist to use:

1. Make certain that neither your sales and customer service personnel nor your promotional materials "talk down" to the older consumer.

2. Train company staff to take your older customers' complaints seriously rather than dismissing them to senility or feeble-mindedness.

3. Recognize that most older adults have the ability to learn how to use the latest in sophisticated products or services (such as computers and automated teller machines). Therefore, do not overlook the potential to market these innovations to the mature consumer.

4. Develop appropriate marketing, sales, and customer service strategies which recognize the minor (or major) intellectual losses experienced by some older adults.

5. Consider utilizing the mental skills and talents of the mature consumer in your sales or service efforts.

Misconception 6: Most Older Persons Suffer from Poor Health

Comedian Jimmi Walker was appearing at a Miami Beach hotel. When asked about his audience, Walker said it was composed of "old people and their parents." He added, "If I talk about a subject they don't like, I can hear their aluminum walkers clanging." Walker got himself in trouble with those comments; the hotel was deluged with calls threatening a boycott and demanding his firing. Shortly thereafter, he apologized for his remarks.

Although Walker may have been joking, his statement illustrates how people often associate the older population with illness, medical equipment, and nursing homes. In short, they assume most silver-haired Americans must be either sick, institutionalized, or both.

You might be surprised by the kinds of people prone to holding this belief, including health care personnel such as physicians and hospital workers. Some of these individuals unwittingly get a distorted picture of the older population because most of their contact is with those who are sick.

Example: I was invited to address the executive staff of a very progressive hospital system. The meeting planner said one of the things she wanted me to do was present an accurate picture of the mature citizen. This meant a discussion of the "healthy" old. The idea was to familiarize hospital management with the opportunities it had to serve the many "well" seniors in the community. Apparently, this was a group which management had lost sight of, since the healthy old were rarely seen in the hospital.

Danger: If most of your contact is with one type of older customer (such as those who are sick), you can become blinded to the opportunity of serving other segments of this market.

Poor Health: By Whose Standards?

Interestingly enough, many mature Americans also vastly overestimate the degree to which their peers suffer from poor health. What makes this even more ironic is that most older adults regard their own individual health as being somewhere between good and excellent!

What is the overall health of the older population? As a group, mature adults do indeed require and receive more medical services and supplies than the younger population. However, *most older adults do not suffer from debilitating diseases which incapacitate them.*

Key Point: Opportunities for you to market products and services to the mature consumer which are *not* health-related may be greater than you think.

When looking at the older population's health status, you should also be aware of this: During any given year, only a small percentage of those over 50 is responsible for a large amount of the care received by the group. Furthermore, it is also a small group that accounts for a major portion of the mature market's health care costs. And, most of these costs occur during the last year or two of a person's life. *Thus, the majority of older adults will remain relatively healthy until their last years.*

Remember: To succeed in the mature market, your business must recognize that most older adults will remain self-sufficient throughout the greater part of their retirement years. During that time, they represent a viable and valuable consumer market with whom you should maintain contact.

Health-Awareness Checklist

How can you determine if your company's marketing strategy reflects an accurate perception of the overall health status of the mature market? Here are a few questions you should ask yourself.

1. Have you fully explored the possibility of providing health care products and services which serve the "healthy" old?
2. If your company provides products or services which are not health-related, have you fully pursued the potential to market these products to the older customer?
3. Does your advertising ever include the healthy old?
4. Do your marketing, sales, and customer service staffs realize that most older Americans are not chronically ill or institutionalized?

Misconception 7: Older Adults Keep to Themselves

She writes about 4,000 letters a year to both friends and strangers. Every day, she plays the organ at her church's daily Mass, as she has done for nearly 40 years. She serves as the entertainment coordinator for a local nursing home facility. Since 1964, she has written a weekly column for the local newspaper.

Who is this woman? She's Charlotte Pitts of New London, New Hampshire. Known as the "Purple Lady" because of her fondness for wearing purple-colored clothing, Charlotte is in her eighties. A retired teacher, she has earned dozens of awards and accolades for her tireless efforts to serve her community and state. While Charlotte's busy schedule may be extraordinary for someone her age, her lifestyle does have much in common with many of our nation's mature adults.

Volunteerism and Older Americans

Far from being isolated or withdrawn, *millions of today's older Americans are socially active, involved in causes, and taking on responsibilities.*

A good example of this is in volunteerism. According to a recent Gallup survey, 44 percent of our nation's 89 million volunteers are over the age of 50.[16] Indeed, one of the major reasons for the achievements and success enjoyed by the American Association of Retired Persons (AARP) has been its ability to utilize the skills of over 300,000 volunteers. Many other programs in both government and the private sector have similarly attracted a sizable number of older volunteers.

Tip: The older American volunteer represents a great resource for your marketing or customer service activities.

Older Americans are also very active in church and synagogue functions, political campaigns, civic associations, the arts, special interest groups (such as garden, chess, travel and bridge clubs), and community service organizations. Some service organizations have even had to launch drives to attract younger people because their ranks are virtually overstocked with gray Americans.

Tip: Community groups and service clubs offer an effective channel to reaching a cluster of older consumers.

Love and Friendship—Still the Same for Young and Old

In addition to group involvement, many 50 + ers are also engaged in meaningful personal relationships with both family and friends. This includes romantic relationships as well. In fact, studies show that older Americans experience the same physiological and psychological feelings when they fall in love as do teenagers! This includes sweaty palms, heart palpitations, an inability to concentrate, and anxiety when away from their romantic partner.[17] In the same vein, the majority of older Americans continue to have sexual desires and abilities and to remain sexually active.

Remember: As long as they stay healthy, most persons who were socially active in the past will continue to be so in their later years. This includes maintaining a network of relationships with a variety of individuals and groups.

Tips on Reaching the Mature Market Via the "Social" Route

Is your company being sabotaged by the aging = social isolation belief? Here are a few things you can do to reach those over 50.

1. Focus your distribution strategy not only on reaching mature consumers on a one-to-one basis but also by reaching them through other channels such as groups, clubs, family, and friends.

2. Solicit the assistance of older volunteers or workers.

3. Consider developing and implementing marketing campaigns that bring mature adults together in a social context.

Misconception 8: Mature Adults Aren't Physically Active

Arlitt Allsup walks five miles every day in just under 70 minutes. What makes this even more impressive is that Allsup is in his 80s!

Allsup is a club member at Dr. Kenneth Cooper's Dallas Aerobic Center. You may recall Dr. Cooper as the man who developed aerobics, the exercise program which has become so popular in the United States. As a dedicated walker, Allsup subscribes to Dr. Cooper's belief that man doesn't stop exercising because he gets too old, but gets "too old" because he stops exercising."[18]

Athletic Americans: Staying Active as They Age

Obviously, not all older Americans are like Arlitt Allsup. However, they are not sedentary either. Actually, *many* mature adults are physically active. And while it is true that the *kind of activity* an older person might engage in may change, the ability to get involved and be competitive usually does not.

Example: Take the case of the Kids and Kubs softball teams of the Three-Quarter Century Club in St. Petersburg, Florida. For almost 60 years, these teams have been competing three times a week between November and March. As you might expect, the 35 members of each team are all age 75 or over.

Getting Off the Rocker: Popular Activities for 50+ers

What about the overall mature adult population's interest in fitness? As Figure 1-1 illustrates, many older Americans are avid sports participants. Their favorite pastimes include exercise walking, golfing, swimming and bicycling. A 1987 Gallup poll found that nearly half (47 percent) of those 65 and over regularly engage in some form of exercise.[19]

While jogging is not among the most popular forms of activity for the mature market, it certainly has its share of participants, some of whom are marathon runners. An associate of mine, Terry Dugan, has actually encouraged older adults to be marathon runners. To inspire those over 50 to participate in fitness activities, Terry has given them T-shirts which proclaim, "I'm Off my Rocker." The T-shirt features a picture of a rocking chair with a line though it.

One more word about physical fitness and mature Americans: The increasing participation in such activity has given birth to a number of events and organizations. For example, we now have the National Seniors Sports Association, Masters Swimming and Tennis programs, the Senior Golf tour, and various Senior Games and Senior Olympics held at sites throughout the country.

1986 SPORTS PARTICIPATION

Females 55+

	Participants (in millions)	As percent of all participants
1. Exercise Walking	8.5	15.9%
2. Swimming	4.0	5.5
3. Bicycling	2.4	4.7
4. Camping	1.8	4.4
5. Fishing	1.6	3.7
6. Bowling	1.5	4.5
7. Exercising with Equipment	1.4	4.5
8. Motor Boating	1.3	5.0
9. Golf	1.2	6.0
10. Aerobic Exercising	1.1	5.0

Males 55+

	Participants (in millions)	As percent of all participants
1. Exercise Walking	5.5	10.3%
2. Fishing	3.6	8.2
3. Golf	2.9	14.4
4. Swimming	2.9	3.9
5. Bicycling	1.9	3.9
6. Camping	1.9	4.6
7. Motor Boating	1.7	7.3
8. Hunting/Shooting	1.6	7.7
9. Bowling	1.5	4.4
10. Exercising with Equipment	1.1	3.4

Source: National Sporting Goods Association © 1987

FIGURE 1–1

Keep in Mind: Retiree "wellness" will be among the major trends of the future.

Key Points to Remember About Physical Fitness and the Mature Market

Will the belief that most older Americans aren't interested in physical fitness activities limit your company's mature market opportunities? Don't let it!

- Realize that most older Americans have the ability to be physically active and competitive.

- Recognize that the 50+ population's interest in—and need for—health promotion activities will boom over the next 10 to 15 years.
- Consider the potential for developing and marketing athletic and recreational products, competitive events, and sporting activities for the mature population.

Marketing Checklist: The Eight Deadly Misconceptions

1. Mature adults are all the same.
2. Mature adults think of themselves as being "old."
3. Older adults aren't an important consumer segment.
4. Mature adults won't try something new.
5. Older persons have impaired mental faculties.
6. Most older persons suffer from poor health.
7. Older adults keep to themselves.
8. Mature adults aren't physically active.

Chapter Wrap-up

To maximize your company's chances for success in marketing to and serving the older consumer, you must

- Train and monitor your marketing, sales, and customer service staffs to assure they do not believe—or act upon—the eight misconceptions.
- Possess a thorough understanding of the mature market.
- Remain open-minded to the many possibilities that may exist to serve the broad spectrum of older customers.

———

1. Hall, Elizabeth, interview with Bernice, Neugarten, "Acting One's Age: New Rules for the Old," *Psychology Today*, April 1980, p. 78.

2. Bernard Baruch quoted in the *New York Times*, June 6, 1984.

3. "Older is later, study says," *Marketing News*, August 16, 1985, p. 8.

4. Harris, Sydney J., "You aren't as old as your 'inside' age," The Philadelphia Inquirer, August 24, 1985, p. 9-A.

5. Satchel Paige quoted in the *New York Times*, June 8, 1984.

6. Logan, Joe, "New 'Easy' sound gets a mixed reception," *The Philadelphia Inquirer*, February 13, 1988, p. 1-D.

7. Linden, Fabian. *Midlife and Beyond: The $800 Billion Over-Fifty Market.* New York: Consumer Research Center, The Conference Board, Inc., 1985.

8. United States Department of Labor, "Consumer Expenditure Survey: Results from 1985," Table 3, p. 1.

9. Cassidy, Lee, "Living, Not Dying," *American Demographics*, April 1988, p. 4.

10. "Misdirected advertising prevents marketers from taking bite from 'golden apple' of maturity market," *Marketing News*, October 26, 1984, p. 19.

11. Nestlebaum, Karen, "Meetings for Seniors: How to Roll Out the Red Carpet to Better Service the Mature Persons' Market," *Meetings & Conventions*, January 1985, pp. 93-96.

12. "The Geromarket 1987 Omnibus Study," Goldring & Company, Inc., July 1987, Age Table 122, pgs. 1-2.

13. Henig, Robin Marantz. *The Myth of Senility.* Garden City, New York: Anchor Press/Doubleday, 1981.

14. "Business Issues in an Aging America," a report from The Travelers Insurance Companies, 1982, p. 6.

15. "Gray Humor," *The Philadelphia Inquirer*, January 16, 1986, p. 2-E.

16. Hoyt, Mary Finch, "Helping others can make you feel better, too," *USA Weekend*, September 12-14, 1986, p. 17.

17. Bulcroft, Kris, and Margaret O'Conner-Roden, "Never Too Late," *Psychology Today*, June 1986, pp. 66-69.

18. Higdon, Hal, "Newest research tells us: If You Want Long Life—Exercise!" *50 Plus*, August 1986, p. 17.

19. Toufexis, Anastasia, "Grays on the Go," *Time*, February 22, 1988, p. 79.

Chapter **2**

Recognizing and Capitalizing on Key Trends

In recent years, corporate America has increasingly turned to trend analysis and forecasting as a means of achieving or ensuring future prosperity. If your organization is seeking to capture the mature market, it will surely need to engage in this activity. In particular, you will have to be keenly aware of those specific trends directly related to the aging of America. By identifying such trends, your business will place itself in the best position to

1. respond to consumer needs and concerns
2. develop new products and services
3. reposition or modify established products and services
4. determine new or emerging segments within the mature market

Over the past few years, I have steadfastly tracked the mature market and have identified six major trends which are taking place in that arena. These trends will have a profound impact on the mature population and those who seek to serve them.

Keep in Mind: Those organizations that both recognize and capitalize on these trends will most likely be the ones to succeed in the increasingly competitive battle to capture a significant share of the mature market.

Trend 1: Growth of the "Oldest Old" Population

Shortly before addressing an audience in Peoria, Illinois, I was interviewed by a newspaper reporter. Our conversation touched upon the tremendous growth in America's older population. The reporter then told me something which really illustrated the point. Apparently, his newspaper used to do a special story whenever someone in town reached the age of 100. Recently, however, the paper had discontinued that policy. Why? Too many people were reaching the century mark! The newspaper now covers these stories on a select basis only.

What's true for Peoria is also true for the rest of America. During the past few decades there has been a spectacular growth in the number of persons age 85 and over, including, of course, those over 100. Today there are more than 25,000 centenarians in the United States.

Of even greater significance is the fact that the 85 + group, also known as the "oldest old," will continue to experience tremendous growth over the next several years. By the year 2000, it is expected that over 5 million people will be age 85 and over, a figure more than double the size of the group today. This group will constitute about 15 percent of the over-65 population, a considerably higher percentage than the 5 percent representation they had in 1950. As Figure 2-1 shows, this trend is one which marketers can virtually

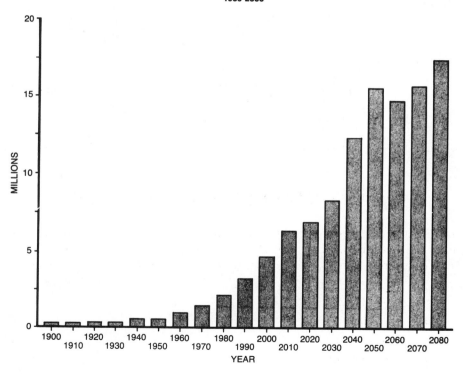

**ACTUAL AND PROJECTED INCREASE IN POPULATION
85 YEARS AND OLDER:
1900-2080**

SOURCE: Taueber, Cynthia M., U.S. Bureau of the Census. "America in Transition: An Aging Society." *Current Population Reports* Series P-23, No. 128 (September 1983).

Spencer, Gregory, U.S. Bureau of the Census. "Projections of the Population of the United States, by Age, Sex, and Race: 1983 to 2080." *Current Population Reports* Series P-25, No. 952 (May 1984).

FIGURE 2–1

bank on not just until the year 2000, but for many decades beyond, because of further decreases expected in the mortality rate and the aging of the baby boomers.

Health Care Services: A Growing Need for the 85+

What implications does this trend have for business over the next 10 to 15 years? To a great extent, this question can be answered by examining the health status of today's 85 + population. While a sizable percentage of this group is able to function independently, many others are not. For example, almost one quarter of the group is institutionalized, and nearly half of those who are not have difficulty in performing at least one of such routine activities as bathing, dressing, eating, or walking.[1] In addition, the 85 + segment has the highest hospital utilization rate of any age group.

Keep in Mind: The belief that many older persons suffer from poor health comes closest to being accurate if one looks only at those over 85 rather than at the entire mature market.

A growing population of persons over 85 means an increasing need for hospital and nursing home services and supplies. However, it will also create an even greater demand for *home* and *community-based* health and social services. There are two important reasons for this:

1. Growth of the 85 + population is expected to far surpass the number of nursing home beds available to serve this group.

2. Increasing public and private sector efforts to control health care spending will shift most of the elderly's care to home and community-based settings.

Special Services Needed by the Oldest Old

Without a doubt, most older Americans want to—and will—remain as independent as possible, and that includes a large number of those 85 and over. This latter group, too, will grow in number over the next several decades. For these individuals, there is and will be a need for such things as

- transportation
- appropriate housing
- financial and legal assistance
- specialty foods
- social activities
- preventive health services

- drugs and medications for managing chronic conditions such as diabetes, hypertension, and arthritis

Note: Unlike the dependent elderly, who will also need some of these services, the independent 85 + group will likely have more say about which services they actually obtain and use.

How Marketers Can Respond to the Growing 85+ Population Trend

Marketers should keep four important ideas in mind in developing successful strategies that respond to this trend:

1. The majority of the oldest old are—and will continue to be— women, especially those who live alone.
2. Like the rest of the mature market, the nature and composition of the 85 + group will continue to change; over time, for example, the aggregate group should be more educated and informed, more independent, have more income, and be more accepting of technology than are its members today.
3. Children and other relatives of the 85 + group will continue to play a significant role in their choice of products and services.
4. Older adults *without children* will be especially in need of assistance in order to prevent their institutionalization.

Awareness Checklist for Marketers

1. How much primary and secondary market research data have you obtained on both the current 85 + group and the 75 to 84-year-old group which will soon join their ranks?
2. Is your organization tracking the business impact which a rapidly growing 85 + population is having in specific states having large concentrations of these citizens (such as California, Florida, Illinois, and New York)?
3. What activities have you undertaken or planned to identify products or services which your company could provide to meet the needs of the growing age 85 + group or their families?
4. If your company is *not* a health care provider, what plans have you made to develop relationships with—and products for—such organizations, since they undoubtedly will play a major role in serving the 85 + group?

Trend 2: Caregiver Crisis—Children Who Care for Elderly Parents

A few years ago, a good friend of mine, Evelyn, learned that her father had Alzheimer's disease. His condition was fairly advanced and was expected to become progressively worse. For several months thereafter, Evelyn regularly drove about 30 miles to her father's home to assist him in managing various aspects of his life.

As her father's mental capabilities deteriorated, Evelyn found it dangerous to leave him alone. She invited him to move in with her and her husband. Soon, this also became too difficult and stressful, so Evelyn found it necessary to place her father in a nursing home. After searching without success for months, Evelyn was able to locate the proper facility for her father.

Evelyn's efforts to help her father are not unusual. In fact, *up to 80 percent of all older parents are assisted by their children in times of need.* At such times, these children assume the role of family "caregiver." The ability of adult children to act as caregivers for their parents is being seriously threatened, however. This phenomenon marks another important trend which characterizes the mature market. I refer to it as the "caregiver crisis."

Three Main Reasons for the Caregiver Crisis

Why is the caregiver crisis occurring? There are three principal reasons. First, the need for adult children to assume the caregiver role is increasing dramatically. Second, there is a growing demand to control health care costs. Third, it is becoming considerably more difficult for people to be caregivers. Let's take a look at each of these factors.

The major force behind the increased need for family caregiving is the growth in the size of the mature market, especially the age 70+ population. Aging brings with it the increased probability that a person will develop a serious health problem. While those in their fifties and sixties are at a high risk of having such conditions, the 70+ group finds itself particularly vulnerable. These older individuals, especially women, are also less likely to have spouses due to separation, divorce, or death. This increases the likelihood that the child will be called on in times of need.

Key Point: The older a person is, the more likely it is you'll need to consider his or her children in your marketing strategy.

Another force creating an increased need for caregiving is the emphasis now being placed on controlling health care costs. Both government and private industry have recognized that medical care and social services can be provided much more cost effectively *outside* of a hospital or nursing home setting. *Result:* Various health insurance programs such as Medicare recently have been redesigned to discourage institutional care. This has greatly increased the need for home care services. As higher health care users, it is often the older group which requires these services; and it is their children who assist them by either providing or obtaining the help that's necessary.

Note: The caregiver crisis will be a major force in contributing to the skyrocketing demand for home and community-based products and services.

The other reason for the caregiver crisis is that it is becoming much more difficult to caregive. Studies have consistently shown that when children are called upon to assist their older parents, *it is the daughter (or daughter-in-law) who usually assumes the caregiver role.* Unlike the past, however, many of these women are likely to be in the work force. For example, among the 55 + population, the only segment whose labor force participation rate has *increased* since 1950 is that of women ages 55-64. Having a job and serving as a caregiver is extremely difficult, especially for women in full-time, management-level positions.

Key Point: The child you will probably need to market to is the middle-aged daughter.

Caregiving is becoming more difficult because *many of the caregivers are themselves members of the mature market.* As Figure 2-2 illustrates, since the beginning of this century, there has been a significant increase in the number of persons who have reached age 80 + in relation to those who are 60 through 64. In fact, 10 percent of those over 65 have at least one surviving parent.

According to the National Center for Health Services Research, a third of all caregivers are in the older age brackets. Senator John Heinz has aptly described this phenomenon as one in which "we're already seeing grandparents caring for great-grandparents."[2] The stresses and demands of caregiving can make it a formidable task for someone of any age, but especially for one who is in this group.

Tip: The caregiver crisis offers you an opportunity to serve the *caregiver* as well as the care receiver.

The Phenomenon of the "Sandwich" Generation

What is also making caregiving more difficult is the "sandwich" generation phenomenon. The "sandwich" generation refers to those people in their middle years who may have both children and parents to care for at the same time. The stresses which these caregivers must endure can be enormous.

Note: The physical/emotional abuse of as many as 1 million older Americans—by their families—is, in part, a result of the stresses of caregiving.

NUMBER OF PERSONS AGE 80 AND OLDER PER 100 PERSONS
AGE 60 THROUGH 64
ACTUAL AND PROJECTED
1900–2030

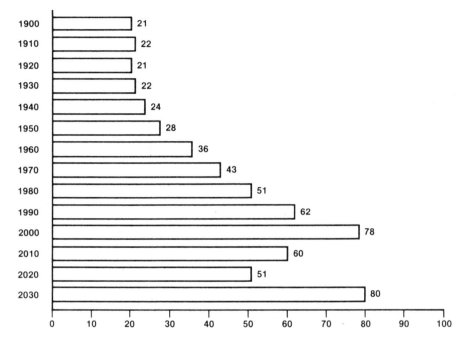

SOURCE: U.S. Bureau of the Census, reported in *Chartbook on Aging in America, 1981 White House Conference on Aging*
and Hoover, Sally, *Supplement to Chartbook on Aging in America.*

FIGURE 2–2

Why the Caregiver Crisis Is Likely to Worsen

You can expect the caregiver crisis to worsen over the next several years.
Why? For several reasons:

1. More and more women are entering the work force and staying in
   it longer, something which seriously endangers their ability to
   caregive.

2. The rising 85 + population coupled with an expected decline in
   the mortality rate will create a vast shortage of nursing home beds,
   thereby increasing the need for family-based care.

3. Young adults, ages 18-34, are spending more years at home with their parents rather than moving out, a factor which can lead to sandwich generation stresses.

4. Many women are having children later in life, making them prime candidates for future sandwich generation problems.

5. Many baby boomers are opting to have no children or small families, which is likely to reduce the supply of caregivers in the future.

Anticipated increases in our life expectancy should also exacerbate the caregiver crisis. Because people will be living longer, those who need an adult child's assistance will be needing that help for more years than ever before. Recent research by Princeton University demographer Jane L. Menken and her colleagues indicates that, for the first time, American women may well expect to spend more years caring for an aging parent than for a dependent child.[3] Increased life expectancy may also create the role of the "double generation caregiver"— someone responsible for assisting both an older parent and a grandparent at the same time!

Keep in Mind: Caring for an elderly parent—now commonly referred to as "eldercare"—will become a major societal concern within the next five to ten years and will remain so for many years thereafter.

Tips for Marketers: Six Ways to Respond to the Caregiving Trend

1. Research and evaluate the needs that caregiving is creating for the adult children found within your company and the markets you serve.

2. Track key business, employment, social, and legislative developments that relate to family caregiving and the sandwich generation.

3. Give serious consideration to developing products and services intended for caregivers as well as their parents.

4. Establish lines of communication with the caregivers.

5. Learn as much as you can about those most likely to be your caregiver customers, namely, middle-aged women.

6. Investigate the potential for developing linkages with adult grandchildren, since it's likely that their role as caregivers will escalate in the years ahead.

One final note: Some businesses will find that the caregiver crisis offers them the chance to serve another customer . . . the employer. Many corporations are beginning to realize the heavy toll that caregiving takes in the work place. The New York Business Group on Health, for example, reported that employees involved in assisting a parent through an acute or chronic problem can adversely affect corporate job performance, productivity, and attendance.[4] The physical and emotional difficulties of caregiving may also require one to seek medical attention. This can cause an employer's health care costs to rise. Several companies, most notably The Travelers Corporation and IBM, have begun to use outside resources to help themselves and their employees deal with the problems of eldercare.

Trend 3: Reentering the Work Force After Retirement

My neighbor recently took advantage of an "early-out" retirement program offered by the DuPont Company. Encouraged by the special incentives, he joined some 11,200 employees in accepting the company's offer. Today, this man works as a part-time consultant sharing his managerial and administrative skills with other employers.

My neighbor's story is indicative of a trend that is likely to intensify over the next several years: older workers retiring from one job and then returning to the work force to pursue other employment opportunities. Why is this happening? There are two major reasons: personal needs and changes in society.

How Personal Needs Prompt Retirees to Return to Work

The average retirement age has been dropping for decades. Many people are now retiring in their mid-to-late fifties. With the increasing possibility of reaching their eighties, nineties, and even hundreds, these individuals now have the potential of spending *more than one-third of their lives in retirement.* Indeed, as Figure 2-3 shows, the average male spent just 3 percent of his lifetime—about 1 year—in retirement in 1900. By 1980, that figure had increased to 19 percent, or 13½ years in retirement. These numbers continue to grow.

It isn't just more years of life in retirement. It is more *quality* years. That's because most of the golden years are likely to be spent in relatively good health. It is the recognition of this which is driving many men and women to seek employment opportunities after retirement.

Note: Most retirees will need to do much more than play golf, watch TV, read, or visit the family to enjoy the 20 or more years which they may very likely live after retirement.

Many retirees or pre-retirees are also learning that retirement can bring with it an abrupt change in lifestyle, which if not planned for, can lead to

LIFECYCLE DISTRIBUTION OF EDUCATION, LABOR FORCE PARTICIPATION, RETIREMENT, AND WORK IN THE HOME: 1900-1980

Subject	Year					
	1900	1940	1950	1960	1970	1980
	Number of years spent in activity					
Male						
Average life expectancy.....	46.3	60.8	65.6	66.6	67.1	70.0
Retirement/work at home......	1.2	9.1	10.1	10.2	12.1	13.6
Labor force participation......	32.1	38.1	41.5	41.1	37.8	38.8
Education..................	8.0	8.6	9.0	10.3	12.2	12.6
Pre-school.................	5.0	5.0	5.0	5.0	5.0	5.0
Female						
Average life expectancy.....	48.3	65.2	71.1	73.1	74.7	77.4
Retirement/work at home......	29.0	39.4	41.4	37.1	35.3	30.6
Labor force participation......	6.3	12.1	15.1	20.1	22.3	29.4
Education..................	8.0	8.7	9.6	10.9	12.1	12.4
Pre-school.................	5.0	5.0	5.0	5.0	5.0	5.0
	Percent distribution by activity type					
Male						
Average life expectancy.....	100	100	100	100	100	100
Retirement/work at home......	3	15	15	15	18	19
Labor force participation......	69	63	63	62	56	55
Education..................	17	14	14	15	18	18
Pre-school.................	11	8	8	8	7	8
Female						
Average life expectancy.....	100	100	100	100	100	100
Retirement/work at home......	60	60	58	51	47	40
Labor force participation......	13	19	21	27	30	38
Education..................	17	13	14	15	16	16
Pre-school.................	10	8	7	7	7	6

SOURCE: U.S. Bureau of the Census. "Educational Attainment in the United States: March 1981 and 1980." *Current Population Reports* Series P-20, No. 390 (August 1984) (median years of school for persons 25 years or older, 1940-1980).

Best, Fred. "Work Sharing: Issues, Policy Options, and Prospects." Upjohn Institute for Employment Research, 1981, page 8 (1900 estimates of median years of school for persons 25 years or older).

National Center for Health Statistics. *Vital Statistics of the United States, 1984.* Vol. 2, Section 6, March 1987 (life expectancy data).

Smith, Shirley J. "Revised Worklife Tables Reflect 1979-1980 Experience." *Monthly Labor Review* Vol. 108, No. 8 (August 1985) (worklife estimates).

FIGURE 2–3

boredom, depression, and even death. Dr. Peter G. Hanson, author of the book *The Joy of Stress*, has said that "the sudden silence gained by retiring from a demanding job into a life of idleness usually causes death or senility within two years unless new stresses and interests can be found."[5] The fear of such consequences, or the actual experience of boredom and depression after retirement, is prompting many persons to go back to work.

Tip: The increasing number of current or upcoming retirees will create business opportunities for organizations which can retrain older workers, conduct pre-retirement career planning courses, or place retirees in new jobs.

Retirees are also reentering the work force to pursue interests or undertake challenges which they could not engage in during prior employment. *Example:* New business start-ups. According to the Bureau of Labor Statistics, more than a million people over 60 were self-employed in nonagricultural occupations in 1985. Many of these individuals are entrepreneurs. For example, the fifth largest auto rental firm in the United States, Ugly Duckling, was started by Thomas Duck at age 63 during his retirement. Experts such as Jeffry A. Timmons, professor of entrepreneurial studies at Babson College in Massachusetts, have already identified a shift toward older, rather than younger, entrepreneurs.[6]

Tip: Marketers looking for franchisees or individuals to run new business ventures may find some retirees are excellent candidates to consider.

Note: Some businesses, particularly those which are small and service industry-oriented (such as consulting firms) may find themselves competing with "second career" retirees. With reduced income needs, a lifetime of experience, and greater accumulated capital, these retirees may be able to outdistance their competitors.

There are also other personal factors prompting retirees to return to work. They include:

- the need for day-to-day income (caused by loss of a job or a change in marital status)
- the desire to supplement a pension and/or Social Security check
- the need to obtain health care benefits lost upon retirement
- the desire to share one's experience with other individuals and organizations

The growing size of the retiree population coupled with its higher educational levels will increase the impact that these factors have on the numbers of older persons entering the work force.

Tip: Keep these motivational factors and needs in mind whether seeking to recruit retirees or to market to them.

Societal Changes: Older Workers Fill a Gap in the Work Place

Most organizations have not actively recruited older workers. In fact, small firms, rather than large ones, have been more willing to hire such individuals. However, several developments occurring within our society are likely to reverse this phenomenon.

To begin with, the rising number of retirees is becoming a resource pool which many employers can ill-afford to ignore. This is particularly true in the service industries, which traditionally have drawn their labor force from the teenage population. Companies in the fast food and supermarket industries, for instance, are increasingly looking to older workers for assistance because the "baby bust" has created a shortage of teenagers. McDonald's "McMasters Program," which recruits and trains older workers, is one example of this.

Key Point: The growing supply of retirees who will want to work (representing *increased demand*) coupled with the diminished number of teenagers available to work (representing *reduced supply*) provides a sound economic basis for hiring older workers.

Businesses are also beginning to witness the benefits of hiring older workers. Companies like McDonalds, The Travelers Insurance Company, Bankers Life and Casualty, and IBM are reporting that the work ethics of older workers set a good example for their younger employees. Moreover, older workers can be hired on a part-time or contractual basis. This provides management with flexibility in scheduling the work hours of the older employee. It also enables the organization to reduce or eliminate the need for paying employee benefits to these individuals, a major cost savings.

Tip: Your company will do best if it looks at retirees as both valuable prospective customers *and* sales/customer service employees.

Three Reasons for the Work Force Reentry Trend

The trend toward persons reentering the work force after retirement will continue to gain strength for several reasons:

- Senior organizations, older adult employment services, and satisfied employers will continue to promote the hiring of older workers.
- Continuing education programs and retraining efforts will increase in number and participation.
- Government will encourage the movement of retirees into the work force to:
    1. help preserve the solvency of the Social Security/Medicare trust funds
    2. bolster tax revenues
    3. continue the push toward privately funded retirement programs
    4. discourage age discrimination

Most of the work performed by the retiree will be on a part-time basis, a preference of both the retiree and the employer.

The continuing influx of retirees into the work force will redefine that part of life which most businesses have historically considered the rocking chair years. Indeed, over the next several decades, we will see the age boundaries between school, work, and leisure disappear as older persons move in and out of these activities throughout their later years.

How to Gauge If Your Company Is Responding to the Work Force Reentry Trend

Is your company prepared to capitalize on the work force reentry trend? The following questions will help you find out.

1. What is your organization's policy regarding the retaining, retraining, or hiring of older workers?

2. What image does the public, especially those over 50, have of your company's attitude toward older workers or older persons?

3. Have you evaluated if and how retirees could be used in your company's efforts to attract and serve the mature market?

4. What relationship and lines of communication do you have with your own retirees?

5. How often does your marketing department seek the counsel of the human resource staff to learn more about (a) the needs, motivations, and concerns of the most accessible mature consumers to you . . . your older workers and retirees, (b) the appropriateness of your communications to retirees, and (c) the possibilities for recruiting/utilizing your retirees in a specific marketing program?

Trend 4: Consumerism—A Growing Concern of the Mature Market

She stood at the fast-food counter, looked at her hamburger, and forcefully asked, "Where's the beef?" She was 82-year-old Clara Peller, the star of a Wendy's TV commercial. Clara's feisty performance notwithstanding, most older consumers have not been so outspoken. This has been most characteristic of the age 65 + group. Studies have shown that the older group tends to complain less than younger shoppers and that seniors are less likely to be assertive when complaining, or persistent when seeking problem resolutions.

The composition and self-concept of the mature market is changing, however. And with these changes, we're beginning to see the emergence of a different breed of older consumers. *More often than ever before, these consumers are voicing their opinions and concerns to the business community.* What's more, there is every reason to believe that this phenomenon will intensify during the next several decades. This increasing activism among the nation's oldest consumers depicts another mature market trend: consumerism.

What's behind the consumerism movement? There are primarily two major forces: education and mass communication.

How Education Affects Consumerism

The more educated a person is, the more likely he or she is to be a prudent, informed, and assertive consumer. This is one major reason why most older shoppers have been less savvy in the marketplace: they have had less education. Today, however, many Americans are entering their retirement years with higher levels of educational attainment than either their parents or their older brothers and sisters. As the chart in Figure 2-4 shows, there is a significant difference among the educational attainment of mature market members age 75 + , 65-74, and 55-64. In short, *the younger the age cohort, the more educated the group is.*

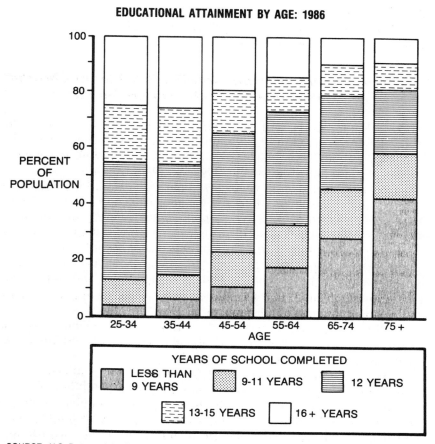

EDUCATIONAL ATTAINMENT BY AGE: 1986

SOURCE: U.S. Bureau of the Census. Unpublished data from the March 1986 Current Population Survey.

FIGURE 2–4

Note: In general, the younger a member of the mature market is, the more likely it is that he or she will possess the educational skills necessary to be an informed and discriminating consumer.

Mature Americans are also seeking to advance their education at both the formal level and through continuing education programs. For example, according to the U.S. Department of Education, nearly 3 million people age 55 and over took adult education courses in the year ending May 1984.

Note: Adult education programs will help provide many of today's 50+ population with the tools for consumerism which they were unable to acquire earlier in life.

Indeed, the mature market represents the fastest growing group of adult education participants. In fact, one of the most successful adult education programs for the over-50 group, Elderhostel, enrolls more than 150,000 students each year at schools and colleges throughout the United States, Canada, and numerous countries overseas.

Tip: The mature market represents an excellent target for educational programming and publications.

Mass Communication: Routine Provider of Consumer Information to the Mature Market

Today's American receives more information in 30 days than our ancestors 100 years ago received in a lifetime! The principal reason for this has been the major strides made in mass communications during this century. One beneficiary of such progress has been the mature adult.

Over the last several years, a number of publications have arisen that are specifically targeted to the older reader. These include *New Choices* (formerly called *50 Plus*), *Mature Outlook*, *Golden Years*, and *Modern Maturity*—the AARP magazine with millions of readers. Many of these publications have large and growing circulations. *More important*: They routinely provide their readers with valuable consumer guidance on such topics as estate planning, financial services, medical insurance, and travel. And they give them information on how to recognize unfair business practices, register complaints, and obtain outside assistance.

Tip: If you want to learn more about the mature consumer's product/service concerns and the advice he or she is receiving about them, read publications targeted to the mature market.

Many of today's mature citizens, especially the younger ones, are also large readers of general newspapers and magazines. And they're heavy users of the broadcast media. For example, a significant number of 50+ers subscribe to *Changing Times*, *Consumers Digest*, *U.S. News and World Report*, and *Reader's Digest*. They regularly listen to local and network news programs, magazine-style shows like "60 Minutes" and "20/20," and TV/radio talk shows.[7] All of these media provide the mature adult with more consumer-oriented information and strategies than ever before!

Warning: If you don't educate the older consumer about your product or service, there's a good chance that someone else will. In that case, you leave yourself open to the possibility of being placed in a reactive or defensive posture.

Business Implications of the Consumerism Trend

What are the business implications of this trend? For one thing, it means that more older persons than ever before are being equipped with the tools necessary to make them better consumers. Furthermore, over the next several years, the gap in educational achievement between the mature market and the under-50 age group will significantly narrow. As a result, businesses may begin to see little difference between the behavior of older customers and younger ones.

Your company should anticipate that mature consumers will

- ask more questions and lodge more complaints than in the past
- be more aggressive in challenging your company's business practices
- become more tenacious in their efforts to have you meet their needs and demands

Checklist for Marketers: Are You Responding to the Consumerism Trend?

Successful companies will both recognize and respond to the increased consumer capabilities of the mature market. Here are a few questions you should ask to see if your company is responding to this trend.

1. Are you monitoring the concerns and complaints registered by older consumers (and their advocates) about your company and your industry?
2. Have you developed products, services, promotional programs, and customer service initiatives which address these complaints?
3. How quickly and satisfactorily do you resolve complaints made by individual older customers?
4. Have you developed and sufficiently publicized booklets, toll-free lines, presentations, or other communications vehicles which assist the older customer in understanding or using your products or services?
5. What efforts have you made to utilize older persons on a consumer advisory panel?

Trend 5: Clout—The Emergence of Senior Power

50 Plus magazine called him "Champion of the Elderly."[8] Claude Pepper, the octogenarian Florida Congressman, has certainly worked hard to earn that reputation. Since 1928, he has vigorously supported a variety of causes that benefit older Americans. His efforts have had a substantial impact on legislation affecting Social Security, Medicare, age discrimination, Alzheimer's disease research, and a host of other issues.

Perhaps of greatest significance, however, is that Pepper's efforts have helped older Americans realize that they have a powerful voice in the Congress and throughout the United States. In fact, Pepper and his actions have been a catalyst for generating a belief found among many mature adults today—a belief that they have power—*senior power*. This senior power is displayed most vividly in the political arena.

Why Older Adults Have Clout

Why have older Americans gained such power? The major reason is that *they vote*. As Figure 2-5 illustrates, the group of persons ages 55-74 has a higher voter participation rate than all other age groups. In fact, in the 1986 election, almost 40 percent of all voters were age 55 or older! What may be most eye-opening about all of this is that persons age 75 + actually have a higher voter participation rate than those 25-34—a major portion of the baby boom generation.

Key Point: In gaining political support for a legislative issue your business supports, it may be more important for you to reach seniors with your message than those in their twenties and thirties.

Active electoral participation by the mature adult population is clearly having an impact on our legislators, both nationally and locally. Strong congressional support of Social Security and Medicare has become commonplace. This is especially true during the months before election day. Senator John H. Chafee of Rhode Island may have best characterized the phenomenon of senior clout when he said, "Anything that comes up for the elderly, everybody's for. They vote and they vote as a bloc."[9]

While I don't agree with Senator Chafee's comments that older persons vote as a bloc—for example, polls show that in the 1986 election the age 60 + vote was nearly split between Democratic and Republican candidates—I can understand how one might get that impression. For over the past few years, the older population has taken on an apparent image of unification. This perception has largely been created because, for the first time in our history, *older Americans have developed strong and mammoth-size organizations to represent them*. This legion of organized older citizens is also responsible for the growing clout of the mature market.

NUMBER AND PERCENTAGE OF PERSONS WHO REPORTED VOTING IN NATIONAL ELECTIONS, BY AGE GROUP: 1980-1986
(numbers in thousands—excludes people in institutions)

Age group	1980		1982		1984		1986	
	Number	Percent	Number	Percent	Number	Percent	Number	Percent
18-plus ..	93,066	59.2	80,310	48.5	101,878	59.9	79,954	46.0
18-19	2,788	34.2	1,468	18.3	2,596	35.1	1,201	16.9
20-24	8,438	42.2	5,671	27.2	8,811	42.8	4,580	23.7
25-34	19,498	54.6	15,667	40.4	21,978	54.5	14,720	35.1
35-44	16,460	64.4	14,676	52.2	19,514	63.5	16,283	49.3
45-54	15,174	67.5	13,350	60.1	15,035	67.5	12,544	54.8
55-64	15,031	71.3	14,141	64.4	15,889	72.1	13,761	62.7
65-74	10,622	69.3	10,312	64.8	11,761	71.8	11,117	65.1
75-plus ..	5,055	57.6	5,024	51.9	6,294	61.2	5,748	54.0

SOURCES: U.S. Bureau of the Census. "Voting and Registration in the Election of November 1980." *Current Population Reports* Series P-20, No. 370 (April 1982).

U.S. Bureau of the Census. "Voting and Registration in the Election of November 1982." *Current Population Reports* Series P-20, No, 383 (November 1983).

U.S. Bureau of the Census. "Voting and Registration in the Election of November 1984." *Current Population Reports* Series P-20, No. 405 (March 1986).

U.S. Bureau of the Census. Unpublished data from the November 1986 Current Population Survey.

FIGURE 2–5

The American Association of Retired Persons (AARP): The Giant Among the 50+ Groups

The American Association of Retired Persons (AARP) has played the giant's role in organizing and representing older Americans. The organization has some 30 million members and adds almost 30,000 new ones every week. At its headquarters in Washington, D.C., AARP staff actively monitor key national and local issues of importance to its constituency: those 50 and over. Through representatives at the federal level and in the state capitals, the group also engages in lobbying efforts to promote the causes it supports. AARP's political stances have had an impact on a number of key legislative votes.

Tip: On legislative issues affecting your marketing to older consumers, look for the AARP position; its influence can be profound.

The Herculean efforts of the AARP have also made many older Americans aware of their individual and collective clout. In addition, one of the organization's current initiatives, AARP/VOTE, should surely do much to further the older American's involvement and influence in the political arena.

AARP/VOTE is a grassroots campaign intended to encourage greater voter participation and heightened public awareness of key legislative issues. While the effort is also seeking to reach younger Americans, its primary focus is on AARP members.

Keep in Mind: In tracking the mature market and identifying the group's needs, AARP is the organization you should monitor most closely.

More and More Clout:
Other Active Organizations

While AARP may be the Goliath of organizations for older Americans, it is certainly not the only group representing this populace. For example, two other groups, the National Council of Senior Citizens and the National Committee to Preserve Social Security and Medicare, rank among the largest nonprofit organizations in America. The National Council has local chapters and has been extremely active in issues of concern to seniors. The National Committee, headed by former Congressman James Roosevelt, is especially vociferous about health care and Social Security matters. Both groups regularly track the voting records of congressmen and report this information to their members through newsletters and other mailings.

Other important organizations include the National Council on the Aging, the Older Women's League, and the Gray Panthers. Maggie Kuhn, the octogenarian leader of the latter group, may well be the female counterpart to Claude Pepper. Through her personal dynamism and dedication, the Gray Panthers has grown to over 100 chapters with more than 80,000 members. Moreover, the group has been very instrumental in effecting governmental, legislative, social, and commercial reforms which combat ageism, promote intergenerational relationships, and protect the older consumer.

Warning: Despite their apparent similarity in purpose, advocacy organizations representing older Americans often have different viewpoints and/or philosophical positions. Therefore, do not make the mistake of assuming one group's agenda necessarily represents that of the other groups or, for that matter, the individual members of the mature market.

Key Point: Your company needs to recognize that the clout of the mature market will only get stronger.

Remember: The aging of the baby boomers will have a staggering effect on the growth of senior power.

What Senior Power Means to the Marketer

What does this trend mean to you? It means that the nation's mature population will have an increasing impact on determining which people are elected or chosen to serve the public's interest and how those individuals may vote on various legislative issues. This, of course, is likely to have a profound effect on the activities and priorities of government, business, and industry. Thus, at both the national and local levels, mature market clout may

- stimulate or squelch your company's business opportunities, and/or
- alter the way in which your company is licensed, regulated, marketed, operated, or financed (especially when serving the mature consumer)

Responding to the Senior Power Trend: A Five-Step Checklist for Marketers

To prosper in an aging America, here are five actions that your company should take:

1. Track the senior organizations' priorities and causes both locally and nationally.
2. Establish an ongoing dialogue with local and national advocacy groups which represent older adults.
3. Identify the key politicians, legislative committees, and government agencies whose focus is on older Americans; monitor their activities and develop active lines of communication with them.
4. Whenever appropriate, assume a proactive and highly visible posture in addressing issues of concern to the mature adult.
5. Strive to flow in the direction of senior power, rather than against it.

Trend 6: Catering to Mature Consumers

For $7.50 a year, a Mature Outlook membership "can make your best years even better." So says the club's brochure, which also mentions that the nominal fee entitles both husband and wife to Mature Outlook magazines and newsletters, travel and vacation discounts, savings on Sears/Allstate products, plus numerous other benefits. What's the catch? Only one . . . you have to be 50 years of age or older to join.

Begun in 1984, Sears' Mature Outlook program has about a million members. But Sears isn't the only business that's reaching out to attract the mature adult. Dozens of organizations have introduced special programs or packages for the older consumer. These marketers are participating in another important trend: the *wooing of the mature market*. I call this trend . . . catering.

Five Reasons Why Businesses Cater to Mature Consumers

Why are businesses catering to the mature consumer? There are at least five good reasons.

1. *The mature market has much discretionary income.* Many advertisers have finally recognized the discretionary spending power held by the age 50 + group. As William B. Strauss, former executive director of Mature Outlook has said, "These people have money and the time to consider what you offer them."[10] His perspective is clearly on target.

2. *Mature adults often have more time to spend their money.* Strauss' comment about older adults having time is another factor prompting businesses to cater to this group. Americans are now living longer and healthier—yet they're retiring earlier.

The travel/leisure industry has certainly recognized this. Numerous hotel chains, cruise operators, airlines, car rental firms, and other businesses have developed special promotional programs for the mature consumer. They know that many 50 + ers have the time to travel and are able to do so during off-peak periods. They also know that mature consumers represent a very important customer base, especially for vacation travel. In fact, the mature market accounts for roughly 80 percent of all pleasure travelers.

Tip: The flexible time schedule available to many members of the mature market lends itself to special promotions during off-season or off-peak time periods.

3. *The 50 + market represents a large customer base.* It is the realization that mature adults are a vital customer segment which is causing businesses like those in travel and leisure to cater to them. In health care, for example, hospitals and medical insurers are offering fantastic programs in an attempt to increase or retain their share of older customers. For example, one hospital in Ohio offers the following free services to members of its seniors club:

- personal financial counseling on health care
- assistance in filling out insurance forms
- subscriptions to health publications
- installation of an emergency response system in the home
- special speedy registration for admission to all of the hospital's services

What's more, members pay nothing to join the club!

The Ohio hospital's program is far from unusual. Similar giveaways can be found in the financial services industry where the mature market contributes a substantial percentage of the money deposited into personal savings and checking accounts.

Warning: The proliferation of these giveaway programs will severely lessen their market impact and any competitive edge sought. This will be especially true in the more urbanized areas.

4. *Mature adults are a large and rapidly growing group of consumers.* The mature market includes more than 62 million people and its ranks will grow rapidly over the next several decades. Thus, we see a variety of companies—from department stores to supermarket chains to real estate developers—offering special promotions, products, and services to the older consumer. A number of these businesses are also developing strategic plans that include specific opportunities to serve a grayer population.

Warning: The unswerving growth of the mature market demands that you develop both a short-term and long-term strategy to serve it.

5. *Mature adults can have a profound influence on legislative and economic developments.* The fifth reason for catering to mature consumers is their growing influence on the political and business climates. This is of special significance to organizations like public utilities, whose rates and activities are regulated by the state. Virtually all gas and electric utility companies have developed special programs for older persons. While these programs are usually intended to help the low-income members of the group, they also serve to enhance a utility's image with other, more activist seniors.

Remember: Providing special services for low-income seniors may, in itself, be a subtle yet effective strategy for wooing other segments of the mature market.

Catering to the Mature Market of the Future

Catering to the mature market will become even more pronounced over the next several years. That's because the five forces which are behind this trend will gain strength. Evidence of this is abounding. In my business activities, I continue to hear from, and assist, more companies who want to initiate perks for the older consumer. I also hear about other companies who want to court this market. Even the mass media are heralding the intensification of this trend as we now see more news coverage of aging issues, reports of new mature market products/services, commercials featuring older adults, and successful TV programs (the "Golden Girls") and films (*Cocoon*) about the over-50 population.

How to Respond to the Catering Trend: Four Suggestions for Marketers

How does your company successfully respond to the catering phenomenon? Here are four suggestions.

1. *Realize that most older consumers will expect to be catered to by the business community.* The myriad of promotional programs now available for the mature market plus the group's growing awareness of its clout will assure this.

Keep in Mind: The baby boomers—a generation of consumers that has always been catered to—will undoubtedly fortify this mindset when they join the mature market.

2. *Plan to do some form of catering.* If your company is to succeed in the mature market, it better plan on doing some form of catering. If you don't, odds are that your rivals will. And, other factors being equal, a *special* program, product, service, or promotion may yield the competitive edge needed to capture a bigger share of this market.

Key Point: Special promotions or programs for the mature market should be carefully researched and planned. They should *not* merely be knee-jerk reactions to competitors' programs. They should be as distinctive as possible so that a unique selling proposition is clearly established. This will be most easily accomplished by shifting the focus away from pricing discounts or giveaways to the special value, benefits, or features of your product or service. The latter will be much more difficult for your competitors to imitate . . . especially within a short time frame.

3. *Recognize the cooperative opportunities offered by this trend.* Courting of the mature market by a variety of industries may also offer your company an opportunity. Specifically, it may enable you to work collaboratively with companies in noncompeting industries who are equally interested in the older consumer.

Warning: As the competition for the mature market gets hotter, this strategy may become more of a necessity than an option.

4. *Be careful about the way in which you cater.* The introduction of special programs and benefits for the mature market has begun to spark some heated debate. At issue is whether or not the public and private sectors are giving away too much to the older generations at the expense of the young.

Caution: If your company also serves the younger consumer, you may have to be very careful in your approach to catering. In the years ahead, it is quite possible that younger customers may react unkindly to companies that offer spectacular discounts and giveaways only to those who are over 50, 60, 65, and so on.

Marketing Checklist: The Six Trends

There are six key trends that will affect your marketing to the mature consumer over the next several years:

1. The number of persons ages 85 and over will increase substantially.

2. The ability of adult children to provide assistance to their parents when in need (i.e., family caregiving) will become increasingly more difficult.

3. More retirees will seek—and find—employment in their later years than ever before.

4. Older persons will become much more knowledgeable, inquisitive, outspoken, and assertive consumers.

5. Mature adults will have an increasingly larger influence in the political and legislative arenas.

6. The business community will continue to develop more promotional programs, products, and services that cater to members of the mature market.

Chapter Wrap-up

To maximize your company's chances for success in marketing to the mature consumer, you must:

- Thoroughly understand and track these six trends.
- Develop short- and long-term responses that capitalize on each trend.
- Adopt (or maintain) a marketing posture that is risk-taking, proactive, progressive, and innovative.

One final thought: In his book, *Megatrends: Ten New Directions Transforming Our Lives*, John Naisbitt advises his readers to make sure they work for a company which has a long-range view of the future. If not, warns Naisbitt, they may find themselves "in a company that is dying in a growing industry."[11] I can think of no better reason why you and your company had better pay close attention to these six mature market trends!

---

1. Dawson, Deborah, Gerry Hendershot, and John Fulton, "Aging in the Eighties: Functional Limitations of Individuals Age 65 Years and Over," *Advance Data Number 133*, National Center for Health Statistics, June 10, 1987.

2. Rovner, Julie, "Long-Term Health Care," *Wilmington News Journal*, June 15, 1986, p. H1.

3. "Family Ties," *American Demographics*, April 1986, p. 11.

4. "Employer Support for Employee Caregivers," *The New York Business Group on Health, Inc. Newsletter*, Volume 6 Number 2.

5. Sifford, Darrell, "Making stress work for you- as it did one author," *The Philadelphia Inquirer*, November 24, 1986, p.2-E.

6. Croft, Nancy L., "It's Never Too Late," *Nation's Business*, September 1986, p. 19.

7. Mediamark Research Inc. (MRI), Spring 1987. Mediamark Research, Inc.

8. Sinclair, Molly, "Champion of the Elderly," *50 Plus*, November 1984, p. 37.

9. Green, Charles, "Congress acts to safeguard Social Security, Medicare," *The Philadelphia Inquirer*, July 23, 1986, p. 4-A.

10. Brown, Paul B., "Last Year It Was Yuppies—This Year It's Their Parents," *Business Week*, March 10, 1986, p. 72.

11. Naisbitt, John. *Megatrends: Ten New Directions Transforming Our Lives*. New York: Warner Books, Inc., 1982, p. 96.

2

The Eight Keys to Successfully Marketing to and Serving Mature Consumers

Without question, your organization will need to have a thorough understanding of the 50+ population and relevant trends to prosper in an aging America. At the core of your efforts, however, must be the adoption of what I call the "eight keys"—eight strategies which, if properly understood and applied, will help you successfully market to and serve the mature consumer.

These eight keys are based upon the genuine success stories of several organizations whose mature market achievements have been exceptional. These nine organizations represent a variety of products, services, and industries. They serve different groups of older customers. They are scattered throughout the United States. Yet, despite their diversity, these organizations have at least three things in common:

1. They have an outstanding record of success in marketing to and/or serving the older consumer.

2. They have an impressive track record of mature market performance.

3. They have applied to perfection one or more of the eight strategies.

The eight keys presented in Part II are not only based upon the lessons learned from these nine exemplary organizations. They also reflect what has been gleaned from a wealth of other information sources including:

- The experiences of clients and colleagues
- Interviews with others involved in developing products, services, and marketing/customer service programs for the mature market
- The tracking of various organizations which have served or employed older adults
- Primary, secondary, and syndicated research studies on the mature market

Within each chapter of Part II, you'll find a profile of one member of our prestigious group of nine success stories. (Chapter 4 discusses *two* of these organizations.) You'll see what each has done to help it capture the mature market. The primary focus, however, will be on *how the application of a specific key* has contributed to the organization's success.

Each chapter also provides strategies, techniques, and suggestions with which to implement the eight keys. Numerous examples demonstrate how several astute marketers have already incorporated some of these recommendations into their marketing programs.

Although application of one or more of these eight keys is critical to mature market success, these strategies should not be perceived as the "last word" in marketing to older consumers. Clearly, this would be an oversimplification; rather, you should look upon each of them as being a fundamental part of any successful mature market program.

Keep in Mind: It is the *execution* of these eight strategies—and not simply an awareness or understanding of them—which will enable your company to prosper in an aging America.

Chapter **3**

Key 1: Emphasize and Demonstrate the Value of Your Product or Service

Airstream, Inc.'s Three-Point Strategy for Successfully Marketing Travel Trailers to Mature Adults

Its recreational vehicles (RVs) are among the most expensive sold in the United States. Prices for its travel trailers range from about $22,000 to $48,000, nearly three times the industry average. The company owns about 70 percent of the luxury end of the travel trailer market. And more than 70 percent of its customers are over 50!

Who is this company? It's Airstream Inc., a subsidiary of Thor Industries in Jackson Center, Ohio. For over 50 years, Airstream's sleek, "silver-bullet" travel trailers have moved down the highways of America . . . and the world. Along with them have traveled some of the most faithful, older customers you'll ever find. In fact, among the company's large number of repeat buyers are a great many above age 70, a few of whom have bought up to eighteen Airstreams.

Airstream's success in developing an affinity between its trailers and the mature market is due to the company's consistent *emphasis and demonstration of the value of its products to the older consumer*: the essence of Key 1.

Airstream has attracted not only the upper-income group to its travel trailers, but the middle-income 50+ers too. Among its RV owners you'll find people who've been schoolteachers, electricians, police officers, and military personnel, as well as doctors, lawyers, and corporate executives.

Airstream has been able to do this by employing a marketing strategy whose foundation is supported by three essential underpinnings:

- product durability
- product quality
- lifestyle fulfillment

These three elements are emphasized in all of the company's promotional efforts and demonstrated by its travel trailers' performance and Airstream's reputation for customer satisfaction.

Steve Krivian, director of marketing services for Airstream, describes these three underpinnings as the points on the ends of a marketing triangle. According to Krivian, these three factors added together form the perception of value and prestige that many mature consumers associate with the Airstream product. Let's briefly examine Airstream's marketing strategy by looking at each of the three critical factors.

1. Product Durability

Over the past 50 years, Airstream has built more than 100,000 RVs. About 60,000 are still on the road. Krivian says a major reason for this is the vehicle's durability. As an example, Airsteam's RVs use far more aluminum than virtually all other travel trailers, which results in less rusting than iron. This enables Airstream's RVs to survive the many tests of time. There are actually a few Airstreams around today that were built in 1936.

In addition, Airstream's travel trailers are assembled in a very exacting and painstaking way. Shunning the mass production process, the company puts each vehicle together in a customized, rigidly controlled manner. As a result, Airstream produces only about 80 travel trailers a month, a number far less than others in the industry. This attention to detail and craftmanship is a powerful marketing tool for emphasizing that Airstream products last longer than its competitors.

The best promoters of this product attribute are the RV owners themselves. Evidence of this is found in the high resale value of the RVs. In fact, a large number of used Airstreams are purchased by first-time buyers who ultimately "move up to" a brand-new Airstream.

2. Product Quality

In a recent questionnaire, Airstream owners were asked what were the most important things which Airstream Inc. had to pay attention to for the next five years. The customers were asked to make their selections from a menu of possible responses including quality, resale value, prestige, durability, comfort, and fuel efficiency. Which factor did they choose most often? *Quality.*

Airstream has learned that product quality is something which is particularly important to older customers. As Krivian points out, "They've had a lifetime of experience in judging what they like and don't like." As a result, the company pays a great deal of attention to this all-important attribute. Airstream has learned which specific attributes are associated with the consumer's perception of quality and has dedicated itself to providing them. (See Figure 3-1.)

Thus, Airstream travel trailers are equipped with such conveniences and creature comforts as a microwave oven, garbage compactor, stereo, TV system, and ice maker. Top-grade materials are used in its RVs such as high-quality wood, which is covered, preserved, and fit to achieve durability, comfort, and aesthetic appeal. The company also backs up its products with an outstanding warranty and service network.

3. Lifestyle Fulfillment

Airstream, Inc.'s founder, Wally Byam, developed a marketing strategy which equated his product with the personal aspirations of its potential buyers: prestige, luxury travel, adventure, development of stronger social ties, and so forth. Thus, an Airstream wasn't perceived as just a piece of hardware, it was considered a reflection of its owner—a way of expressing one's personality, interests, or lifestyle needs.

From this entrepreneurial vision, Airstream has fashioned a marketing program which associates its RVs with the actualization of people's innermost desires. This strategy is manifested in its advertising through the use of such sayings as "building dreams is our business," "making dreams come true since the 1930s," and getting into the Airstream "way of life." (See Figure 3-2.)

Perhaps more than anything else, the Wally Byam Caravan Club demonstrates how those who buy an Airstream RV get more than just a piece of transportation. Created over 30 years ago, the caravan club has more than 18,000 members representing about 60 percent of Airstream's RV owners. (See Figure 3-3.) The club brings together Airstream owners from a myriad of backgrounds and locations to socialize and share their most apparent common interests: travel and Airstreams.

According to Krivian, the Wally Byam Caravan Club has given the customer a strong reason for buying an Airstream which transcends the product's inherent attributes, namely, a social club and a "family" network that provide pleasure to the "empty nesters" after their children have left home. The club and other promotional efforts have played a tremendous role in the company's ability to develop a large and faithful following of older customers.

Putting It All Together

By emphasizing product durability, product quality, and the lifestyle satisfaction which its travel trailers help fulfill, Airstream Inc. has achieved great success in the mature market. To a large extent, this is due to Airstream's

Everywhere you look, you see the Airstream touch.

Don't let the sleek, smooth lines of an Airstream travel trailer fool you. It is the result of over 50 years of experience constantly refining and evolving the design of an Airstream based on the travel experiences of our over 100,000 customers. Airstream's thoughtfulness, ingenuity and efficiency of design may very well surprise you. The result is a level of convenience and sophisticated design unmatched by any other travel trailer.

Like the design of an airplane or luxury boat, Airstream "integrates" its storage and features into our design so that they are carefully hidden by and become part of the total structure. Like the normally hidden "one touch" step — or the power cord storage compartment. Another example most people often aren't aware of is the blanket storage tray located beneath the lift up mattress and above the underbed storage areas of the twin bed 31', 32' and 34' trailers.

You'll find features tucked way in many locations where you might not expect it — like the lock box, or large area under the wardrobe of the 31', 32' and 34' trailers, even under the arm rests of our front lounge.

Dometic
quality leisure line products

FIGURE 3–1

52

Making dreams come true since the 1930's.

Airstream has been making dreams come true since the 1930's. Although the basic concept has never changed, constant innovation and refinement have made today's Airstream motorhomes the best ever — for quality, dependability, and long life.

With an Airstream motorhome, you will discover a freedom you have never known before. You can go where you want, go when you want with no deadlines to meet, no reservations to make. You can enjoy your own food, relax in your own living room, sleep in your own bed. It's like taking your home with you wherever you travel. Of course wherever you take that home, it's nice to know you'll probably find good neighbors — other Airstream owners just like you.

There's simply no better way to travel than motorhoming. And no better value motorhome to travel in than Airstream. Test drive one today and start making your own dreams come true. Airstream. First we set the standard. Now we've raised it.

A. Lake Louise in Canada's Banff National Reserve.
B. Lake Placid, N.Y. hosted the WBCCI International Rally with 3,975 families attending.
C. Touring at Banff Springs, Alberta.

Airstream

Airstream, Inc. • Jackson Center, Ohio 45334 • (513) 596-6111

FIGURE 3–2

FIGURE 3–3   A Wally Byam Caravan Club Outing

recognition that to attract and retain an older customer, a company needs to emphasize and demonstrate the value of its product or service to that customer. As Krivian says, "The mature market is a very sophisticated market. We have a tremendous respect for our customers and their wealth of experience. They've been around and they're savvy—so they know what value and quality are when they go out and make their purchase."

Why Using a "Low Price" Strategy to Attract Mature Consumers May Fall Short of Your Marketing Expectations

Unlike Airstream, Inc., many businesses approach the mature market with the notion that the best way to market to the older customer is by focusing entirely upon the price of their product or service. The most common strategy is to offer the older customer either no-cost or low-cost services. The latter is often in the form of age-related discounts; for example, if you're 55 and over and you shop at Store X, you'll automatically have 10 percent taken off your bill.

In some cases, there may indeed be a sound basis for a low-priced strategy.

For example, offering discounted prices or giveaways can be an effective way to motivate the older customer to try your product or service. It's also a strategy which may be implemented fairly quickly or easily. *But by pursuing this as a singular approach, many marketers face the danger of severely limiting their mature market success.*

Three Factors Beyond Pricing That Influence Older Consumers to Buy

A marketing strategy built solely upon pricing—in particular, low pricing—oversimplifies the decision-making process engaged in by most older consumers. There may be several other factors beyond a product's price that play a role in determining whether the mature consumer will buy what your company sells. Here are three of these factors.

1. *Product attributes.* It is the durability of Airstream's travel trailers which, *in part*, accounts for that product's appeal with the mature market. Durability, however, is but one of many attributes that may affect an older consumer's decision to buy a product or service. Comfort, safety, reliability, and competence are others which may be equally important to those over 50.

The travel/leisure industry provides another good illustration of this. *Example*: In the past few years, luxury van conversions have become quite popular. In addition to amenities like luggage racks, stereo systems, and fancy paint jobs, these vans are noted for such creature comforts as captain's chairs, a couch that unfolds into a bed, and plenty of space for seven or eight people. These features have made the vans a favorite of many members of the mature market.

Convenience and product quality can also be of major importance to the older customer. *Example*: At the Seniors' World Fair in Atlantic City, New Jersey, were a number of exhibitors who were displaying products and services they offered to the older customer. One of the exhibitors was a large, budget hotel chain which had a special promotion for the mature traveler. While I was speaking with a representative from the company, a woman in her sixties approached the exhibit booth. As she read the sign on the exhibit booth, the woman looked at the hotel representative and asked, "Excuse me, you're from Hotel X, right?" The woman from the hotel chain nodded her head in agreeement. The woman then said, "I just want to tell

you that my husband and I—we are seniors—but we do not stay at your hotel." Somewhat surprised, the hotel representative asked why not. "Well,"
the older woman replied, "when my husband and I travel, we like to stay at
places that have good restaurants. We don't like the food at your restaurants."

Taken aback, the woman from the hotel asked, "Well then, where do
you stay?" "My husband and I stay at the Hilton," the older woman re-
marked. "That's a lot more expensive than our hotel," responded the sales
representative. The older woman smiled and said, "I know, but let me point
this out to you. When my husband and I travel in a strange city, we don't like
to wander around at night looking for places to eat. We like to eat in a good
quality restaurant with good service. And we prefer that it be conveniently
located right where we're staying. Because of that, we're willing to spend the
extra money to stay at the Hilton."

2. *Attitudes of the sales or customer service staff.* Having grown up in
an era before self-service gas stations and convenience stores, the older consumer tends to place a high value on customer service. For example, in a
recent study conducted by the AARP, mature adults identified friendliness,
patience, and personal interest of bank employees as very important factors
in their choice of a bank.[1]

A related survey by Payment Systems, Inc. of Tampa, Florida reinforces
this notion. The survey found that persons over 65 with incomes under
$25,000 were almost three times as likely to open their primary checking ac-
count at a bank that showed greater personal concern for its customers than
were an affluent group ages 40 and younger with annual incomes over
$40,000! The younger group was also twice as likely to choose a bank that
had lower fees.[2]

Note: The older customer's high regard for service cuts across a variety
of industries. For example, in a recent retail-oriented survey, mature consumers listed poor customer service as their *number one* shopping barrier.[3]
Studies also indicate that in purchasing food, clothing, home furnishings, or
general merchandise, mature consumers are more concerned with product
attributes and the personal interaction aspect of their shopping experience
than they are with the price of the goods being offered.

3. *Emotional considerations.* Emotional considerations can also influence a mature consumer's buying decision. These include the desire to fulfill
lifelong aspirations, gain prestige, or receive the "royal treatment."

Key Point: These emotional "hot buttons"—striking at the heart of the
individual's innermost desires—are often interwoven into the customer's
perception of product quality. Lavish cruises, health resort vacations, and
luxury auto purchases are manifestations of this phenomenon in the older
customer.

Marketing Checklist: Factors Beyond Price Which May Influence the Mature Consumer's Purchasing Decision

- Product attributes
- Attitudes of sales and customer service employees
- Emotional considerations

Pricing Strategies Can Be Easy to Dislodge

In his book, *Marketing: A Strategic Perspective*, James M. Hulbert presents some important ideas on successful marketing. When discussing pricing strategy, Hulbert makes the point that adding benefits or value is always better than competing on price. This is because only one competitor can be the price leader, and just one competitive breakthrough can destroy that strategy.[4]

This is particularly applicable to the mature market. Today, members of that segment are being offered specially priced benefits by a myriad of marketers. At one time or another, each of these programs was novel. However, most of these discount-type initiatives have since been matched or surpassed by other organizations who jumped on the bandwagon with a "me-too" strategy. Thus, the originator of each program no longer possesses the distinct competitive advantage once held.

This lack of a distinct competitive advantage or unique selling proposition (USP) presents another major problem for the marketer.

Key Point: Without a USP, the older consumer may find it difficult, if not impossible, to differentiate between the marketer's product and other ones offered by competitors.

Example: A somewhat related problem has affected marketers of health maintenance organizations, or HMOs. When the HMO concept was first introduced, all a marketer needed to do to differentiate his product was compare it to traditional indemnity insurance plans (for example, Blue Cross-Blue Shield coverage). The marketer could then point out the advantages of the HMO product . . . in particular, its lower costs.

Now that HMOs have become more widely accepted and available, a marketer must do more than simply distinguish his product from indemnity insurance; he must differentiate it from other HMOs which may be competing in the same market. In addition, he must also differentiate it from the many new indemnity insurance programs which recently have been introduced. Some of these programs are equal to or less than the cost of an HMO product.

Unfortunately, most HMO marketers have not done this, thereby creating what Arthur Sturm of the Sturm Communications Group in Chicago calls the "Vanilla Ice Cream Phenomenon," or VICP.[5] In highly saturated markets, the VICP has also made it difficult for some HMOs to market their special insurance programs for age 65+ individuals. Under such circumstances, many seniors have found it hard to "sort out" all the differences among the competing HMOs.

Caution: By focusing on a price-oriented mature market strategy, marketers may subject themselves to at least four potential problems:

1. They may give the mature consumer little information from which to distinguish their product/service in a highly competitive and glutted marketplace.

2. They run the risk of generating confusion in the mind of the mature consumer about their product's benefits and attributes.

3. They diminish or obscure the value of any other special features or benefits their product or service may offer to the mature consumer.

4. Even if they are the first to introduce a "lowest-price" strategy, their leadership status may be derailed when competitors hop on the "me-too" bandwagon.

Keep in Mind: A mature market strategy which focuses solely on low pricing is also unlikely to build loyalty among the older consumers it attracts. This is because *the older consumers most drawn to low-priced products, services, or retailers tend to be those with lower incomes.* Unless they are given some other reason to use what you have to offer, these individuals will—out of sheer economic necessity—change brands or stores as soon as they can find a better price someplace else.

Some Older Consumers Are Suspicious of the Special Price Breaks

Example: A marketer attending one of my midwest seminars described the aerobics program her health care center had developed for retirees in the community. The program charged $1 admission for each of 14 aerobics classes attended. The organization thought the nominal fee was an appropriate one to charge the older persons for this activity.

Much to the center's surprise, however, community residents did not respond to the low fee. In fact, no one showed up for the classes until the fee was raised! Why? When the retirees heard about the program's low fee, they apparently began to question how good it was. Thus, the "no-show" response.

Such a reaction to special giveaways and deep discounts shouldn't come as a surprise. Many mature consumers associate low-budget prices with products of dubious quality. For these shoppers, it's worth paying more if you can be certain you'll be receiving quality.

Value: The Road to Long-Term Success

Several potential dangers and limitations are posed by a mature market strategy which is singularly focused on pricing. Frank Forbes, director of membership services operations for the American Association of Retired Persons (AARP) comments: "I think seniors today are looking for value. Certainly they are looking for a fair price. But I think that they are willing to weigh the value in its total context and not just look at value in terms of price alone. And it seems to me that the worst sham possible is to sacrifice quality for a price."[6]

Forbes ought to know. He and his staff oversee the activities of service providers that offer products and services to AARP's 30 + million members.

Key Point: To succeed in the mature market over the long haul, your company will have to place its emphasis on your product's value to the older customer. This is particularly true if you expect to capture the most coveted of older consumers . . . those with a substantial amount of discretionary income.

Remember: The more affluent and more educated members of the mature market possess spending power and consumer skills which allow them to be among the most discriminating of shoppers. For this group, price is—and will be—only one of many measures used to determine if your product is worth buying. Such buying behavior will undoubtedly characterize many of tomorrow's mature consumers as well.

How to Emphasize and Demonstrate Your Product's Value to Mature Consumers

Make Customer Service a Top Priority

While a low price may stimulate many older consumers to try your product, it is unlikely that you'll build brand loyalty if that's all you have to offer. Providing the mature market with outstanding customer service, however, can make a difference. Here are a few suggestions on how you can improve or enhance your customer service.

Provide Employee Training

Members of your sales and service staffs need to be educated on how to best serve the older customer. Companies like Ramada Inns and Publix Supermarkets are among those that have provided such specialized training or guidance. Ramada, for example, has produced a videotape which highlights ways in which the hotel chain's employees can better serve the mature traveler. At Publix, employees are instructed on how to make things easier for the older shopper. This includes teaching checkout clerks to give some of the stores' older customers two light bags to carry their groceries in rather than just one heavy one.

Offer In-Depth Information and Guidance

In today's rapidly changing marketplace, consumers are being barraged with an array of product and service options from which to choose.

Key Point: It is more important than ever for your company to explain to older consumers how your product or service works, what makes your product different, and what it can do for the customer.

Example: One organization that has done this is the Fallon Community Health Plan, an HMO in Worcester, Massachusetts. Before enrolling older persons in its "Senior Plan," Fallon's staff takes the time to educate them about the program's strengths and weaknesses. By utilizing this approach, Fallon creates reasonable expectations about what the program can and cannot do. Not surprisingly, Senior Plan has had a high level of customer satisfaction and a very low dropout rate. It also has more members than any other plan of its kind in New England.[7]

Provide Easily Accessible Toll-Free Numbers

One way to show your commitment to serving the older customer in the best way possible is to install toll-free lines, which can be used to provide product information and to take complaints. They should be properly and adequately staffed and operate during convenient hours of the day.

Example: Whirlpool Corporation offers a toll-free COOL-LINE 24 hours a day to answer consumer questions. The company receives numerous calls from older adults. The comments made by many seniors prompted Whirlpool to modify some of its appliances so they could be easier to operate for those with limitations in strength or vision.[8]

Demonstrate Care and Interest *After* the Service Is Delivered

In his book, *The IBM Way*, Buck Rodgers, former vice president of marketing at IBM, advises readers to work hard to get a new customer, but to work *even harder* to hold a customer.[9] Indeed, one of the major reasons behind IBM's success has been its ability to provide a high level of service *after* the sale.

Older customers are especially appreciative of efforts to ascertain their satisfaction with your product or service. There are many creative and unobtrusive ways to do this. *Example:* Presbyterian Hospital in Albuquerque, New Mexico has used what it calls "after-care cards." These personalized notes are sent to the hospital's post-operative patients (many of whom are over 50) soon after their discharge. The card gives the names of nurses whom the individual (or his family) can call if he or she has any concerns or questions. This program has been extremely well received by the hospital's patients and nurses.

Example: Grand Circle Travel offers another example of how interest in the older consumer can be shown after the service has been delivered. The tour operator asks each of its travelers to complete an evaluation form (citing both the negative and the positive) at the end of his or her trip. This kind of "after-care" concern may, in part, explain why Grand Circle has been able to successfully serve the mature traveler for almost 30 years.

Encourage the Mature Market to Experience the Value of Your Product or Service

There are a number of techniques you can employ to stimulate the older customer to use (and reuse) your product or service. Here are a few ideas:

Free Trials. Providing taste tests, product samples, or product demonstrations is an effective technique. General Foods' Sanka® beverage is frequently offered to older persons who attend large seniors' events such as AARP conventions and retirement expos. Thorneburg Hosiery Co. of North Carolina offers older adults a free pair of its Thor-Lo® Padds® socks if they participate in its HealthWalk program.

Special Distribution Systems. By using toll-free telephone numbers, home delivery, or conveniently situated retail locations, you can also make it easier for the older adult to experience your product. Medicine Shoppe, Inc. in St. Louis, for instance, typically locates its drug stores near supermarkets or post offices: places where older customers frequently visit. General Foods, meanwhile, has run promotions in which it sends a free one-ounce sample jar of its Brim Roasted Buds® decaffeinated coffee directly to the older shopper's door if he or she calls a special toll-free number.

Incentives for Product Loyalty. By rewarding those who use your product or service, you'll also increase the likelihood that older customers will use and reuse what you have to offer. *Example:* Senior Vacation Hotels of St. Petersburg, Florida allows its repeat travelers to become members of its "exclusive Alumni Club." Members receive special treatment including free trips to local attractions, free TVs for their room, and complimentary tickets to dinner theaters. This is one of the reasons why the vast majority of the hotel's business comes from repeat guests.

Coupons. As a group, older consumers are large coupon clippers and users. A number of consumer packaged goods manufacturers have been successful in using this approach.

Marketing Checklist: How to Make It Easy for the Older Customer to Experience Your Product's Value

- Free trials
- Special distribution systems
- Incentives for product loyalty
- Coupons

Use a "Value-Added" Approach

Your product or service will command greater value to the mature adult if you can show that, in buying it, the customer will receive other tangible or intangible benefits. Several organizations have developed special programs which revolve around this "value-added" approach. For example, "Lifestyle Members" of Gateway Federal Savings and Loan's "The Statesman's Club" (in Cincinnati) may gain access to an IBM personal computer, a software program that helps plan and monitor the budget, financial planning seminars, a lending library, and a host of other benefits. While this club isn't limited to those over 50, the large account balances required for membership tend to attract older depositors.

Important Point: Value-added benefits need *not* be limited to club-oriented programs. In fact, they can be tied into a specific product or service just as well.

Stress the Special Capabilities of Your Product and/or Your Organization

Make the mature consumer aware of what special capabilities your products and/or your organization have. One good way to do this, of course, is through advertising. The ad in Figure 3-4 demonstrates how this can be done. It features Heinz's Alba High Calcium Hot Cocoa®. This ad—which was quite successful for Heinz—places its emphasis on several important qualities of Alba:

1. It has more calcium than the leading hot cocoas.
2. It is low in calories.
3. It tastes delicious.
4. It is good for your bones.

Keep in Mind: An emphasis on bringing about positive, healthful outcomes or experiences represents an excellent way to demonstrate the value of your product or service to the older consumer.

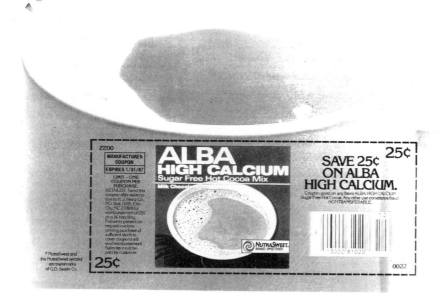

Great taste that's good to the bone.

If you're a woman over the age of 45, you need 1000 to 1500 milligrams of calcium a day to keep your bones strong.

Unfortunately, one out of two women your age receives less than 70% of that requirement.

FOODS HIGH IN CALCIUM	SIZE	CALCIUM	CALORIES
ALBA HIGH CALCIUM	1 cup	323 mg.	60
Skim Milk	1 cup	302 mg.	86
Whole Milk	1 cup	291 mg.	150
Plain Yogurt	8 oz.	274 mg.	139
Cheddar Cheese	1 oz.	204 mg.	114
Ice Cream	1 cup	176 mg.	269

That's where delicious ALBA® HIGH CALCIUM hot cocoa can help.

We changed the name to ALBA HIGH CALCIUM, because it's the only hot cocoa that has more calcium than an 8-ounce glass of milk. In fact, it has more than *twice* the calcium of the leading hot cocoas.

Perhaps best of all, ALBA HIGH CALCIUM is sweetened with *NutraSweet*.* So you get a healthy dose of calcium and a rich, chocolate taste for just 60 calories.

Treat yourself to ALBA HIGH CALCIUM. It's the only hot cocoa this good, to the bone.

The delicious source of calcium.

Heinz

FIGURE 3–4

Actively Support Pro-Consumer Organizations

By associating or working with pro-consumer groups, your company gains several advantages.

- You may learn more about the older consumer's specific needs and concerns.

- You may improve your customer service capabilities.
- You may enhance your reputation in the eyes of the mature market.

The latter benefit has frequently been observed in the focus groups in which I've participated. During many of these groups, participants have elevated the credibility and trustworthiness of a business simply because it has some connection to an advocacy organization representing older Americans.

Tip: Prime examples of groups worth affiliating with are the Society of Consumer Affairs Professionals (SOCAP) and local area agencies on aging.

Example: One company that has done an excellent job in working with consumer advocacy organizations on older adult initiatives is Florida Power and Light (FP&L). In addition to working on projects with such pro-consumer groups as the Better Business Bureau, the State Attorney General's Office, and the Red Cross, FP&L has frequently collaborated with the Florida State and County Offices on Aging. Like the "Information and Referral Brochure" it developed with the Area Agency on Aging of Broward County, *many of FP&L's projects are designed to help older Floridians be more informed consumers.* In addition, several of FP&L's employees are also members of SOCAP.

Marketing Checklist: Five Ways to Emphasize and Demonstrate Your Product or Service's Value to the Mature Consumer

1. Make customer service a top priority.
2. Make it easy for the mature consumer to *experience* the value of your product or service.
3. Give the older customer something more than just your product or service.
4. Promote the special capabilities of your product and/or your organization.
5. Actively support organizations which are committed to assisting the consumer . . . especially the older consumer.

Chapter Wrap-up

For your company to achieve long-term mature market success, you must *emphasize and demonstrate the value* of your product or service to the older consumer. By pursuing this strategy, you will:

1. Build customer loyalty.

2. Avoid the pitfalls and limitations of a price-focused strategy.

3. Attract and serve those segments of the mature market most likely to bring you the greatest financial success (the middle and upper income 50+ers).

A few more words about item number 3. Obviously, it is vitally important that the consumer needs of the lower income members of the mature market be met as well. If businesses are to do this, however, most of them will have to develop and maintain profitable product lines that serve other consumer groups. This includes the other members of the mature market.

Keep in Mind: By offering special discounts to older consumers, marketers may be establishing an unwise precedent. Should the 76-million baby boomers expect—and obtain—such discounts when they get older, these marketers may find it difficult to serve enough regular-paying customers to make their businesses profitable.

---

1. *Older Bank Customers: An Expanding Market* (Leader's Guide). Washington, D.C.: American Bankers Association, 1985.

2. Edmondson, Brad, "Grumpies at Chase Manhattan," *American Demographics*, February 1987, p. 20.

3. St. Clair, Jeffrey J. *Changing Perspectives on the Mature Consumer Market: An Executive Summary*. Columbus, Ohio: Meretrends/Retail Planning Associates, Inc./Ernst & Whinney, 1988.

4. Hulbert, James M. *Marketing: A Strategic Perspective*. Katonah, NY: Impact Publishing Company, 1985.

5. Sturm, Arthur, "Time for Move to Chocolate HMO," *Advertising Age*, September 15, 1986, p. 48

6. Personal telephone conversation with Frank Forbes, June 1987.

7. Personal telephone conversation with Christy W. Bell, executive director of Fallon Community Health Plan, February 1988.

8. "Ways to Keep Senior Customers Happy," *Selling To Seniors*, October 1987, p. 4.

9. Rodgers, Buck. *The IBM Way*. New York: Harper & Row, 1986.

Chapter **4**

Key 2: Address the Needs and Concerns of the Mature Consumer

Two Success Stories: Companies Who Found a Niche in the Mature Market

At first glance, they appear to be markedly dissimilar. One is a clothing manufacturer, and the other, a mail-order company. One has 32,000 employees, and the other, has less than 100. One began doing business in 1850, and the other began in 1982. One is on the East Coast, the other, in California.

Yet for all their differences, these two companies share at least three major things in common. First, they have identified a similar need among mature consumers. Second, they have met that need with a fine group of products. Third, they have achieved outstanding mature market success.

Who are these companies? Comfortably Yours® and Levi Strauss & Co. Together, they represent classic examples of how both businesses and older customers can profit when marketers employ Key 2: address the needs and concerns of the mature consumer. Let's look at how each of these companies has applied this strategy to perfection.

Comfortably Yours: Products That Guarantee "Comfort" to the Consumer

In the early 1980s Elaine Adler perceived an unmet need. She was looking for a birthday gift for her mother who would soon be 80. But in searching through various catalogs, Ms. Adler discovered that there were very few items appropriate for a woman her mother's age. Most of the catalog items were emphasizing stylishness; what her mother really needed was something to make her more *comfortable*.

Determined to meet this need and armed with her previous direct marketing experience, Elaine Adler began Comfortably Yours in 1982, mailing a 32-page booklet to 250,000 prospective buyers. Today more than 22 million Comfortably Yours catalogs are sent out each year. Each contains about 50 pages and identifies more than 300 products. And company sales—about $300,000 in the fall of 1982—now equal nearly $18 million a year.

Over 1 million people have bought Comfortably Yours' products. Of this group, about 60 percent are members of the mature market. In addition, many of the company's younger customers have not only purchased Comfortably Yours' products for themselves . . . but for their age 50 + parents as well.

Product Line with Unique Distinctions

Comfortably Yours' products are intended for those who want the make the activities of daily living easier, healthier, and safer. But the major benefit offered by its products is comfort. Indeed, the company guarantees it!

Products are geared to a variety of groups. For the pregnant woman, there's a cushiony, twin-pillow set to make sitting or sleeping easier. For concerned parents, there's a transportable intercom unit to monitor the activities of the newborn baby. For men on the go, there's a non-fog mirror which makes it possible to shave while showering.

Although most products in the Comfortably Yours' catalog can be used by younger adults, many of the items it offers are of greatest benefit to older consumers. This is because these products are best suited for people who've experienced such health problems as arthritis, declining vision or strength, frequent back pain, and reduced mobility or circulation. Such problems are much more likely to occur with aging.

The company's catalog features numerous products to help compensate for physical limitations. For example. because arthritis can impair manual dexterity and strength, Comfortably Yours® features a number of products with Velcro tabs for easier closing. Catalogs have also offered BIOCURVE™ pens specially designed to make it easier to write and deep-grooved rubber grips to make it easier to turn door knobs. (See Figure 4-1.) Other products have included lightweight snippers and large-handled scissors to permit easy cutting, and rubberized gloves that make it easy to grip anything from a jar lid to a rake. (See Figure 4-2.)

Sensitivity to Customer Needs

Comfortably Yours' success in serving older customers has been built on more than just providing specialized products that serve that group. It has also been a result of the company's ongoing sensitivity to the needs of the

FIGURE 4–1 Comfortably Yours Biocurve™ Pen

older adult market. Products like the rubberized gloves, for example, have been introduced based upon customer requests. In fact, Comfortably Yours was the first mail-order company to offer incontinence products . . . something also prompted by customer letters.

Other products sold by the company have been developed by persons with specialized health needs. One such product is the Exer-Trim™. This device is an exercise platform constructed of solid wood and foam rubber. De-

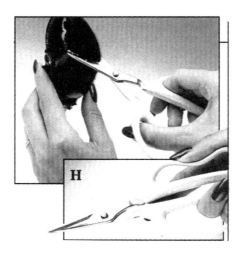

FIGURE 4–2 Comfortably Yours Scissors

signed by a man who had undergone bypass surgery, the Exer-Trim™ allows the user to walk or run on it while being cushioned against the impact stress which can cause knee and back injuries. According to Louisa Budd, Ms. Adler's long-time assistant, the Exer-Trim™ is made for an older person because it is "geared toward someone who really doesn't want to go on a treadmill or bounce on a rebounder." The popular product is a classic example of how Comfortably Yours has addressed the needs of those who want to exercise but who must contend with physical limitations.

Sensitivity to the needs and concerns of older customers also extends to the innovative layout and copy found in Comfortably Yours' catalogs. From the beginning, this has been Elaine Adler's mandate. The catalogs use large print type to make it easier for people to read. In addition, products are organized by "comfort" categories (such as "Travel Comforts" and "Health and Exercise Comforts") to make them easier to find.

Lengthy descriptions of each item are also provided in the catalogs to help the reader understand more easily what the product is and the purpose that it serves. Graphics and conversational copy are used to present the products in an upbeat, informative way. This latter technique helps people feel comfortable with their need for some of the specialized items offered . . . items which some catalogs have described in a way that makes people feel disabled . . . even if they are not.

Marketers seeking to emulate Comfortably Yours' mature market success would do well to read the following words, excerpted from a letter Ms. Adler wrote to her customers in one of Comfortably Yours' catalogs:

> Thank you for telling me how you feel about our products and service. Roberta, Lee, Kitty, and Joanne are just a few of our ladies who were recently complimented for the way they 'helped' you. I am proud to say all my staff are attuned to your needs.
>
> I try to respond to all my personal mail. I learn a lot from all of your comments and understand some of your particular needs.

Levi Strauss & Co.: Dressing Comfortably for Older Males

In 1978, Levi Strauss & Co. conducted a nationwide market research study to establish a profile of the American male apparel purchaser. From this study, a major consumer segment emerged which accounted for about 25 percent of the male population in America. Unlike Levi's faithful clan of denim jeans customers, this group purchased large quantities of dress slacks. Primarily over the age of 45, these men were also much older than the denim loyalists.

From the results of the survey, Levi's was able to ascertain the needs of this large group of older male shoppers. They were men looking for comfortable, easy-to-care-for slacks at reasonable prices. Other characteristics of this older dress slacks consumer also surfaced from the survey. For example, the profile identified him as a mainstream individual who was

- value conscious
- not a fashion maven, but someone who *did* want to look neat
- interested in wearing traditional-looking slacks with conservative colors like navy, tan, and gray
- interested in wearing slacks for both work and social occasions

After closely examining these findings, Levi's began the task of filling the apparel needs of this huge potential customer base. It was out of this research and development process that Levi's® Action Slacks were introduced in 1978.

Meeting the Needs for Comfort and Easy Care

Action Slacks were designed with the older male's expressed desire for comfort kept clearly in mind. As a result, Action Slacks were specially cut for the less lean, mature body. The pants were made to "give" or stretch with an expandable waistband and fabric that enabled the wearer to sit or move around easily in them.

In keeping with the second major need voiced by the identified consumer segment, Action Slacks were made so they would be easy to care for. Thus, the slacks were designed so they could be put in the washing machine but still come out looking as if they'd been dry cleaned. Other preferences stated by the prospective older buyer were also met. For example, the slacks were offered in traditional fabric colors. They were also reasonably priced: higher than the cost of low-budget brands, but well below the cost of the designer labels.

Levi's also positioned Action Slacks to be consistent with the major needs expressed by its would-be purchasers. Promotional copy placed a major emphasis on the slacks' level of comfort. Advertisements declared "these may be the most comfortable slacks you've ever worn." To this day, that message remains the mainstay of the Action Slacks' advertising campaign. (See Figure 4-3.)

Back in 1978, millions of men's dress slacks were sold in America. Very few of them, however, were Levi's. Today, Levi Strauss & Co. owns one of the largest shares of the men's dress slack market, with Action Slacks accounting for $100 million in company sales annually. More than five million pairs of Action Slacks are sold each year and over 75 million pairs have been sold since they were first introduced. While a significant number of these slacks have been purchased by younger men, by far the largest group of customers has been men over 45.

What has been the basis for Levi Strauss' outstanding achievement? First, the company identified some unmet needs felt primarily by a large number of mature consumers, in this case, men. As Steve Goldstein, a director of consumer marketing for Levi's, says, "We saw a void in a product cate-

Levi's® Action Slacks are top performers

Comfort, style, and lasting good looks—that's what you want in slacks you can look and feel good in, day in and day out. And because the soil resistant Visa® fabric is Sta-Prest,® the creases in these Levi's Action Slacks stay just-pressed perfect, washing after washing. Tailored with a unique hidden Action waistband, these may be the most comfortable slacks you've ever worn. And they come in so many colors, only the fit and comfort are the same every day.

$00

FIGURE 4–3

gory which would bring two very important attributes to this older, maturing market segment. Attribute number one was comfort and attribute number two was ease of care." Second, Levi's designed and marketed products which fulfilled those needs in a consistently superior way.

It is this two-step process: identifying the special needs of older consumers—and fulfilling them well—which helps breed mature market success.

Ten Needs and Concerns of the Mature Market

Given the heterogeneity of the mature market, it is impossible to lump together a menu of common needs and concerns applicable to the entire 50 + population. But it *is* possible to identify several needs and concerns which are likely to be felt—at one time or another —by a large number of older adults.

Here are ten of these needs. You'll also find examples of organizations that have—in one way or another—developed programs, products, or services to meet those needs. These organizations range from nonprofit associations to "Mom-and-Pop" businesses to Fortune 500 companies.

Keep these three thoughts in mind:

- These needs are certainly not the only ones felt by individual older adults; they are, however, among the most important and the most prevalent needs of the overall 50 + population.
- Each of these ten needs represents a relatively untapped window of opportunity.
- The number of 50 + ers having these needs should be even greater in the years ahead.

1. Adjustment to Life in the Later Years

Increasing life expectancy and the continuing trend toward early retirement have resulted in a growing need for older adults to plan for, and adjust to, their later years of life. This is particularly important since many people may now look forward to spending more years of their lives in retirement than in any other phase of life.

While many persons adapt well to life in the "second 50" (as Roger Enberg of the Institute of Medicine at the National Academy of Sciences calls it), others find the going is tough. In his book *Success Over 60*, Albert M. Myers says most people who have not adequately prepared for their golden years will die within six years of their retirement.[1]

It isn't just retirees who may face emotional difficulties in the later years. Spouses of retirees, widows and widowers, and other unmarrieds may also find this period unsettling if they're not prepared to handle it. For many older women this may pose a particular challenge, since the typical American wife may expect to outlive her husband by at least seven years.

Healthwise, Inc. of Boise, Idaho is one organization that has developed programs to help older Americans function well during their retirement years.

Example: One Healthwise program, Growing Wiser, is especially designed to promote mental well-being. Through the use of workshops and a training manual, Growing Wiser helps attendees:

- improve and protect their memory
- maintain a high level of mental vitality
- cope with life changes and the loss of loved ones
- communicate more effectively
- maintain their independence

Growing Wiser has been presented through various hospitals and community organizations. The program has earned several prestigious awards including the 1986 U.S. Department of Health and Human Service's Community Health Promotion award.

2. Money Management/Financial Security

Most members of the mature market will begin to experience a decline in median income after the peak earning years, ages 45-54. This drop in income is either generated, or furthered, by retirement from the work force.

With the reduction in income, money management and financial security become major concerns for many mature adults. For example, the 1985 Prime Life Generation survey of Americans ages 50-64 found that a majority of those polled were worried that inflation would reduce their standard of living during retirement.[2] Indeed, inflation, declining health, loss of a spouse, and changes in Social Security, Medicare, or pension benefits are all potential events that can seriously jeopardize one's security and independence in the later years.

Two organizations that have sought to help the mature market better manage its money are the National Council on Aging (NCOA) and Puget Sound Savings Bank in Seattle, Washington. NCOA has provided valuable information on financial management to mid-life women through its "Facing Our Future" workshops. These workshops have been held around the country and feature discussions on such money matters as IRAs and pensions, savings and small investments, budgeting and the financial aspects of divorce, widowhood, and retirement.

NCOA's targeting of mature women makes good sense for at least three reasons:

- Older women tend to worry more about their finances than men.
- Many older women are less familiar with money management since that task has typically been delegated to the adult male.
- Older women stand a much greater chance of having to manage money in the later years of life because of their longer life expectancy.

Note: Separation or divorce after age 50 can also create money management problems for older women (for example, those who become part of the "displaced homemaker" group).

Since 1984, Savings Bank of Puget Sound has conducted year-round public seminars and workshops on money management for mature consumers within its service areas. These seminars, along with a quarterly newsletter, counsel older adults on such financial matters as estate planning, understanding annuities, protecting assets during health care crises, and comprehending the impact of tax changes.

3. Home Maintenance Services

The majority of older adults prefer to remain in their own homes throughout the retirement years, and most of them do. For many of these individuals, maintaining a home can be a major problem. To begin with, older persons tend to live in older homes. Such homes generally require more upkeep and repair. Then, too, the physical demands of home maintenance, particularly external tasks (such as painting, lawn care, and snow removal), become extremely difficult. Finally, many older homeowners are women who live alone. They may lack the health, strength, or mechanical skills necessary to maintain their homes.

Example: Geri-Pare is a private, nonprofit agency based in Brooklyn, New York, which assists older people in need of minor home repairs and modifications. Geri-Pare utilizes retirees to perform a variety of tasks including replacing door locks, installing grab bars, fixing minor plumbing leaks, repairing small appliances, and lowering light switches.

4. Transportation Services

As they age, many older persons find their transportation needs increase significantly. For some, declining health means they can no longer drive, or that they can drive only on a limited basis (such as during the day). For others, alternative forms of transportation (like buses and cabs) may be too costly, too infrequent, or unavailable. Regardless of the reason, transportation problems make it very difficult for a large number of older adults who need to do such things as see their families, go food shopping, visit doctors, or run errands.

Example: C-PALS is a privately held, Iowa-based company that seeks to solve the transportation needs of the older population. C-PALS' customers are each escorted by a licensed chauffeur who not only takes them where they want to go but also performs minor chores like carrying in the groceries or taking out the trash. Individuals pay a fixed annual fee which entitles them to use C-PALS' services on a 24-hour basis up to three times a week. Additional fees are charged for excess waiting time or the handling of heavier chores.

5. Legal Assistance

Overall, the 50+ group's need for legal guidance transcends that of the younger population. Aside from such generic situations as civil suits, divorces, and real estate settlements, members of the mature market are liable to have certain age-related legal needs. These include setting up trusts, writing or revising wills, handling age discrimination problems, drawing up prenuptial agreements for second marriages, or tackling Social Security benefits disputes. In addition, adult children may also need assistance in obtaining the power of attorney for an older parent, or in settling a difficult estate.

In recognizing the specialized and increasing legal needs and concerns of a growing older population, a few firms have set up businesses which specialize in "elder law." *Example:* Through its two California-based offices, Gilfix Associates provides legal counsel to 50+ers and their adult children especially in the area of estate planning. More than 70 percent of the firm's clients are over the age of 50.

6. Companionship

The likelihood of being single becomes much greater after 50 due to separation, divorce, or death. This is especially true for women. For many mature adults, the desire to find a companion with whom they can live, socialize, and/or travel is strong. A number of creative programs have sprung up in order to fill this need.

Example: People Match is a program that was established in 1983 by Heritage Home Health, a for-profit home health agency in Bristol, New Hampshire. People Match uses a videotape and a sophisticated questionnaire to match home seekers with older homeowners who live alone. The home seekers may be young or old. Users of People Match pay a $300 fee for the service. The program has assisted many persons and has also generated additional business for Heritage's primary service . . . home health care.

Example: Travel Companion Exchange, Inc. (TCE) of Amityville, New York has been matching up single travelers for several years. About half of its members are over 50. In exchange for an annual fee, members of TCE can choose potential travel mates based on listings in the firm's newsletter. Like People Match, TCE uses personality profiles to facilitate the selection of companions. Interestingly, the majority of TCE's pairings are between men and women rather than travel partners of the same sex!

7. Health Care Services and Programs

On average, the 50+ age group utilizes more health care services than does the rest of the population. This is especially true of those over 75. For this reason, members of the mature market may, at one time or another, be in need of a wide range of health care services and products provided by physicians, pharamacists, nurses, hospitals, home health agencies, nursing homes, and medical equipment suppliers.

In addition to these acute and long-term care services and products, health prevention and promotion activities are of major importance to the over-50 population. The benefits of such activities have clearly been documented. In one longitudinal study of some 17,000 Harvard alumni, for example, Dr. Ralph Paffenbarger of the Stanford University School of Medicine and his team of researchers found that regular exercise can extend life by about two years. The study's results also proved that regular exercise decreases the risk of mortality from all diseases.[3]

While many businesses are treating the 50+ population's acute and long-term health care needs, a much smaller group of organizations is presently filling the mature market's fitness-related needs.

Example: One organization that is doing this is the Newport Athletic úlub (NAC) in Newport, Rhode Island. NAC has established an "Inner Circle" club for mature adults. For the cost of an initiation fee and monthly dues, the club offers exercise programs developed especially for its members. These include water exercise classes and low-impact, slower-paced aerobics classes. The club's marketing director also makes presentations on fitness to local seniors groups.

8. Adaptive Products

As Comfortably Yours and Levi Strauss & Co. illustrate, there is a significant number of older persons who can benefit from products that are slightly modified to suit their specialized needs. In one study funded by the Administration on Aging, Martech Associates and the Gallup Organization found that noninstitutionalized persons ages 55+ identified several problem areas of daily living. All of these lend themselves to the development of adaptive products.[4] The most common of these problems included:

- Opening medicine packages
- Reading product labels

- Reaching high things
- Fastening buttons, snaps, or zippers
- Vacuuming or dusting
- Walking up and down stairs
- Cleaning bathtubs and sinks
- Washing and waxing floors
- Carrying purchases home

Several businesses have already introduced adaptive products which respond to older market needs. In recognition of the large number of mature adults with visual problems, G.K. Hall began marketing large-print books in 1971. Since then, other companies, including Doubleday & Company and Senior Service Corporation, have become large-print book publishers. Similarly, Whirlpool Corporation's "Customized Series" line of washers and dryers features large-size graphics for controls and knobs as well as instructions printed in large type. These appliances, originally intended to help those with visual limitations, have been well received by the entire population.

Keep in Mind: Many adaptive products, if properly designed, can have universal appeal and so can be successfully marketed to all consumers.

Other companies such as Wilson Sporting Goods (easy-grip golf clubs), Oreck Corporation (lightweight vacuum cleaners), AT&T (handsets that increase the volume of an incoming voice), and Selchow-Righter (large-sized tiles for its Scrabble® game) have also developed and marketed modified products to meet needs that are felt most commonly by members of the mature market.

9. Medical Insurance/Medical Information

Because they are more likely to require health care services than are younger persons, those over 50 must be protected against the cost of major medical expenses. This need is particularly great among those under age 65 who lack employer-provided insurance. It is also necessary for most Medicare enrollees, the majority of whom are over 65. Although Medicare covers most of the 65+ group, it typically pays for less than half of the older adult's medical expenses. Therefore, the majority of Medicare eligibles need to purchase additional "Medigap" coverage.

While Medigap insurance covers some of the expenses not paid for by Medicare, there are other, sizable expenses for which it provides no coverage. Included among these noncovered services are the costs associated with a long-term nursing stay. In fact, more than 500,000 Americans drop below the poverty line each year because of these costs.

A number of health insurers have developed policies which help insure against the cost of a long-term nursing home stay.

Example: Pioneers in this field were Acsia Insurance Services of Daly City, California and AMEX Life Assurance Company (formerly Firemen's Fund American Life Insurance Company). Back in 1974, Acsia saw the gap in nursing home coverage and developed a policy to fill it. Through the assistance and expertise of underwriter, AMEX, Acsia now markets its insurance product in more than 40 states. With over 60,000 policyholders, Acsia and AMEX rank among the industry leaders in selling this form of this insurance protection.[5]

Most older consumers are also in need of information which can help them sort out the ever-increasing variety of health care options and insurance programs available.

Example: One organization which has made a consistent effort to do this is The People's Medical Society of Emmaus, Pennyslvania. Founded in 1983, the society publishes newsletters, booklets, and books on health care consumerism and prudent health care shopping. Well over half of the group's 50,000 members are over age 50.

10. Special Diets

Changes in lifestyle, health, and/or family size are likely to bring about the mature adult's need to observe a new or modified dietary regimen. According to a study by the Campbell's Soup Company, a number of concerns influence the older consumer's dietary needs and food preferences.[6] These include the desire to

- maintain good health and independence
- control various health problems (such as hypertension, diabetes, and cholesterol)
- minimize food preparation time
- purchase appropriately sized portions

All of the above concerns create an expanding need for a wide range of food and beverage products. Several food manufacturers, including Campbell's (for example, its reduced-salt soups), have developed products with the older dieter in mind. Libby, McNeil and Libby Co.'s line of low-sugar fruits, "Libby Lite®," has been very successful with the mature market. Denny's restaurants have also fared well with their low-cholesterol, smaller-portion menu choices. And the Kroger Company supermarket chain has found the mature market receptive to its innovative marketing of precooked meats, which offer purchasers convenience as well as smaller portion sizes.

Marketing Checklist: Ten Mature Market Needs

1. Adjustment to life in the later years
2. Money management/financial security

   3. Home maintenance services
   4. Transportation services
   5. Legal assistance
   6. Companionship
   7. Health care services and programs
   8. Adaptive products
   9. Medical insurance/medical information
  10. Special diets

How to Identify the Needs of *Your* Target Market

So far we've looked at some of the most widespread needs and concerns of the mature market and the ways in which those needs are presently being addressed. Here are six ways you can identify the specific needs and concerns of the older consumers *your business* wants to target.

1. Use Primary Research Techniques

Budgetary considerations aside, *there is no better and more accurate way to identify the needs of the older consumer than through conducting your own primary research.* It is simply the best way to "reality test" the mature market. After all, what better way to know what older consumers need than to *ask them!*

Primary Research Approaches

There are many ways to obtain information about the 50+ group by using primary research techniques. Let's look at some of the options available.

Telephone Surveys. Telephone surveys represent an excellent way to obtain valuable information about the mature market's needs and concerns. Survey sizes and sampling techniques can be constructed to yield findings that can be generalized to the overall older population. Furthermore, the costs may be minimal in consideration of the volume of useful and reliable data received.

Dr. Arlene Weissman—a respected and knowledgeable marketing researcher with Tillinghast, a Towers Perrin company—believes that telephone research is probably the *best* way for most organizations to identify the mature market's needs. Dr. Weissman does utter one caveat, however, on the conduct of mature market telephone surveys: *make sure the survey participants know right from the outset of the conversation that your purpose is to solicit their feedback, and not to sell them anything.* While most older persons are more than happy to share their opinions, they are generally "turned off" by telephone sales pitches.[7]

Note: The cost to conduct meaningful, statistically valid telephone surveys may be beyond your budgetary parameters. However, you'll see that there are many other techniques which can be used to uncover the mature market's needs.

Focus Groups. While focus groups (that is, meetings involving a moderator and about eight to ten panelists) are limited in that they cannot provide information which can be generalized to an entire group of 50+ers, they do provide an outstanding, cost-effective way of obtaining feedback from the mature market. Focus groups also offer a few other advantages. For example, they

- allow the researchers to meet face-to-face with the older adult, thereby enhancing the communications process
- allow participants to "brainstorm," thereby increasing the likelihood that fresh ideas and new perspectives will be elicited
- initiate a personal relationship with individuals who might later be used in other aspects of the marketing effort (for example, as members of an advisory council)

The following points should be kept in mind when conducting focus groups with the mature market:

- Be prepared to provide transportation to and from the meeting site, as this can be a problem for some older members of the mature market.
- Be as clear as possible up front about what the purpose of the focus group is and what the participant's role is, since for many 50+ers this may be a novel experience.
- Be as concrete as you can about the product and service ideas you want to test; don't expect the attendees to conceptualize these for you.
- When appropriate, try to recruit a majority of women for your groups since (a) this reflects the demographic profile of the mature market in most geographic areas, and (b) many older women (particularly those over 65) tend to be less outspoken when among a group with older men.
- Ask potential recruits if they've been in a focus group within the last month.

Note: Some persons are focus group "professionals" who frequently participate to partake of meals, cash, or other incentives.

Example: One organization which has effectively used qualitative research (i.e., focus groups) with the mature market is Barnett Banks of Florida, Inc. Barnett used the findings from several focus groups it conducted with older adults to design its "Senior Partners®" program. Targeted to customers age 55 +, Senior Partners has been an extremely successful program for the bank.

Note: A variation of the focus group technique is the "two-way" focus group. This involves a panel made up not only of older adults, but also of those who produce or provide services to them. The dialogue which occurs during these groups often generates invaluable feedback and ideas.

Mail Surveys. Some marketers learn about the mature market's needs through direct mail surveys.

Example: Retirement Centers of America (RCA) is one of the largest developers of retirement and life-care housing in the country. RCA sends out about 10,000 questionnaires to retirees in the specific area that it's considering for development. About 6 percent of these surveys are completed and returned. RCA then uses the findings to determine the key design and service features needed for the communities it establishes.

Note: One other benefit that RCA has found in using this form of research is that it helps educate prospects about the concepts of life-care and retirement housing.

For budget-conscious marketers, mail surveys tend to be a less desirable research technique regardless of what consumer market is being targeted. Response rates generally are low. Thus, it typically will require a larger expenditure to gain a meaningful supply of data. In addition, there is no dialogue to help assure that the respondent understands the questions. Further, it may not be possible to generalize the results since those who do respond to these surveys may not be representative of the total group.

There may be another key impediment to conducting this kind of survey if you're targeting the mature market: Some older individuals may have difficulty reading the copy due to visual problems.

Important: If you decide to use the mail survey approach, *make sure that such things as the type size, spacing, and colors chosen are appropriate for the older reader.*

Personal Interviews. Personal interviews can clearly uncover needs and concerns of the mature consumer. Unfortunately, this technique is usually quite costly from both a financial and a human resources standpoint. *A Cost-Effective Alternative:* Utilize your customer service and sales staff. With proper training, these individuals can encourage older consumers to provide your company with valuable feedback and ideas. This can be done when someone inquires about your product or service in person, by mail, or over the telephone.

Employee/Retiree Feedback. There's value in getting employees involved in various organizational activities like marketing and customer service. There is no doubt that, given the proper encouragement and reinforcement, your employees can generate some of the best business ideas and information.

Keep in Mind: An extremely valuable member of your company is *the retired employee.* While all employees possess the ability to generate ideas and feedback, the retiree holds two additional advantages when it comes to capturing the mature market. First, he or she is a member of the mature market. (This, of course, may also be characteristic of your older workers, thereby giving them an equally important advantage.) Second, since most retirees are able to spend more time in community activities than others, they often are in a better position to gauge "grassroots" opinions. This is especially important if you need to know what their peers may be thinking about your company and/or its products and services.

Example: One company that knows this quite well is the Ford Motor Company. Ford uses its retirees to offer suggestions for new car models. They do this through a retiree advisory committee which meets a few times each year. The committee's feedback has helped Ford make modifications in car design that take into account some of the special needs and concerns of the older automobile buyer.

Keep in Mind: Your older workers are also an excellent source for feedback and ideas. As *readily accessible* members of the mature market, they can share their firsthand perspectives on what needs and concerns age 50+ consumers have. It is surprising that so many corporate marketers overlook this invaluable resource.

2. Build and Analyze Mature Market Customer Information Systems

Many companies seem to know little about their existing base of older customers.

Example: I met with a large insurance company and a growing communications firm. Both wanted to increase their share of the mature market. Yet neither could tell me much of anything about what the characteristics were of their present older customers. They knew they *had* older customers, but that was pretty much it!

Perhaps there is a reasonable explanation for the above two companies' lack of internal data on their older customers. Let's face it, until recently, the mature market wasn't even recognized as a market segment worth tracking. All that's changed, however.

Marketers should develop a system which compiles information about their older customers. You should be able to answer some or all of the following questions:

1. What is the demographic and geographic makeup of my older customers?

2. Which of our products or services do they use the most?
3. How much do they spend on our products?
4. How do they find out about our products?
5. Where do they typically purchase our products?
6. How often do they register complaints about our products?
7. What do they tend to complain about?

This internal research and analysis serves at least three purposes:

- It can help identify gaps in your mature market data base which need to be filled.
- It can help you better service your existing older customers and cross-sell other products to them.
- It can help you develop strategies that will generate new mature market customers.

Tip: Syndicated products that measure consumer purchase and media behavior may be able to help you identify your over-50 customer base and analyze their current purchasing of your products. They also might tell you which of your competitors' products are being used by older consumers. Products such as Information Resources, Inc.'s InfoScan™, for example, are especially valuable to companies that have little or no direct contact with the actual consumers of their products. Businesses that routinely *do* come into contact with the consumers of their products (such as banks, hospitals, and insurance companies) may be able to obtain this information more easily since they maintain individual customer accounts.

3. Pay Attention to Your Customers' Comments

Your older customers can be your greatest source for uncovering the mature market's needs and concerns.

Key Point: Telephone calls, letters, and face-to-face contact all can elicit valuable input . . . if your business steadfastly listens to the comments, records them, and acts upon them when possible. As we saw, Comfortably Yours repeatedly invites its customers to provide feedback and ideas. Needs expressed by these customers have resulted in a number of successful new products.

Note: The real beauty of gaining feedback from your older customers is that it is so inexpensive!

Cavett Robert, founder of the National Speakers Association, tells a great story that illustrates this point perfectly. It's about a little boy who walks into a grocery store and asks the grocer if he can use the telephone. After the grocer grants him approval, the boy dials a number and says the following:

Mrs. Johnson, do you have a gardener? (Pause) Oh, you *do*. Well, I'm an extremely good gardener. (Pause) "Yes, ma'am, I understand you have a gardener, but I'm *really good*. I do the edging. . . . (Pause) Yes, ma'am, I understand. You're happy with your gardener. OK, thanks a lot.

The boy then hangs up the phone and starts whistling as he heads out of the store. At this point, the grocer stops him and says, "Gee, son, I'm sorry you didn't get the job." To which the boy quickly responds, "I got the job!" The grocer says, "You did not!" The boy then says, "Yes, I did, sir, you don't understand. You see, I'm her gardener. I'm just checking to see how good I'm doing!"

Tip: Businesses that successfully market to any customer—regardless of age—should also regularly check to see "how good they're doing."

4. Use Role-Playing Exercises

One of the best ways to find out about an older consumer's needs and concerns is to "walk a mile in his (or her) shoes." A few years ago, industrial designer Pat Moore did this so she could learn what it was like to be an 85-year old woman. During a three-year period, Moore disguised herself using costumes and make-up. She wrapped her legs in ace bandages to slow her gait, used ear plugs to dull her hearing, and taped her fingers to simulate arthritis. Moore's many experiences, sad and joyful, have since been chronicled in her book, *Disguised: A True Story.*[8]

You don't have to go to the same lengths as Pat Moore to get a firsthand impression of what some of the needs of the mature market might be.

Example: A practical approach has been used by Meridian Bancorp of Pennsylvania. Many employees in Meridian's 180 branch offices in Pennsylvania and Delaware have attended a full-day workshop to sensitize them to the needs and concerns of some older customers. The workshop uses several techniques such as having the trainees work under various physical handicaps which might affect an older customer. This training program (which was actually developed by the AARP and the American Bankers Association) has been well received.

Warning: If you're planning on doing a role-playing exercise, a few words of caution are in order, particularly if you decide to focus on the health problems that may accompany aging. While it's important to understand the needs of those older customers with physical problems, this approach may prove to be counterproductive if not handled carefully. The danger is that, by focusing on some limitations that may occur with aging, you may unwittingly reinforce myths about the overall older consumer group; i.e., that they are all alike, or that they all have physical handicaps. For this reason, any role-playing exercise that focuses on the less-healthy old should be balanced by messages that identify this group as but one segment of the large and diverse mature market.

5. Read Mature Market Publications

One great way to spot older consumer needs and concerns is to read publications that are specifically targeted to this group. This technique is vastly underutilized. First, examine the editorial content. What subjects are frequently discussed? What new issues seem to be getting coverage? What concerns are cited? What advice is given?

Note: This technique is similar to the "content-analysis" methodology used by such organizations as The Naisbitt Group.

Second, use a less obvious, but sometimes even more revealing approach—read the "Letters to the Editor" column. You can pick up some wonderful ideas and concerns from scanning this section. Keep in mind that the writer's comments are likely to reflect the opinions of thousands of others who didn't bother to write.

Example: Issues of *New Choices* magazine have included letters from readers expressing a need for (1) ways to help people enjoy life as a single, (2) advice on managing financial affairs as an older widow, and (3) ideas on how to dress fashionably in the mature years. *New Choices* responds to these and similar letters with relevant articles. Couldn't your business benefit from learning about the needs expressed by older consumers in mature market publications?

6. Take Advantage of Secondary/Syndicated Research

A wealth of information about the mature market's needs and concerns is available from secondary and syndicated research studies. This may have been published by popular and professional media, government agencies, trade and professional organizations, academic and research institutions, marketing research firms, seniors organizations, and so forth. In many cases, it will cost you less to purchase this information than what you'd have to pay to conduct your own research.

Tip: The Consumer Expenditure Survey, which is released by the Department of Labor's Bureau of Labor Statistics, is a particularly useful secondary research source. Conducted on an annual basis, it is the only national survey that provides complete data on household expenditures and the demographic characteristics of those households. By looking at this information, you can get a better idea of the needs and purchasing behavior of current and upcoming mature market households.

Example: One organization that benefitted from utilizing secondary research is Commonwealth National Bank of Harrisburg, Pennsylvania. The bank used information gleaned from some national studies on financial services and the older customer to put together its mature market strategy. Along with some localized, market-specific data, the bank was able to develop its "62 PLUS" program. In little more than two years, Commonwealth

National has developed more than 1,000 new banking relationships with households headed by older persons. More important, these new customers have accounted for about $14 million in new deposits to the bank![9]

Keep in Mind: In some cases, data from secondary/syndicated sources may provide you with all the mature market information you need.

Marketing Checklist:
Six Ways to Identify Mature Market Needs

1. Use primary research techniques.
2. Build and analyze mature market customer information systems.
3. Pay attention to your customers' comments.
4. Use role-playing exercises.
5. Read the mature market publications.
6. Use secondary and syndicated research information.

Chapter Wrap-up

To succeed in the mature market, your business must address the needs and concerns of the older consumer. While many of these needs may be similar to those of younger consumers, others will be quite different. By following the techniques laid out in this chapter, you will equip yourself with some of the best methodologies to identify and meet those specific needs.

Many concerns are shared by a large group of older adults. These needs are likely to be even greater in the future. Thus, they represent definite, long-term business opportunities for many companies. In fact, those who satisfy these needs *today* will likely be among the most successful companies in the "grayer" world of tomorrow.

Caution: While the importance of identifying and meeting customer needs among the entire consumer population is something that has been stressed repeatedly during the past few years, I can't tell you how many times I've helped (or heard about) a company that tried to fashion a successful mature market program in an ivory tower. While this approach may appear to be time-saving and cost effective, odds are that—in the final analysis—it will prove to be quite the opposite.

Remember: Over the long-run, few, if any, businesses will develop successful programs for the 50+ market by employing "seat-of-the-pants" marketing strategies.

1. Myers, Albert and Christopher Anderson. *Success After 60*. New York: Summit Books, 1986.

2. *The Prime Life Generation: A Report Describing the Characteristics and Attitudes of Americans 50 to 64 Years of Age*. Washington, D.C.: American Council of Life Insurance and the Health Insurance Association of America, 1985.

3. Higdon, Hal, "Newest research tells us: If You Want Long Life—Exercise!," *50 Plus*, August 1986, p. 17.

4. Tenhoor, William, and Anita Shalit, "Independence for the Elderly: The Challenge to Technology and Business," *Aging*, 1985, No. 349, p. 27.

5. Personal telephone conversation with Fred Lebe, director of services, Acsia Insurance, June 1987.

6. Eastlack, Joseph O., "Trends in Food and Nutrition in the Mature Market," a presentation at the American Psychological Association 93rd annual convention, Los Angeles, CA, August, 1985.

7. Personal telephone conversation with Arlene Weissman, July 1987.

8. Moore, Pat with Charles Paul Conn. *Disguised: A True Story*. Waco, TX: Word Books, 1985.

9. Personal telephone conversation with Carolyn Troxell, manager of marketing, Commonwealth National Bank, June 1987.

Chapter 5

Key 3: Promote the Positive Attributes of Older Adults and Aging

New Choices: The Magazine That Stresses the Positive Aspects of Growing Older

With a 41 percent increase in advertising revenues between 1985 and 1986, and an 18 percent increase in advertising pages during that period, this publication was ranked fourth by *Adweek* magazine among the hottest smaller magazines in America.

Its paid circulation has risen steadily upward; in three years its circulation grew by 51 percent. Today, a half million paying subscribers read this publication, which reaches more than 1.5 million people. What is this magazine? It's *New Choices*, a Reader's Digest publication.*

Why has *New Choices* achieved such dramatic and impressive growth? There are a number of reasons, one of which is the magazine's high editorial quality. *New Choices* has received several awards for journalistic excellence.

Another major reason why *New Choices* has been so successful in increasing its subscriber base—and its advertising revenues—is because of the magazine's upbeat view of what life can be, and often *is* like, for those in their second 50 years. It is in celebrating life after 50 that *New Choices* magazine has utilized and benefitted from another effective mature market strategy, namely key 3: Promote the *positive* attributes of older adults and aging.

---

*Note: Prior to December 1988, *New Choices* magazine was known as *50 Plus*.

The Magazine's Message: It's OK to Be Over 50

New Choices conveys a positive message about the 50+ years in all of its printed materials. Current or potential advertisers, for example, are sent the results of market research studies which tout the buying power and active lifestyle of its readers. A newsletter that presents similar information about the overall mature market is also sent out to the advertising community.

The major recipients of *New Choices'* positive message about aging, however, are its subscribers. In each issue of the magazine you'll find a recurring message: *Despite all the negatives our society has often associated with growing older, it's OK to be over 50.* In fact, to have reached 50 is an achievement which one can feel good about. As *New Choices'* editor, Bard Lindeman, says, "It means that you have been a survivor . . . a successful survivor in most cases."

Through articles, graphics, and high-spirited editorial comments, *New Choices'* readers are applauded for having reached a point in life at which they can take pride in their accomplishments: the successful management of families, careers, homes, and/or finances. In a society that too often has revered the young while shutting out or ignoring the old, *New Choices* magazine seeks to make its readers feel downright good about aging.

Enjoying and Promoting the Good Life

New Choices doesn't just make its readers feel good about being over 50. It also shows them how exciting and fulfilling life in the mature years can be. (See Figure 5-1.) Thus, you'll find lively articles about such topics as sex and romance, exotic vacations, beauty tips, and high fashion.

One way the magazine does this is by reporting on specific people who are enjoying their 50+ years. From celebrities such as Bill Cosby and President Reagan to the not-so-famous, *New Choices* uses these individuals as role models to encourage and inspire its readers. According to Lindeman, this presentation of role models is one of the magazine's vital missions. These leaders of what Lindeman calls the "great gray legion" often influence the lives of his readers.

The 50+ Years: A Time for Growth and Achievement

New Choices also believes the 50+ years represent a time of "new beginnings." Reflecting this upbeat posture, the magazine often presents articles about older adults who have taken up new challenges or causes, or who have continued to excel in their later years. Each year, for example, the publication selects and salutes a team of All-American, 50+ athletes. It regularly

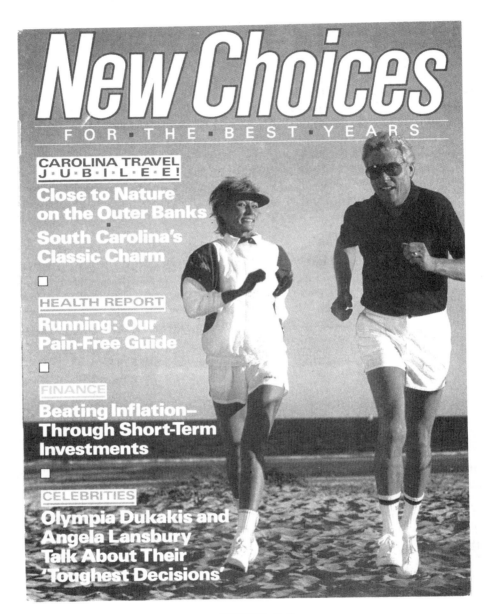

FIGURE 5–1

reports on mature adults who've gone back to school, successfully battled diseases, or participated in important societal events (national peace marches, for example).

Another way *New Choices* illustrates the growth and achievements of older Americans is through its "second career" stories. In these articles, individual retirees and career changers are profiled. (See Figure 5-2.) Some of these people voluntarily left the work force or changed jobs. Others, however, were more or less pressured to do so.

In one article, *New Choices* presents the story of a man who decided, at the age of 55, to produce an investment newsletter. Previously, he had been a printer, an employee in a Las Vegas casino, and a college professor. He had never earned more than $25,000 a year. The newsletter, however, has been so successful that it has made the man a millionaire. In reporting this story, *New Choices* engaged in its familiar "you, too, can do it style," by specifically highlighting the millionaire's following comments in the margin: "Anyone could do what I've done. It's an open game."

"Youth Creep": You're As Young As You Feel

Bard Lindeman and *New Choices* have recognized a new phenomenon in America called "youth creep." It's a phenomenon that describes the changing attitude many older people today have about aging. Youth creep reflects the belief that many people age 50+ still feel young and vibrant—much younger than their chronological years.

In sensing, monitoring, and reporting on the pulse of a changing mature market, *New Choices* has clearly established itself as the magazine industry's outspoken promoters and motivators of the over-50 population. By debunking the myths —while stressing the positive aspects of older adults and of aging—*New Choices* brings a message that more and more represents the anthem mature America wants to hear.

As Bard Lindeman advises, "There is a whole lot of living waiting for the 50+ person to reach out and grab. But it won't come up your street; it won't come into your driveway. You've got to go out and get it. And that, in a nutshell, is our editorial theme." It is also the tenet upon which much of *New Choices'* success has been built.

Why It Pays to Promote the Benefits of Aging

Most Mature Americans Like Being Their Age

Of all age groups, it is those over 50 who have lived to see and hear the most negative stereotyping about aging and growing old. Because of this, you might think that they'd be depressed about being older. Yet, this is simply not the case. On the contrary, *most older Americans feel good about their maturity*. In fact, they tend to feel better about their lives than do younger persons.

Example: A recent *USA Weekend* poll showed that, compared to younger adults, those over 50 were happier with their friendships, their

Wendell's pinstripe suits
may be gone, but not
his love for business.

SECOND CAREERS

Goodbye Board Room, Hello Main Street

*Wendell Gooch gave up
a Chicago bank
vice-presidency to publish
two small newspapers in
a rural Indiana town.
His headlines have
never been brighter*

by LES LINDEMAN

PHOTOGRAPHS BY PAM SPAULDING

FIGURE 5–2   A typical feature in *New Choices*

financial situations, their marriages or closest personal relationships, and
their overall lives. In addition, the survey found most people over 50
preferred to be their present age including half of those 75 and over![1]

Comedian George Burns may be the paragon of the high-spirited older
group. His attitude represents what may be the ultimate in optimism about

being old and growing older. George has already booked himself to perform at the London Palladium on his birthday in 1996, the year he turns 100. He has also written a book called *How to Live to Be 100 or More* (New York: Putnam, 1983). Expressing his cheerful outlook on life in the later years, George says that, "Once you've lived to be 100, you've really got it made. That's because not that many people die after 100."[2]

Implication: By presenting the positive aspects of aging, you actually mirror the way in which most 50 + ers see themselves and want to be seen by others. This clears the way for establishing rapport and building credibility with the older consumer. That, in turn, can help generate an interest in—and demand for—the products or services you offer.

Aging Attractively: The Mindset of Tomorrow's Older Consumer

For the first time in our history, people are beginning to view aging and gray hair as attractive. Older models, like Kaylan Pickford, appear in advertisements. Celebrities such as Pat Boone and Debbie Reynolds, both of whom are over 50, have developed fitness tapes. Joan Collins, the 53-year-old star of the TV series, "Dynasty," has been proclaimed as the sexiest woman in America. A 1986 *Ladies Home Journal* poll conducted by the Roper Organization showed that John Forsythe, Robert Redford, Paul Newman, Clint Eastwood, and Burt Reynolds—all of whom are over 50—were the sexiest men in America.[3]

In part, this appreciation for the over-50 population is due to the efforts of publications like *New Choices*. It is also due to Madison Avenue's heightened awareness of the mature adult's purchasing power.

Another major factor fueling this phenomenon is the aging of the baby boomers. In 1986, the first of the 76 million members of this group turned 40. As they grow closer and closer to middle age themselves, the boomers are apparently beginning to develop a greater acceptance of, and appreciation for, the older generation. Many members of the latter group, of course, are their parents.

Keep in Mind: More than any other group, the baby boomers will look to perceive themselves—and aging—in positive ways. In the process, they will do whatever they can to grow old youthfully.

Tip: If you expect to successfully sell and serve the enormous 50 + group of tomorrow—replete with its mass of graying baby boomers—you'll almost certainly have to focus on the positive attributes of older adults and aging. If for no other reason, then, it makes good business sense to utilize this strategy *now*.

As the great French author, Victor Hugo, once wrote: "Nothing, not all the armies of the world, can stop an idea whose time has come."[4] In this case, the idea is that aging can be beautiful. And it *will* be for sure, in the twenty-first century!

How to Promote the Positive Attributes of Older Adults and Aging in Your Marketing Program

Realize What the Positive Attributes Are

Any marketer who wants to successfully employ this mature market strategy must first recognize what some of the positive attributes of aging—and our older population—are. Unfortunately, this is not obvious to everyone . . . especially because of the conventional way in which our youth-oriented culture has been accustomed to viewing its elders. Below are listed four of them.

More Control Over One's Time. A couple of years ago, I was in a cab heading toward the airport in Denver. In the cab with me was an older gentleman who looked to be in his mid-to-late sixties. We struck up a conversation about traveling and the man began to talk about his Eastern Airlines' "Get-Up-and-Go" passport. He and his wife had recently purchased two of these passports.

With much delight, the man told me how often he was able to put his Eastern passport to good use. He then cheerfully explained to me how he had used it to get to Denver. Apparently, he had taken a flight out of Phoenix, his hometown, late in the evening. He then flew into Atlanta, Georgia, arriving there sometime in the wee hours of the night. After waiting at the airport for several hours, he caught a flight to Denver and reached his destination the next morning.

As I thought about what this man had done, a burning question entered my mind. Why didn't he just fly from Phoenix to Denver? Wouldn't that have made a lot more sense? When I asked him this, he responded quickly with a smile. "I know what you mean," he said. "A few years ago, when I was still working, I was in the same rat race you're in. I would have never thought to do this. But now my situation has changed. I have much more time at my disposal. As it happens, Eastern doesn't have a direct flight from Phoenix to Denver, so I had to go by way of Atlanta. But that's OK, because now I don't mind taking a little extra time to do things."

Point: Many older Americans—especially those who have retired— have more control over their time than at any other period in their lives. This opens the door to some special marketing opportunities.

Wisdom, Experience, and Maturity. Darrell Sifford, a columnist with *The Philadelphia Inquirer*, once wrote an article in which he shared with readers the things he knew about life when he was 30. Sifford then went on to say, "But I'm not 30 anymore. I'm 55, and almost daily I realize how much I didn't know when I was 30—and how much I still have to learn."[5]

It takes a lot of living and experience to develop the skills and insights needed to handle effectively the day-to-day challenges and responsibilities of life. Perhaps this is why, in past times, it was the oldest person in town who was recognized as the village sage. Maybe G. Stanley Hall, a 19th century scientist put it best when he said, "There is a certain maturity of judgment about men, things, causes, and life generally that nothing in the world but years can bring—a real wisdom that only age can teach."[6]

Note: America's older population represents an enormous pool of wisdom and experience which, regrettably, has often been overlooked in modern times. (Chapter 6 tells you how to use this information to fashion a successful marketing strategy.)

Achievement/Accomplishment. It takes many years of sweat and toil to achieve anything of substance in life. Thus, it should come as no surprise that over 90 percent of those listed in *Who's Who in America* are over 40, including a substantial number of persons age 50+. Similarly, the overwhelming majority of millionaires in America (approximately 75 percent) are over 50.

Keep in Mind: As *New Choices* magazine reminds us, the later years of life also provide a time in which one can set and meet *new* personal goals, whether for business or pleasure.

The Opportunity to Give to Others. One of the most wonderful aspects of aging is that it's a time when people can give of themselves to society. Older Americans do this in a big way and they derive much personal joy in the process.

As volunteers, 50+ers are actively involved in a wide spectrum of political, social, and spiritual causes. The Retired Senior Volunteer Program, for instance, utilized the collective skills of some 350,000 persons around the country to donate 67 million service hours in 1985. In a similar demonstration of its willingness to help mankind, the 50+ group donates large sums of money to charitable causes.

Mature adults find their later years also give them the opportunity to give back to society in other ways too. Often this is through the pursuit of social service careers in fields like nursing and teaching.

Example: A couple of years ago, the senior vice president of a highly successful Fortune 500 company resigned from his position to become the president of a relatively small agricultural college. The new job required that he take a cut in salary. One reason he was motivated to take the position, however, was because he liked the academic environment's care and concern for people. Using his sharply honed business skills, he will now work to strengthen this college's image and reputation as well as assure its long-term prosperity.

Keep in Mind: It's especially important to remember this "giving back to society" mindset if your organization is involved in the fields of higher education, health and social services, fund-raising, or human resources.

Marketing Checklist: Four Positive Attributes of Aging or Older Americans

- More control over one's time
- Wisdom and experience

- History of achievement/accomplishment
- Desire to give to others

Develop Products or Services That Focus on the Positive Attributes

Opportunities abound for creative marketers who not only recognize the positive attributes of aging, but who *respond* to them by developing new products and services. Here is one innovative organization that did.

Sophisticated Seniors: A "Glamorous" Approach to Selling

The founders of Sophisticated Seniors—a geriatric nurse and a nursing home administrator—began their business in 1985 after discovering a niche in the senior fashion world. From personal experience, they had learned that the mobile shopping services that brought clothes to seniors in nursing homes were not meeting the needs of the residents. For one thing, these shopping services were selling clothes that were institutional, unattractive, or inappropriate. For another, they were displaying their wares in an unappealing and uninviting manner to prospective customers. With this in mind, Sophisticated Seniors went about developing a mobile shopping service of its own.

Unlike its competitors, Sophisticated Seniors uses a *glamorous* approach to selling clothes to nursing home residents. It does this in several ways. It offers its customers a cheerful and stylish array of clothing and jewelry. It also uses eye-catching displays and mannequins to exhibit its goods attractively.

Of greatest significance, however, are the company's fashion shows. These shows are held "on location" using recruits selected from among the nursing facility's residents. Many of the the event's participants are over 80. Donning colorful and coordinated outfits, these senior models walk down a runway to the cheers and applause of their fellow residents.

Reaction to the Sophisticated Seniors' concept has been so good that the company now serves close to 100 sites. These include retirement centers, senior housing units, and senior centers as well as nursing homes. In addition, the business has developed a line of adaptive clothing for handicapped or bed-ridden patients.

Key Point: Most older persons, no matter what their age or lifestyle, want to look and feel their best for as long as possible. And, with the right clothing and jewelry, there's no reason why they can't! This is as true for the typical nursing home resident as it is for those who regularly frequent the shopping malls.

Note: The opportunity to market products and services that make a person look and feel good extends long into the retirement years.

Modify Your Existing Products to Reflect the Positive Aspects of Life After 50

Existing products or services can be adapted to capitalize on some of the positive attributes of older adults and aging. A number of overnight campgrounds, for example, have developed vacations for the mature market by capitalizing on the more flexible schedule of the retiree population . . . and the zest which many 50+ers have for traveling and meeting new people. Using the same facilities as those offered to youngsters, these programs have been modified to reflect the interests, preferences, capabilities, and pace of the mature market.

Campground owners have benefitted from these programs in at least two ways:

- They have developed a new market for their facilities.
- They have found a means of offsetting the ill-effects of the "baby bust" which has reduced the number of younger campers.

Several airlines, hotels, tour operators, supermarkets, department stores, and universities have realized similar benefits in adapting their programs and services to accommodate the many older consumers who have flexible schedules.

Strategically Position Your Products to Portray the Benefits of Maturity

You can enhance your mature market opportunities by strategically positioning your products or services to reflect the positive attributes of older adults or aging.

Example: International Games Inc.® of Joliet, Illinois, perhaps best known for its Uno® card game, also sells another parlor card game, Skip-Bo®. Part of the company's strategy is to market the game to adults over 50. As a result, International Games has developed an advertising campaign specifically targeted to the older consumer. Both the strategy and the advertising campaign have been very successful as Skip-Bo® has sold well to the mature market. A quick look at International Games' advertising technique illustrates one of the reasons behind this success.

In one ad, three older adults are seen seated at a table with huge smiles on their faces as they gasp at one of the playing cards drawn. Underneath them is the cover of a Skip-Bo box and the big, boldly printed message, "Not for the retiring type." Beneath this are the words, "Nothing goes with good times and good company like a great card game." (See Figure 5-3.)

Note: Skip-Bo's advertisement positions its product well for the mature market by focusing on several positive characteristics of older adults:

FIGURE 5-3

- First, the ad shows the 50+ group is active and likes to socialize.
- Second, it shows the mature adult enjoys playing games and having fun.
- Third, the ad reinforces the credo that 50+ers are capable of participating in activities that require brain power.

This theme represents a potent and positive statement about the mature market—that older adults are no less active, fun, and intellectually capable than other age groups. With a picture and a few words, International Games debunks a number of myths about aging and portrays older Americans in the upbeat way they typically see themselves.

Tip: Use of upbeat advertising messages and campaigns is one of the most effective means of implementing Key 3.

Sponsor Programs and Activities That Demonstrate the Appeal of Being 50+

There are many ways in which your business can get involved in activities that tout both the positive attributes of aging and the mature adult. Here are a few examples of this.

Example 1: "We Still Are" Upbeat Ad

"People ask us what we used to be. I tell them 'We Still Are!' " says a Pfizer ad. (See Figure 5-4). Pfizer has been using former film star Alice Faye to present this upbeat message to older adults for several years. Through slide shows, a film, and numerous public presentations, Ms. Faye has encouraged older adults to remain physically and socially active. She has also given them advice on how to do this. Still fit, trim, and active in her seventies, Alice Faye is a wonderful example of how vibrant older Americans can be. She serves as an ideal role model and booster for her peers.

Example 2: "Senior Smarts"

Senior Smarts is an annual competition held in Florida. The event features teams of age 60+ Floridians who test their knowledge of such diverse topics as music, science, politics, mathematics, geography, and current events. As a sponsor of "Senior Smarts," Morrison's Cafeteria is one organization that has given its support to events that reflect the intellectual capabilities of the mature adult.

Note: The ABC-TV game show, "Jeopardy," has introduced a similar competition with its championship tournament for seniors.

Example 3: "Time of Your Life" Expo

Since 1984, Opportunities and Services for Seniors, Inc. of Los Angeles has presented the "Time of Your Life®" Expo in California. Time of Your Life is the largest exposition and entertainment event for age 50+ adults in southern California. In 1987, more than 42,000 older adults attended the festivities which were sponsored by CIGNA Healthplans of California, KABC-TV, American Savings and Loan Association, and Heritage Park Communities.

Time of Your Life Expo is an upbeat extravaganza which celebrates the mature years. Attendees enjoy numerous entertainers including celebrities from their era. They attend educational seminars, see exhibits and demonstrations, and learn about a variety of consumer products and services. The event also features door prizes and contests, one of which is the "Remarkable Seniors Recognition Program."

People ask us what we used to be

I tell them 'We Still Are!'

Alice Faye

Enjoy these years...you've earned them

As Alice Faye says in her new film "We Still Are!", it's important to do at least one interesting thing every day. And if nothing interesting is happening, make something happen. You can greatly increase your chances of living a longer, more satisfying life by maintaining a regular schedule of enjoyable activities, eating sensibly, getting regular exercise, not smoking, and following doctors' orders.

Alice Faye shows the way

"I'm responsible for me. I've just turned 71 and I feel young. I swim every day and never do the same thing two days a week. If there's anything unusual with my body I go right to the doctor."

Health Care information—an important product brought to you by Pfizer

Pfizer and Alice Faye have teamed up to offer a health care program for mature individuals, including the new film "We Still Are!", a delightful blend of scenes from some of Ms. Faye's favorite movies woven together with practical advice to help you achieve and maintain good health.

Pfizer

Pharmaceuticals •
A Partner in Quality,
Cost-Effective Healthcare

FIGURE 5–4

Tip: Even if you don't sponsor these events, they may still be excellent places to exhibit. Expos offer you the chance to meet and speak with thousands of older customers in a positive and nonthreatening environment. They may also allow you to learn more about your competitors and those with whom you might collaborate.

Utilize the Services of Older Workers and Volunteers

By utilizing the services of older workers and volunteers—especially those who are in their retirement years—your company can visibly demonstrate its belief that older adults are (and can be) productive, useful members of our society. In the process, your organization will also benefit from the assistance that these individuals provide.

Example: One company that has utilized the services of older workers is First National Bank of Stamford, Connecticut. First National has a pickup and delivery service that uses retirees as couriers. These couriers visit offices of the bank's customers during normal business hours. There, they may collect deposits or handle loan applications. Customers using this novel and convenient service have praised the older workers for their courteous attitudes and reliability.

Keep in Mind: At least two positive attributes of the retiree population help to make this innovative service possible:

- the group's long history of responsible work experience
- the group's flexible time schedule

Marketing Checklist: How to Promote the Positive Attributes of Older Adults and Aging

1. Recognize what the positives attributes of older Americans and aging are.
2. Develop products and services that focus on the positives.
3. Modify existing products to reflect the positive aspects of life after 50.
4. Strategically position your products to portray the benefits of maturity.
5. Sponsor programs and activities that demonstrate the appeal of being 50+.
6. Utilize the services of older workers and volunteers.

Chapter Wrap-up

To achieve maximum success in marketing to and serving the mature market, you must promote the positive attributes of older Americans and aging. By pursuing this strategy, your business will:

- Reflect the way most older adults see themselves as individuals.
- Be in sync with the way most older adults want to be seen by the business community and society at large
- Pave the way to gaining rapport, credibility, and acceptance among the mature market.
- Expand your base of products and services for the older consumer.

Also keep in mind that America's future members of the mature market (i.e., the baby boomers) will undoubtedly want society to perceive them and aging in an upbeat manner. To thrive over the long-term then, marketers will *have to* portray aging and older Americans in positive ways. Indeed, in the twenty-first century, aging and blue sky may be equal. Businesses who understand this equation today may well find themselves floating in a sea of black ink tomorrow.

Caution: Be careful not to overstate the case in implementing key 3 by portraying the "second 50" years as trouble-free or the closest thing to heaven on earth. By flattering the mature market or exaggerating the joys of aging, you are likely to destroy your credibility with a group that knows only too well the realities of being 50+. Be sure your marketing strategies are guided by at least two important watchwords: sincerity and moderation.

---

1. Crowe, Adell, "What age would we like to be? Look in the mirror and see," *USA Weekend*, February 6-8, 1987, p. 4.

2. Kiester, Edwin, Jr., "Getting a Jump on Living Longer," *50 Plus*, September 1984, p. 17.

3. Barrett, Katherine, and Richard Greene, "America's Favorite Men," *Ladies Home Journal*, November 1986, pp. 67-74.

4. Ries, Al and Jack Trout. *Positioning: The Battle for Your Mind.* New York: McGraw-Hill, Inc., 1981, p. 211.

5. Sifford, Darrell, "At 55, looking back on what one doesn't know at 30," *The Philadelphia Inquirer*, May 4, 1987, p. 2-D.

6. Harper, Fletcher, and Sloan Walker, "Incredible Drive," *Mature Outlook*, March/April 1986, p. 88.

Chapter 6

Key 4: Involve the Older Consumer in Your Mature Market Programs

Survival of the Fittest: How One Hospital Has Flourished Where Others Have Failed

Increased competition, declining admission rates, and cost containment pressures have created havoc in the hospital industry. Dealing with these and other challenges has not been easy for many hospitals. Some facilities have seen their profits reduced substantially. Others have been forced to close their doors; since 1984, more than 200 hospitals have met this fate.

For a hospital with a large volume of Medicare patients (most of whom are age 65 and over), the demands are especially great. Since a change in the law was enacted in 1983, Medicare generally will pay the hospital only a pre-determined, fixed amount regardless of how much it costs the facility to treat a patient. This places the hospital "at risk," since it typically costs more to care for Medicare patients than other individuals.

Despite this difficult business climate and the Medicare payment constraints, Sun Health Corporation's Walter O. Boswell Memorial Hospital in Sun City, Arizona has flourished. The non-profit hospital has done so in a highly competitive health care region and with an extraordinarily large Medicare patient base representing about 85 percent of its overall patient population. In fact, the average age of this hospital's patients is almost 72!

How successful has this hospital been? Within its primary service area, the hospital's market share is an astounding 78 percent. In the adjacent areas, its market share of Medicare patients is 43 percent, which is equal to the *combined* market share held by seven other hospitals serving the area. Through 1987, this hospital has been "in the black" every year since the law on Medicare hospital payments was changed. Since 1984, this facility's net revenues have exceeded its expenses by over $23 million.

A number of factors have contributed to Boswell Memorial Hospital's success, including the facility's

- expertise and experience in treating a variety of medical problems typically associated with the older adult: strokes, heart failure and shock, chronic bronchitis, and emphysema
- reputation for providing high quality care (as evidenced by the extremely high ratings it earns from random surveys of its patients)
- ability to treat patients in a cost-effective manner

There is another major reason for Boswell Memorial Hospital's success: the hospital's ongoing commitment to involving the older adult in its various programs and activities. This commitment reflects another successful strategy used in capturing the mature market. It is Key 4: *involve the older consumer in your mature market programs.*

Boswell's Secret: Get the Community Involved from the Start

As Sun City's population grew in the 1960s, the residents of this retirement community began to perceive a need for a hospital of their own. In the late 1960s, construction of this hospital became a reality.

Sun City's residents were invited to play an integral role in building the hospital. And they heartily responded. Many citizens offered their support by providing feedback, financial contributions, and "hands-on" assistance. Before the first patient was ever admitted for treatment, Boswell Memorial Hospital had already benefitted from its policy of involving older adults in its activities. In November 1970, the hospital opened its doors with about 100 beds. It has grown since then to a 355-bed facility.

Making the Most of Mature Adults in Staff and Managerial Positions

While the size of Boswell Hospital has changed, one thing remains the same: Its steadfast commitment to involve the older population in all of its efforts. Here are a few examples of how this is done.

The Board of Directors. The Board of Directors is comprised of volunteers, all but one retired and over 50, most of whom live within the community.

Board members at Boswell Memorial don't function simply as advisors to the hospital. They are involved in policy setting and in operational activities such as determining what kinds of health care services and educational programs to offer. They also fulfill these roles by participating in many of the hospital committees.

Employees. Many companies today are encouraging their older workers to leave through "early out" programs. This is not the case with Boswell Memorial Hospital, however. While the normal retirement age at the hospital is 65, the organization has no mandatory retirement policy. Indeed, the hospital's oldest employee is a 78-year-old medical librarian.

About 20 percent of Boswell Memorial's paid staff is over the age of 50. These employees represent the whole gamut of job classifications, from entry level jobs, such as food service workers and housekeeping attendants, to the president of the hospital.

Volunteers. A major factor in Boswell Memorial Hospital's success is its outstanding army of older volunteers. In describing this group, *army* is probably the best word to use. Not counting Boswell's Board of Directors, this group includes some 2,000 volunteers, a figure considerably outnumbering the hospital's employee staff. (See Figure 6-1). It is the largest team of hospital volunteers in the state.

What do all these older volunteers do? Just about everything! This includes providing assistance in more than 120 different areas within the hospital and the community. When new residents come to the community, for example, volunteers welcome them and inform them about local health services and how to find a physician. When people visit the hospital, volunteers transport them to and from the parking lot and greet them at the front door. When patients need breakfast or someone to be their advocate, the volunteers are there to help.

Boswell's volunteers also man all of the hospital's information desks. They serve as messengers between patients and their families. They handle mail and code data into computers. They run the gift shop, the thrift shop, and two resident galleries, the latter generating income for the hospital and the artisans and craftsmen in the community. Boswell's older volunteers also help out in less conventional ways. Retired engineers advise on building design and decor. A retired doctor aids those with poor vision. Retired nurses participate in health screening programs.

Many of Boswell's older volunteers also help out with its health education programs. These programs are attended by about 20,000 people a year. During weeks when the hospital offers heart education programs, an older volunteer dresses up in a heart costume. This walking/talking "healthy heart" is affectionately known as "Thumper." (See Figure 6-2). Thumper walks around the hospital giving information on how the heart works and how to keep it healthy. He also provides literature about Boswell's open-heart surgery program.

How Older Adults Can Help Your Business to Thrive—If You Let Them

Obviously, not every business gets its start the way Boswell Memorial Hospital did. Before it was even built, the hospital had gained the interest and sup-

FIGURE 6–1 Volunteers of the Walter O. Boswell Memorial Hospital, Sun City, Arizona

FIGURE 6–2 Boswell Memorial Hospital's "Thumper"

port of those who might use its services the most—the residents of Sun City.

Boswell could have become complacent and forgotten about those in the community who helped the hospital get launched. But it hasn't. The hospital and its parent organization, Sun Health Corporation, continue to deeply involve the older population in their activities. As a result, they thrive.

What can marketers from any business or industry learn from Boswell Memorial Hospital's experience? The words of Pamela K. Meyerhoffer, vice president for Public Affairs at Sun Health Corporation, probably sum this up better than anything else. Says Ms. Meyerhoffer, "The most generic thing is involving mature adults in the determination of when, how, and where the service or product is to be provided . . . be it through focus groups or by actually having them involved in the provision of that product or service as employees and volunteers. Get them into the process because they then become a part of it and adopt it as their own."

Six Reasons to Involve Mature Adults in Your Marketing Program

Almost any business can benefit from involving the mature market in its activities. Here are six reasons why.

Reason 1: To Maximize Your Potential for Success

Earlier in this book, I referred to the Seniors' World Fair in Atlantic City. This event had been billed as "the greatest show in the northeastern United States for and about 50+ adults." It was to be an extravaganza for older Americans, featuring a jazz festival, continuous entertainment, free gifts, lectures, dancing, and a spectacular showcase of exhibits and displays.

As the first event of its kind held in the "graying" Middle-Atlantic region of the United States, the event seemed like one whose time had come. With much fanfare, the promoters of the fair aggressively contacted a multitude of advertisers to become trade show exhibitors.

By the time the fair arrived, everything seemed to be in place. Over 100 exhibitors had booths, the media were alerted, the entertainers were lined up, and the guest lecturers were set to go. Everyone, it seemed, was waiting for a throng of 50+ers to appear. But . . . they never did! The three-day event ended with nowhere near as many 50+ers attending as the 50,000 or so that had been expected.

What went wrong? Here was one major flaw: Although the promoters had strongly committed themselves to involving *exhibitors* in the fair, they hadn't spend nearly as much energy trying to involve the other key group needed for the event's success . . . those over 50. From all appearances, an insufficient amount of effort was spent on:

- soliciting feedback from the area's older adults on how the event could be staged successfully
- inviting 50+ers to participate in planning or working at the fair
- contacting seniors/retiree organizations to obtain help in promoting the event or in providing transportation to it
- publicizing the event at the "grassroots" level

The "Bottom Line": Unfortunately, almost everyone lost out . . . the promoters, the exhibitors, and the many 50+ers who didn't attend what was actually a good fair. If there's a lesson to be learned in all of this, it is this:

Key Point: If you want to enhance the probability that your mature market program will succeed, don't forget to involve the older consumers in it.

Reason 2: To Receive Invaluable Information and Ideas

In their book, *In Search of Excellence*, Thomas J. Peters and Robert H. Waterman, Jr. made several important observations about successful companies. One of these had to do with how close these companies were to their customers. To quote the authors:

> A simple summary of what our research uncovered on the customer attribute is this: the excellent companies really are close to their customers. That's it. Other companies talk about it; the excellent companies do it.[1]

One benefit of involving older consumers in your efforts is that it *does* allow you to get closer to them: to learn about their lifestyles, their goals, their dreams, their social networks, their perceptions, and their problems. It allows you to develop programs, products, and services for the mature consumer that are *market-driven*, not product-driven. It enables you to learn how to reach the mature market with your product or service.

What goes hand in hand with this is that involving the older consumer also puts you in a better position to listen to what he or she needs and wants. As Peters and Waterman stated in their book, "The excellent companies are better listeners. They get a benefit from market closeness that for us was truly unexpected—unexpected, that is, until you think about it. Most of their real innovation comes from the market."[2] No better testimonial of this exists for the mature market than Comfortably Yours. As noted, that direct-mail company picks up some of its best new product ideas by actively soliciting, and listening to, the comments of its customers.

Reason 3: To Enhance Your Credibility and Rapport with the Mature Market

Not surprisingly, most mature adults find it easiest to identify with other persons in their age group. By using older persons, you help create a "he's one of us" feeling among the mature market. Often, this results in greater credibility for your organization and its products.

Utilizing older persons can also strengthen the customer service side of your business.

Example: Western Savings & Loan in Arizona has found that its older employees are more effective at servicing the bank's older customers. Some franchises have made a similar discovery and are now actively courting retirees to sell the products and services they offer to the mature market.

Reason 4: To Help the Older Customer Better Understand Your Product or Service

There is an old Chinese proverb which says, "I hear and I forget. I see and I remember. I do and I understand."

Key Point: The best way to get an older consumer to understand what it is you have to offer is to get him or her to *actively participate* in the effort. The spin-off benefit of this is that it enables the participant to help others better understand what you have to offer.

Boswell Memorial Hospital has clearly benefitted from this phenomenon. Its older volunteers have gained a true knowledge of some of the inner workings of the hospital's programs and services. As emissaries of the hospital, they have been able to relay this information to members of the community.

Reason 5: To Capitalize on Current and Future Employment Trends

The diminished supply of teenagers and young adults is creating a shortage of workers in a number of service-related fields, including the restaurant, supermarket, hospitality, banking, health care, and insurance industries.

Tip: The declining pool of teenagers makes the use of older adults a sensible recruitment and marketing strategy.

A number of companies have recognized the confluence of these two trends. Publix Supermarkets, for example, has a number of retirees who serve as baggers of groceries for its food shoppers. Wendy's International has a large number of older workers who are employed in its restaurants. At Florida's Sea World, older persons perform a number of tasks including marketing and group sales.

Remember: The number of older adults who want to remain active as employees, volunteers, or business owners will continue to increase.

Reason 6: To Reap the Benefits of the Mature Adult's Experience

Older adults have had the opportunity to acquire the skills of a lifetime. These skills can be put to excellent use by your organization. Geri-Pare, the nonprofit agency that handles home repairs for seniors, provides a great example of this. The organization utilizes a staff of retired mechanics to handle its fix-up projects.

Marketing Checklist: Six Reasons for Involving the Mature Adult in Your Business Activities

1. To maximize your potential for success
2. To get invaluable information and ideas
3. To enhance your credibility and rapport with the mature market
4. To help the older customer better understand your product or service
5. To capitalize on current and future employment trends
6. To reap the benefits of the mature adult's experience

How to Involve Older Adults in Your Mature Market Programs

Whether serving as full- or part-time employees, consultants, volunteers, or in some other capacity, those over 50 can be of tremendous value in helping you attract and serve the older customer. Here are four specific ways.

Creating Products and Services

Members of the mature market, whether individually or as part of a group, can play a pivotal role in helping you develop products and services that serve the over-50 consumer. Four organizations that illustrate the almost limitless range of possibilities in this area are Retirement Community Developers, Lutheran General Hospital, Group Health Cooperative, and Clipper Cruise Lines, Inc.

Example 1: Retirement Community Developers (RCD) of Alexandria, Virginia used a focus group of older adults when planning The Charter House, its luxury mid-rise retirement community in Silver Spring, Maryland. The group gave the organization ideas on the design of the facilities, services needed, activities to be offered, and other important matters. The focus group's input was also used to develop advertising and community relations programs. Sensitivity to the mature adult's perspectives has helped The Charter House lease 75 percent of its 217 units in less than two years of operation.

In the meantime, RCD's commitment to mature market involvement continues. The organization is now using focus groups made up of residents of The Charter House to help it revise its advertising messages. Ads approved by the residents have elicited a high response rate from prospective occupants.

Example 2: At Lutheran General Hospital in Park Ridge, Illinois, older adults have been used in videos that educate patients on various medical conditions. The video presenters are not physicians or nurses, but individuals who have personally experienced the condition described. In one video, for example, a former chemotherapy patient helps others about to undergo this procedure to better understand what to expect from it. The hospital's empathetic approach to the videos has been well received.

Note: Lutheran General's initiative illustrates how the mature market can be utilized to develop products which can be of value to consumers *of any age.*

Example 3: Group Health Cooperative of Puget Sound (GHC) in Seattle is one of the oldest and largest HMOs in the United States. Among its more than 300,000 members are many age 50+ers, including over 30,000 Medicare enrollees. One of the reasons behind GHC's success in attracting and retaining older customers lies in its ability to involve them in shaping some of its programs. In 1983, for example, GHC formed a "Senior Caucus" made up of older consumers. Since its inception, the Senior Caucus has been instrumental in helping GHC develop a number of needed programs for seniors, including an innovative long-term care insurance product offered through a partnership with Metropolitan Life Insurance Company.

Example 4: St. Louis' Clipper Cruise Line, Inc. benefitted enormously from calling upon the skills of just one 50+er. This individual, an avid golfer, helped the company put together its golf tour packages. The tours have been very popular among Clipper's older travelers.

Keep in Mind: While your business may be different from the four just mentioned, the ways in which they involve mature adults are applicable to any organization.

Promoting and Advertising

Older adults can also be part of your advertising and promotional campaigns. A few years ago, Ozark Air Lines engaged in an innovative and clever promotional effort which involved the mature market in two different ways. First, Ozark featured a senior in advertising its "Senior Saver Discount Club." (See Figure 6-3.) Then, as the ad copy indicates, the airline stimulated other seniors' involvement by inviting club applicants to send in a photograph of the "special people you visit most."

What made this promotion so savvy was that it

1. used "everyday" seniors with whom people could identify, and,
2. encouraged older persons to play a hands-on, active part in the campaign by asking them to send in personal photos and offering the possibility of a free round-trip ticket

Note: Another outstanding aspect of Ozark's promotion was that it recognized the magnetism of the grandparent-grandchild relationship.

Tip: Contests and sweepstakes are excellent ways to involve the mature market in your promotional activities and generate interest in your products.

Selling Your Products and Services

Using older adults to sell your company's products and services to other 50+ers makes a lot of sense.

Example: One company that does this is the Avon Corporation. A few years ago, I had the opportunity to participate in a promotional program being developed by Avon. During that time, I had the privilege of being introduced to one of Avon's older employees—an 83-year-old woman who was one of the company's top salespersons. Not surprisingly, I learned that this woman was especially good at selling Avon's products to other older women.

Keep in Mind: The mature adult's experience can help you sell your products to other groups, too. For example, Protocall Communications of Ontario, Canada has used older salespersons to represent the ethical products of major pharmaceutical companies. These salespersons are retirees who formerly worked in similar positions at some of the top pharmaceutical companies. Both Protocall and its clients have benefitted from the older sales representatives' drug industry experience.

Who cares about Ozark discounts?

If you're over 60, *you* should. Because membership in the Ozark Air Lines Senior Saver Discount Club entitles you to 10% off any published Ozark fare. Which makes it a great way to see your loved ones more often.

When you join, you also become a member of Ozark's Frequent Flyer program—and get up to 4,000 free bonus miles. You can earn free trips after just 10,000 miles.

Joining is easy. Just call your local Ozark Air Lines office and ask for details. A lifetime membership is just $25. Ask about our companion membership option that allows you to take along a friend or relative.

Incidentally, we'd like to see your loved ones, too. So when you send in your application, please include a picture of the special people you visit most. We may want to use it in an upcoming ad. If we do, we'll say thanks with a free roundtrip ticket for your next visit.

Of course, you don't *have* to share your picture with us to enroll in the club. But we'll be awfully disappointed if you don't.

Pictures become property of Ozark and must have your name, address and phone number on back. Proof of age is required to join the club.

OZARK FLIES YOUR WAY

FIGURE 6–3

Serving Your Customers

Using older adults to serve the age 50+ customer is an excellent business strategy.

Example 1: Royal Cruise Line's approach to doing this is especially innovative. Through its "Host Program," the company uses a select number of men over 50 to socialize, dine, and dance with unattached women passengers who take its cruises. In exchange for their participation, the hosts receive a complimentary cruise and a bar credit. There are several benefits derived from this program:

- It helps even out the male/female ratio on board.
- It makes the cruises more enjoyable.
- It helps Royal Cruise Line attract more older men and women to the trips.

Example 2: WCAU-TV in Philadelphia utilizes the skills of Phyllis Sanders, a woman in her sixties, as its "seniors" reporter. In her reports on the news, Ms. Sanders gives information on social, legislative, and consumer issues that affect the lives of older persons. Her segments have been very popular as have her presentations to community groups.

Marketing Checklist: Four Ways to Involve Older Adults in Your Mature Market Programs

1. Developing your products/services
2. Promoting and advertising your products/services
3. Selling your products/services
4. Serving your older customers

Tips on Recruiting a Mature Market Team

While it's important to know why you need to involve those over 50 and how you can utilize the group, there is another vital consideration: How do you find older adults who can assist you? Here are six suggestions.

Know the Whys and Hows of Your Recruitment Effort Before You Start

Before you can even begin to build or expand your mature market team, you need to ask two questions:

- Why do we want to involve the older adult in our mature market programs?
- How can we involve the older adult in our mature market programs?

By answering these questions, you should be able to determine:

- if involving the older adult is really an appropriate way to achieve your short- and long-term business objectives
- the range of possibilities that exist for your company to involve the mature adult
- the demographic/psychographic characteristics of the older adults you wish to involve
- how you should pursue and "position" the recruitment effort

The benefit of this analytical process is that it helps you determine whom among the mature market you will need to involve.

Know What Motivates the Mature Market to Get Involved and Incorporate This into Your Recruitment Program

There are several reasons why people over 50 get involved in business-related activities. For example, it may be because they

- need the income
- want to test their entrepreneurial abilities
- seek to have their ideas heard or acted upon
- long to share their know-how
- want to keep busy

In recruiting your mature market team, your mission is twofold:

- First, you need to understand the factors which motivate older adults to get involved.
- Second, you need to compare those motivational factors with the results of your self-assessment. In other words, what factors will most likely attract the kinds of 50+ers you want to recruit?

Let's say you want to form a mature market advisory board to enhance the quality of your airline's service to the older consumer. In this case, the people you're looking for may have a greater need for personal input and social contact than for increased income. On the other hand, suppose you want to find older employees to sell your company's financial services and products to 50+ers. In that case, the potential for greater income or a new challenge may be the major stimulus influencing someone's interest in your program.

Keep in Mind: Once you have matched up your company's needs with the most appropriate motivational factors, you will then be able to develop a recruitment program with the "bells and whistles" necessary to make it effective.

Minimize the Barriers to Gaining Involvement

A retiree recently told me about his efforts to obtain part-time employment. At one of the firms he visited, he was asked to file a job application. Much to his dismay, the lengthy application had many detailed questions including one which asked the man to retrace his entire work history back to high school. The job applicant found this "boilerplate" application inappropriate, cumbersome, and insulting for someone of his age and experience. Because of this, he decided not to file for the job.

The man I've just referred to is neither eccentric nor lazy. In fact, he's a healthy, optimistic, and reasonably ambitious person. Undoubtedly, he would have been an excellent part-time worker for the aforementioned company.

Tip: A lengthy job application can become a roadblock to obtaining helpful services from an older person.

There are several other recruitment barriers, many of them generated by the older adult's own apprehensions. For example, some individuals may have concerns about:

- their prior activity-related experience (or lack thereof)
- the amount of time that must be committed to the activity and the responsibilities that go along with it
- activity locations or transportation
- losing income or benefits earned from prior employment
- working with younger employees
- your organization's motives

All of the above barriers can be circumvented, however, if appropriate actions are taken. For example:

- job applications can be simplified and/or shortened to reflect the kind of work involved
- classroom and on-the-job training programs can be used to (1) ease older adults into new activities and (2) help younger persons work more effectively with them
- transportation can be provided to worksites, focus group facilities, and so forth

In addition, consideration can be given to developing programs that allow some persons to work out of their homes or in their immediate neighborhoods. Promotional materials can spell out as clearly as possible the nature of the activity, the company's goals, and the older person's duties. Company representatives can be trained to advise the older applicant on what impact, if any, the activity will have on his or her other sources of income and benefits.

A number of organizations have made a concerted effort to minimize the potential barriers to mature market involvement in their programs.

Example 1: McDonald's conducts an orientation program for older workers recruited through its McMasters Program. Younger employees, meanwhile, attend sensitivity classes to help them better understand and work with their McMasters colleagues.

Example 2: The American Association of Retired Persons provides extensive training to its new volunteers *before* they are sent out in the field to counsel others.

Example 3: Avon's sales opportunities enable older persons to work within their own communities.

Example 4: The Traveler's Insurance Company's Retiree Job Bank offers flexible work schedules to those it hires. The program also allows retirees to work at The Travelers up to 960 hours per year without losing their pension benefits.

Use High Visibility Media to Promote Your Activities

To maximize your recruitment efforts, you should consider publicizing them through communications channels that reach large numbers of older persons. Obviously, the specific promotional vehicles you use will depend upon the nature of your activity. Here are some of the best routes to consider:

- TV, newspaper, and radio ads/public service announcements— mature adults are avid newspaper readers and heavy users of the broadcast media. (They also tend to prefer specific newspaper sections and TV/radio programming.)
- Community and ethnic newspapers—these tend to have a large readership in a very targeted area.
- "Seniors" publications—localized publications, rather than national ones, will generally be the most cost effective to use.
- Company newsletters—this is an excellent way to reach your own older workers and retirees.
- Visual displays—these would include posters, flyers, and highway billboards.

Example: One outstanding example of a creative and successful promotional program for obtaining mature market involvement was The Travelers' "Un-Retirement Party." The Travelers held this party to recruit older persons for its Retiree Job Bank. The party was preceded by a month-long campaign. During this time, the company used press releases, posters, pamphlets, and buttons to inform people about the party. (See Figure 6-4.) The Travelers also operated a booth at Connecticut's Governor's Day, a day-long

"With my schedule, I take a four-day weekend every week I work."

Un-Retire.

Find out how. Come to The Travelers Un-Retirement Party in Hartford, Sat. Nov. 16, 10 AM to 2 PM.

The Travelers Retiree Job Bank offers you flexibility in work hours. All jobs are part-time, and your work schedule often can be tailored to your personal schedule.

So, if you're retired, active, skilled and dependable, consider Un-Retiring at The Travelers.

Learn more. Come to our Un-Retirement Party at The Travelers Plaza Building, 50 Prospect Street:
—Meet Travelers Un-Retirees.

—Try your hand at computers.
—Refreshments served.
—Free parking at The Hartford Club on Prospect St., just east of The Travelers Tower.

For information call: (203) 277-2025

It's never too late for a job at The Travelers.

I'm Un-Retired.
The Travelers

The Travelers Older American Program.
The Travelers Companies, Hartford, Connecticut 06183.

Employment opportunities at The Travelers are equally available to all qualified applicants.
An Equal Opportunity Employer.

Advertising by Hirsch Elliot Inc.

FIGURE 6–4

event that showcases all of the state's services for older adults. As a result, the company attracted 400 retirees to its Job Bank!

Note: Like The Travelers, you can attract older workers by creating part-time, flexible employment opportunities—something that many retirees find appealing.

Use Available Public/Private Resources to Help in Recruiting

One of the best things about obtaining mature market involvement is that you don't have to go about it alone. There are a number of private and public resources available to help you. On the public side, many federal and state agencies have an active interest in helping businesses utilize the skills of older adults. McDonald's, for instance, has obtained the assistance of one of the Maryland Offices on Aging to do its recruiting. A somewhat related effort exists in Hillsborough County, Florida. There, "Working Seniors" helps older workers find unsubsidized employment. Working Seniors is a public-private partnership sponsored by the Hillsborough County Department of Aging Services, the Greater Tampa Chamber of Commerce, and the University of Tampa.

On the private side, a number of firms have sprung up to match older persons with companies who seek to utilize their skills. Operation ABLE (Ability Based on Long Experience) is a private nonprofit agency with offices around the country. Worne & Associates, in Marlton, New Jersey, is a private employment agency which has been placing people over 50 in jobs since 1982. The Ford Modeling Agency's "Classic Women" department has helped supply ad agencies with older models for several years.

Beyond the many service-related firms, there are also several published references available. Some of these provide advice specifically on how to attract and/or utilize the older worker. These include the National Association of State Units on Aging's guide, "Marketing Strategies for Recruiting Older Individuals," and Operation ABLE of Greater Boston's handbook and videotape entitled "A Silver Opportunity." (See Appendix B for a listing of these and other relevant resources.)

Coordinate Your Activities with Other In-House Departments

Inter-departmental communication can be valuable to the marketing effort. Yet this practice is seldom adopted. Where the avenues of communication and collaboration seem to be least open is between the human resources and marketing departments. This is easy to understand since their mature market connection is not readily apparent. However, there are clearly benefits to be realized when these two units collaborate with one another.

Example: Suppose you're in the marketing department of a Fortune 1000 corporation. Your company has just developed a new soft drink. The drink is a low-sugar, no-caffeine beverage targeted primarily to an older audience. What you'd like now are some good ideas on what to name the product. Where can you get them? Well, why not ask your retirees? And who's in the best position to help you reach your retirees? The human resources department, of course!

Note: By working with your human resources department, you may also come up with other creative ways to recruit and involve older adults in your company's business activities—regardless of whether or not the products or services involve the mature market.

Dialogue between the human resource and marketing departments can flow in the other direction, too. Suppose the human resource department decides to do a survey of your company's pensioners: where they're living, what kind of activities they engage in, what their concerns are, and so forth. In that case, you, in the marketing department, might be called upon to submit some specific questions for inclusion in the survey. Ultimately, the answers to these and other survey questions could be shared with you. In all likelihood, some of the data could provide you with information useful in formulating or improving your company's mature market (or other) strategies.

Marketing Checklist:
Suggestions for Recruiting Your Mature Market Team

1. Know the whys and hows of your recruitment effort.
2. Know what motivates the mature adult to get involved and incorporate those factors into your recruitment program.
3. Minimize the barriers to gaining involvement.
4. Use high visibility media to promote your activities.
5. Use available public and private resources to help you tap into the 50+ pool.
6. Coordinate your activities with other in-house departments.

Chapter Wrap-up

To maximize your success with older consumers, you must involve the group in your mature market activities. You'll be best served if you involve the older consumer long before a specific product or service is ever produced. And you'll benefit most if you involve mature adults on an ongoing—rather than a one-shot or intermittent—basis.

There are many ways to involve the mature market beyond those activities that are directly related to the marketing and sales functions. And

50+ers can also be an excellent resource in helping you attract and serve *many* customer populations—not just members of their own group.

Finally, remember that some of the best mature consumers to involve may be found right in your own back yard: They are your own older workers and retirees.

---

1. Peters, Thomas J. and Robert H. Waterman, Jr. *In Search of Excellence: Lessons from America's Best-Run Companies.* New York: Harper & Row, 1982, p. 156.

2. Ibid, p. 193.

Chapter 7

Key 5: Establish Relationships with Key Groups and Influencers

Royal Cruise Line: Catering to Mature Travelers

Since 1974, Royal Cruise Line's ships have taken people to exotic destinations all over the world. To enjoy one of this San Francisco-based cruise line's typical 12- to 14-day vacations, passengers spend upwards of $4,000 per person. Many of these travelers are members of the mature market. In fact, about 75 percent of the 45,000 or so tourists who travel with Royal Cruise Line each year are age 50 +. Royal Cruise Line's ability to attract and serve the middle and upper-income older traveler has made the company one of the most successful and profitable in its industry. How has Royal Cruise Line been able to do this?

Like the other eight organizations profiled in this section of the book, Royal Cruise Line's mature market success is based on several factors. For one thing, the company has developed innovative programs to meet the needs of its prospective customers. For example, it was the first marketer to introduce programs designed to attract single older men to cruise vacations. It also uses its creative skills to develop a number of unique payment plans, including "Crown Credit," an option it offers to those who want to finance the cost of their vacation.

Another reason for Royal Cruise Line's success is that the company is able to meet its customers' expectations by—

- delivering the outstanding food, accommodations, entertainment, culture, activities, and tourist attractions promised in its promotional literature;
- treating its passengers like royalty . . . giving them superior service and catering to their individualized needs; and
- providing special benefits to its repeat customers, a group that represents about one-third of all Royal Cruise Line's travelers!

All of these things combine to make the typical Royal Cruise Line passenger feel that his (or her) vacation was inexpensive when considering the *value* received.

One other specific marketing strategy has contributed to Royal Cruise Line's prosperity. This represents Key 5 in successfully marketing to and serving the mature consumer: *establish relationships with key groups and influencers.*

Reaching the Masses

To attract older travelers to its cruises, Royal Cruise Line works with a variety of individuals and organizations— first and foremost are travel agents. In addition to handling individual reservation requests and deposits, agents help the company interface with the mature market at the grassroots level. They play a vital liaison role: relaying leads, communicating customer comments, and promoting/sponsoring Royal Cruise Line tours for specific groups of 50 + ers who live within well-defined areas.

Royal Cruise Line has also cultivated relationships with organizations and communities which attract older adults such as senior centers, retiree clubs, and adult housing communities. In addition, the company has worked with other groups which, while not made up entirely of older Americans, do tend to have large numbers of age 50 + members (for example, alumni associations). Working with, and marketing to, such groups makes it easier for Royal Cruise Line to attract older tourists. Part of the reason for this lies in the affinity which exists between these individuals and the organizations to which they belong. According to Duncan Beardsley, the company's senior vice president of marketing, this "magnetism of the member to the group" provides a very strong motivation for someone to take a vacation.

There are other key groups and influencers with whom Royal Cruise Line has established a link. Among the most successful have been the mass media—in particular, local newspapers and publications for older adults. As an example, the company has run tours that have been sponsored by *The Salt Lake Tribune, Active Seniors* (a monthly magazine), and *Senior Spectrum Weekly*, a newspaper serving older adults in the Sacramento, California area. Among the benefits of working with these publications is the widespread publicity the tours receive. When the *The Salt Lake Tribune* helped organize a trip, for example, the newspaper mentioned the outing in its Sunday paper. With coverage like this, the cruise became a community event.

The Power of the Pied Piper: Using Satisfied Customers to Entice Newcomers

How does Royal Cruise Line develop new relationships with key groups of importance to older adults? The initial contact generally comes from a satisfied customer. The power of the customer's testimonial not only gives the company access to a group, it also helps close the sale.

A case in point concerns "Sons in Retirement," or SIRS. SIRS is a California-based organization that has about 150 chapters throughout the state. Each of these chapters is made up of retired men who meet monthly. After enjoying a Royal Cruise Line trip, a member of the travel committee of one SIRS group asked his travel agent to find out if an entire SIRS chapter could be booked on a cruise. Through the assistance and support of this SIRS member, a representative from Royal Cruise Line was able to make a presentation about its tours to the chapter. Subsequently, a successful travel program was run with the group.

Royal Cruise Line's experience with SIRS illustrates a major benefit of establishing relationships with group leaders and the organizations they represent: it helps gain powerful third-party endorsements that can lead to *multiple* sales. As Duncan Beardsley puts it, "The individual that is a leader of a group has a respectability or a credibility among the members that is very important to any marketer trying to talk to that group. When one of them decides to go on a trip, 50 of them will follow. It's the Pied Piper syndrome."

Knowing the clout wielded by third-party endorsers, Royal Cruise Line finds ways to incorporate influential people into the marketing of its cruises. Many times these will be opinion leaders within the groups. Take the cruise line's "Senior Class Tour," a program offered to all senior centers in Northern California. To promote this tour, Royal Cruise Line placed a large counter card with brochures in every senior center. Attached to the display was a photo of the group leader for the specific center involved. The company used this approach so prospective tourists could see that someone they knew would be traveling with them.

Royal Cruise Line employs a similar strategy when running its newspaper-sponsored programs. In this case, the company typically seeks out respected media personalities to host its tours—ones whom the mature traveler can identify with. The host of a 1987 program sponsored by the Sacramento-area's *Senior Spectrum Weekly*, for instance, was Don Bloom, the middle-aged, executive editor of the publication. Mr. Bloom's affiliation with the program was conspicuously touted in the flyer used to promote the tour. (See Figure 7-1.)

Making a Good Thing Even Better: Alternative Dining Selections

Groups and influencers don't just help Royal Cruise Line reach clusters of older adults or sell more tours. They also help the company offer *better* cruises. Nothing illustrates this more clearly than its relationship with the American Heart Association (AHA).

Acting upon the advice and assistance of another satisfied customer, a nutritionist, Royal Cruise Line approached AHA a few years ago about developing a menu with items that were lower in calories, fat, and cholesterol.

Announcing
A Unique Transatlantic/European Adventure
Sailing the Warm, Gentle, Southern Atlantic Route

SENIOR SPECTRUM HOSTED DEPARTURE
April 25, 1987
Aboard the Top-Rated *Royal Odyssey*

Launch your springtime on Royal Cruise Line's special Transatlantic/European cruise from San Juan, Puerto Rico, to Lisbon, Portugal. Then complete your two-week vacation on our spectacular 6-night package in the elegant, cosmopolitan city of Lisbon.

COMPLETE 16-DAY
AIR/CRUISE/HOTEL FARES

Air/Cruise/Hotel Fares From San Francisco.

Suite Categories	A-C	$2398
Outside Categories	D-H	$2098
Outside Categories	I-M	$1998
Inside Categories	N-Q	$1898

All fares are per person, double occupancy. Single supplement,(cat. D-Q) $950. 3rd or 4th person: $1560.

YOUR 6-NIGHT POST-CRUISE LISBON
LAND PACKAGE INCLUDES:

- 6 nights at the 5-star Alfa Hotel
- Continental Breakfast each morning
- Passenger booked in a Suite (Category A-C) will receive a hotel suite in Lisbon
- A Royal Cruise Line Hospitality Desk to assist with optional sightseeing tours

Don Bloom is from Woodland and, with his wife Nancy, has traveled to Europe, the Orient, South Pacific, the Caribbean and throughout the United States. Don has been Sports Editor of *The Woodland Democrat* and *The Sacramento Union* and a columnist for *The Sacramento Bee* after starting his newspaper career in 1948. Now Executive Editor of *Senior Spectrum*, Don has written for numerous publications in America and Germany, and his book, "Confessions of a Sportswriter," will be published next summer.

Join Don and Nancy on this fabulous cruise of a lifetime!

Special Bonus Amenities!

★ Discounted Cruise Fare
★ A Hosted Cocktail Party
★ One Bottle of Wine per Stateroom

For reservations and information please contact your local Sacramento Travel Agent, a cruise expert.

Royal Cruise Line

FIGURE 7–1

Through that relationship, Royal Cruise Line became the first cruise line to include alternative dining selections at all breakfasts, lunches, and dinners served on its ships. All of these items are specially prepared in accordance with the AHA's dietary recommendations. A Royal Cruise Line/AHA booklet which includes information about the nutritional content of these menu selections is also provided to cruise passengers. (See Figure 7-2.)

Through its association with AHA, Royal Cruise Line has learned how to better address the dietary needs of the over-50 population. The company has also benefitted from having its alternative menu selections sanctioned by the AHA. Indeed, the credibility it has gained from this effort more than compensates for the time and labor required to develop the program. Says Beardsley, "We could have created something ourselves, but better we did it under the blessing or aegis of an organization that already has credibility in this area—specifically, the American Heart Association. So it was worth the energy to go to them and have them guide us." Not surprisingly, the AHA-approved program has been well received by Royal Cruise line's older travelers.

A Dominant Marketing Tool

To date, more than 150,000 people have experienced a Royal Cruise Line vacation. In the process, the company has built itself a very profitable business. To achieve such success, Royal Cruise Line has had to develop marketing strategies which make its tours appealing to its most likely customers—older Americans with time and money. Among those strategies, the establishment of relationships with groups and influencers has been of particular importance. Says Beardsley, "There's no question it is the dominant marketing tool that we have to get people to travel."

Seven Marketing Benefits of Establishing Relationships

There are a number of benefits to be gained from establishing relationships with key groups and influencers. All of them can help increase the probability that your marketing efforts will be successful. Following are seven of these benefits.

You Can Maximize Your Selling Power

Many businesses develop sales strategies for the mature market as if most 50 + ers were isolated from each other and the rest of society. This "they exist in a vacuum" mentality results in a variety of promotions that target the older consumer on a one-at-a-time basis.

Royal Cruise Line presents

an Exclusive First in Cruising

DINE TO YOUR HEART'S CONTENT

 American Heart Association

The American Heart Association's Plan for Healthful Shipboard Dining Exclusively Aboard the Golden Odyssey, Royal Odyssey and Crown Odyssey

♛ Royal Cruise Line

FIGURE 7-2

Most older adults *do* have frequent contact with specific individuals and groups. While this is especially the case with those in their fifties, sixties, and early seventies, it is also true of the majority of those over 75. To ignore this fact may unnecessarily limit the potential your company has to sell its products and services to:

- groups with large numbers of 50+ers
- groups that have access to large numbers of 50+ers

Example: A client of mine wanted to increase his company's sales. For several years, his company had sold its seniors-oriented product through door-to-door salespeople. While the company gained a significant number of older customers this way, the client now realized that revenues and profits could grow much faster if his staff were also able to sell this product to groups.

Unfortunately, this company faced two major obstacles in trying to broaden its sales approach:

- Its nationwide sales force had little familiarity with either group sales or the groups to whom they should be prospecting.
- One of its competitors had already solidly established a dominant position in group sales. Not surprisingly, that company had also become the industry leader.

After meeting with this client, I was convinced that he'd have an uphill battle in trying to make heavy penetration into the group markets.

Warning: In a competitive marketplace, most businesses cannot afford to restrict their 50+ marketing programs to a one-dimensional level. The best marketing progams will be those that enable products to be sold on both an individual and a group basis.

You Can Develop or Improve Distribution Channels

Personal, one-on-one contact is generally the best way to sell your products to older consumers. But for many businesses, this may be very costly or impractical. By establishing relationships with groups and influencers, however, the "high touch" aspect of marketing to the mature consumer becomes possible. This is because such linkages can often help you reach 50+ers at the grassroots level.

Royal Cruise Line's relationship with travel agents illustrates how linkages can help you reach mature adults at the local level. There are other approaches too. For example, several companies, including Polaroid, Continental American Life Insurance Company, and Combe Pharmaceuticals, have come into closer contact with older consumers by working with Mature Concepts of Berlin, New Jersey. Mature Concepts acts as a liaison between these and other companies and some 4,000 organizations in the mid-Atlantic region. In that capacity, the firm has distributed product samples and coupons to about a half-million older adults.

Important: While some relationships may not enable you to have direct contact with the mature market, they can increase your ability to gain *access* to that market. This is especially valuable when it allows you to reach 50+ers "en masse". Several marketers have capitalized on this opportunity by working directly with groups of older adults and government organizations.

You Can Gain Valuable Insight on the Older Population's Needs

Not too long ago, I had the pleasure of listening to an after-dinner speech given by Ms. Maggie Kuhn, founder of the Gray Panthers. During her talk, Ms. Kuhn presented some marvelous insights on what it's like to be an older American. Any perceptive businessperson in the audience that night could have left the room with several good marketing ideas.

Along with Maggie Kuhn and her Gray Panthers, many other individuals and organizations can help businesses broaden their knowledge of the older consumer. The cultivation of cooperative relationships makes this all possible.

Tip: Marketers can use this information to provide better service to older customers, to improve their products, and to develop new programs and products.

You Can Enhance Your Product's Credibility

Without question, the issue of credibility is of paramount importance when it comes to successfully marketing products and services to the mature market. Very often credibility can be gained through collaborating with other businesses or organizations that are held in high esteem by the mature consumers you are targeting.

Warning: Do not assume that all nonprofit agencies or organizations that work primarily with the 50+ population have credibility. Many older adults may actually dislike some of these groups or be unfamiliar with them.

You Can Increase Your Visibility

Working with other groups and influencers can also help you maximize the exposure which your company, your programs, or your products receive among the mature market. While establishing relationships with members of the mass media provides an obvious illustration of how this could happen, there are other good examples.

   Example: For a few years, Barnett Banks of Florida has been a sponsor of AARP's "55 Alive" driver education program. The bank has gained a tremendous amount of visibility from this activity. In 1986, for example, 33,000 people took the course through Barnett's sponsorship. During the first half of 1987, another 26,000 persons had participated in the program. Initiatives like this have helped Barnett accumulate $4.5 billion in deposits from a large and loyal base of older customers.[1]

You Can Obtain Resources to Develop or Expand Mature Market Programs

Collaboration with groups and influencers can also enable you to acquire staff, facilities, funding, or additional products and services. All of these can be used to help you initiate or broaden the programs you have to serve the mature adult.

   Example: One of the most successful adult education programs in the world, Elderhostel, is built around the organization's relationship with colleges and universities. These facilities provide the courses, the teachers, the housing, and the food for people who attend Elderhostel's programs. Today, Elderhostel works with about 1,000 educational institutions in the United States and foreign countries. Growth in the size of Elderhostel's academic network has been accompanied by consistent increases in the numbers of older adults who take its programs. That group now numbers about 150,000 students a year!

You Can Draw Upon the Powers of Group Participation

By establishing relationships with groups that have significant numbers of older members, you may also increase your ability to attract customers. There is a certain magnetism that often motivates people to participate in activities undertaken by clubs or organizations to which they belong. *This force may be even stronger among members of the mature market.*

   Note: Several analyses of the over-50 population's social behavior have found that, in general, older Americans tend to be group-oriented. Dr. Morris Massey, an expert in the field of human behavior, and author of the book, *The People Puzzle*, has even cited the "group-team" concept as a common value held by older Americans.[2]

   In working with groups and their leaders, you also are more likely to obtain the support necessary to help your program be successful. This has definitely been Royal Cruise Line's experience. Says Duncan Beardsley, "Once an organization makes a commitment that they are going to go on one of our cruises, they're determined to get enough people to make the trip viable.''

Key Point: Relationship building can help your company gain commitments from the groups you work with—something that increases the probability that your marketing efforts *will* be successful.

Marketing Checklist: Seven Benefits of Establishing Relationships with Key Groups and Influencers

You can . . .

1. Maximize your selling power
2. Develop or improve your channels of distribution
3. Increase your knowledge of the older population and its needs
4. Enhance your credibility
5. Increase your visibility
6. Obtain resources to develop or expand your programs
7. Draw upon the powers of group participation

Key Groups and Influential People Who Can Help You Serve the Mature Market

On the following pages, I will identify several groups and influencers that could be important to your organization's mature market-related activities. I'll also provide an example of how each of them has worked with others on such efforts. Figure 7-3 lists these and other important groups and influencers.

Keep in Mind: The groups I discuss are not presented in any particular order of priority; also, the nature of your organization and its objectives will determine:

- which of those mentioned are applicable to your business
- how you will get involved with them

Groups for People Over 50 on the National and Local Level

Older adult groups may be membership-oriented like the American Association of Retired Persons (AARP) and the National Council of Senior Citizens. They may be part of public programs like the Retired Senior Volunteer Pro-

Key Groups and Influencers

- older adult groups and related organizations
- government agencies and related organizations
- religious groups and the clergy
- health care providers, insurers, and associations
- employers, unions, and human resource organizations
- academic institutions
- foundations
- family (e.g., children and grandchildren)
- opinion leaders
- other marketers (e.g., those in non-competing industries)
- service organizations (e.g., the Red Cross, Kiwanis, American Legion)
- clubs and related groups (e.g., alumni associations, bridge clubs, civic associations, gardening clubs, etc.)
- support groups (e.g., family caregiver chapters)
- bank trust officers
- attorneys
- elected officials
- the mass media and media personalities

FIGURE 7–3

gram and the Service Core of Retired Executives. They may be cause or demographically related like the Older Women's League. Or, they may be lifestyle/occupation-oriented such as the National Association for Retired Credit Union People and the National Association of Retired Federal Employees.

The exact nature of the opportunities that may exist to work with these groups varies. They may range from educational programming, to staff assistance, to product/service marketing. Perhaps the best example of the latter concerns AARP and its relationship with companies like the Prudential Insurance Company of America and Olsen-Travelworld, Ltd. Through this relationship, these businesses have been able to offer their services to AARP's 30 + million members.

Key Point: Since many of these groups are found at the local level, they may enable your business to engage in very targeted marketing programs.

Government and Nonprofit Agencies

A myriad of government agencies are involved in providing programs and services which concern older Americans. These organizations exist at all levels: national, state, county, and municipal. They include the Social Security Administration, the Health Care Financing Administration (which administers Medicare and Medicaid), and state and county offices on aging.

In addition, there are a number of private, nonprofit organizations whose principal activities concern older Americans. These include such groups as the National Association of Area Agencies on Aging (NAAA), the American Society on Aging, and trade/professional associations like the Gerontological Society of America.

Tip: While the majority of area agencies on aging are public organizations, there are many others which are private, nonprofits. These groups tend to be more disposed to working with the private sector.

As with the 50+ groups, government agencies may work with the private sector on a broad spectrum of initiatives. In fact, a few of these organizations have been encouraged to enter into public/private sector business-oriented programs.

Example: The Health Care Financing Administration (HCFA) has been aggressively seeking relationships with HMOs and other health-related entities in an effort to control its costs for insuring some 30+ million Medicare enrollees.

Example: The National Association of Area Agencies on Aging (NAAAA) has been among the more visible private, nonprofit organizations that have developed working relationships with the private sector. Southwestern Bell Publications, Aetna Life Insurance and Annuity Company, Hoechst-Roussel Pharmaceuticals, and AT&T Communications are among those businesses which have utilized the resources of the NAAAA and the 600+ area agencies whose interests it represents.

Tip: Regardless of what opportunities may exist to work collaboratively with any of the above organizations, many of them can still provide you with important data, publications, and legislation concerning the older adult. This is particularly true of Congressional offices and committees.

Religious Groups and Clergy

Both religion and religious affiliation are very important to America's older population. Those over 50 are more likely to regard their religious faith as important than are younger persons. They are also more likely to attend church and to represent the membership of specific religious groups. Gallup has found that 41 percent of all Protestants and Jews are age 50+.[3] And, while Catholics tend to be a somewhat younger group, there are still many urban congregations whose memberships are very "gray."

Opportunity: Businesses can work with various religious organizations and clergy at both the national and local level.

Example: Several marketers of travel and health care products/services have developed a relationship in which they serve members of the Catholic Golden Age, a national organization for Catholics age 50+ that has over 350,000 members. Dan Dipert Tours, a very successful marketer of tours for older adults, works with local church leaders. Presbyterian-University of Pennsylvania Medical Center in Philadelphia performs health screening services for some 3,500 church officers and their spouses, 85 percent of whom are 55 or older.

Religious organizations and clergy also represent excellent groups to collaborate with on issues of concern to the older population. Thus, some marketers have wisely invited community religious leaders to attend seminars they've either sponsored or given. These individuals are often in close contact with older adults and their families and can be excellent referral sources.

Tip: Educational marketing is a particularly good approach to interfacing with religious groups and their leaders.

Health Organizations

For those within and outside of the health care industry, organizations such as health providers, insurers, and associations can be excellent groups to build relationships with. In addition to reaching large numbers of 50+ers, these groups are in a good position to understand some of the needs of this group. They also can bring your business increased visibility and credibility. In some instances, they can exert a strong influence on the older adult's consumer behavior.

Tip: This is particularly true of physicians, a group highly respected by many 50+ers.

Example: Lifeline Systems of Watertown, Massachusetts is one company that has benefitted from its relationship with the health care community. In this case, hospitals have become major purchasers of Lifeline's emergency medical system, a product most often used by older adults. Hospitals buy Lifeline's emergency medical systems and then sell or lease them to older adults within their community. To date, Lifeline has sold more than 120,000 of these security systems.

Several marketers have developed relationships with medical associations and/or organizations that fight for the prevention, treatment, and cure of specific diseases (particularly those that commonly affect older adults).

Examples: Thorneburg Hosiery Company has jointly sponsored the HealthWalk program with the American Podiatric Medical Association. The program involves older adult groups throughout America. Also, United Airlines has developed a cause-related marketing effort with the Alzheimer's

Disease and Related Disorders Association (ADRDA). Under this arrangement, people who join United's "Silver Wings Plus" program (for those age 60+) will have some of their membership fee donated to ADRDA.

Employers, Unions, and Human Resource Organizations

A sizable population of 50+ers can be reached through those involved with older workers and retirees. These include mid-size to large corporations, government employers, private/public sector unions, and personnel-related associations like the American Society for Personnel Administration and the International Society of Pre-Retirement Planners.

Employers represent a particularly good channel for marketers to cultivate. That's because an aging America has brought with it a huge increase in the number of older workers and retirees. In some well-established companies, for example, there are almost as many retirees (if not more) than active workers. This has created employer interest in several areas including older worker productivity, health care cost management, or retiree communications.

Tip: Health care costs for older workers and retirees has become a major concern for many American corporations and unions. A huge, relatively untapped opportunity exists for those businesses who have products and services that address this problem.

Several businesses including General Learning Corporation, Whitney Communications, and Retirement Advisors, Inc. have found success in selling publications to employers, who then provide them to their older workers or retirees. These publications offer the pre-retiree or retiree information about topics of concern to the older adult, including the managing of one's personal finances and health. Other businesses have sold health insurance or prescription drug services to employers or unions that have large retiree populations.

Note: Relationships with these groups may also allow you to sell more easily your products and services *directly* to the mature consumer.

Examples: Some employers are now making it possible for insurers to market their long-term care insurance product through the company. Although the employer isn't contributing to the cost of the policy, he is providing the insurer with an implied endorsement and an excellent distribution channel. Another company that has effectively used this strategy is the Government Employees Insurance Company (GEICO). For many years, GEICO, a privately held corporation, has worked closely with the federal government's Office of Personnel Management. Through this relationship, GEICO has sold auto insurance policies to a large group of age 50+ federal workers and retirees.

Tip: Many employers and unions also have retiree clubs. These can often be identified and reached by networking with the above groups.

Academic Institutions

Many colleges and universities engage in activities which, in one way or another, concern older adults. Like Florida International University's Southeast Florida Center on Aging, these activities involve research, education, training, and program development/execution. It is quite likely that your organization can benefit by networking with these institutions.

Example: One company that has tapped into a university's expertise to better serve the older adult is May Department Stores Company. Through the assistance of medical and social service professionals at the Washington University School of Medicine and Jewish Hospital, May Company has been able to present its popular OASIS (Older Adult Service and Information System) educational classes.

Tip: When developing relationships with educational institutions, don't forget to consider the local libraries. In some instances, they can be excellent places to distribute information about your product or service, or something related to it. Elderhostel, for example, sends a copy of its course catalog to every public library and branch facility in the United States and Canada. Libraries can also be good customers for "seniors" publications.

Foundations

A number of foundations, both private and community, provide grants to nonprofit organizations for programs that directly benefit the older population. About 3 percent of the roughly $5.2 billion in grants awarded in 1985 were awarded for programs serving this group.[4] Among the most active grantors have been the The Commonwealth Fund, the AARP Andrus Foundation, the Villers Foundation, and the Retirement Research Foundation.

Foundations generally provide funds for programs that seek to keep older persons independent, active, and involved. One of The Robert Wood Johnson Foundation's projects, for example, awarded grant monies to home health agencies for developing new services that would keep older persons from being prematurely institutionalized.

Note: Grant monies can sometimes be used not only as sources of funding, but also to help develop profitable products/services . . . if they meet the needs of an aging population and benefit the society-at-large. Further, opportunities exist for those external businesses that assist the nonprofit groups in carrying out these programs (market research companies, consulting firms, advertising agencies, and so forth). Given the demographic projections, these opportunities are likely to increase in the years ahead.

Several company-sponsored foundations like those of Johnson & Johnson (The Robert Wood Johnson Foundation), The Travelers Insurance Company, and The Hartford provide generous grants for programs that benefit older Americans. The Committee for Corporate Public Involvement of the life and health insurance industry reports that a number of its member companies have supported senior-oriented programs. The Committee has also singled out attention to the "elderly" as a recommended priority for its members.[5]

Key Point: Even if your business cannot directly work with any of the above foundations and corporate grantors, you can still benefit from learning about their projects. By keeping aware, you may:

- get a better picture of the short- and long-term needs of an aging society

- have the opportunity to witness the successes and failures of experimental programs for older persons

- obtain valuable, secondary research data from which you can develop or modify your own marketing programs

Grandchildren

One of the best relationship strategies is the development of marketing programs that link mature adults and their grandchildren. According to research by R.H. Bruskin Associates, 28 percent of this nation's men and 35 percent of its women have grandchildren.[6] And, they see those grandchildren often. For example, a study funded by the National Institute on Aging (NIA) found that most grandparents see their grandchildren at least monthly. More than one-third see them once a week![7]

When they're not seeing their grandchildren and doing things *with* them, grandparents are often doing things *for* them . . . like buying them toys and clothing.

Note: According to one study, grandparents spent almost $2 billion on toys for their grandchildren in 1985. That was close to 20 percent of the entire toy market.[8] In *50 Plus* magazine's May 1985 Grandparent Survey, more than 85 percent of the 4,000+ persons who responded said they had bought clothing for their grandchildren in the last two years.[9]

Tip: Conducting similar surveys with your older customers may be one good way to develop effective grandparent-grandchild marketing programs.

Several businesses have developed marketing strategies and new products and services that recognize the chemistry of the grandparent-grandchild bond. Most of these are in the toy, clothing, travel, and publishing industries.

Examples: The F.A.O. Schwarz toy store in New York has a "Grandma's Shop." This section of the store carries expensive gifts such as china dolls and fancy dresses for infants. Among publishers, Cahners Publishing has introduced *Grandparents Today*, a closed-circulation magazine sponsored exclusively by toy manufacturer, Fisher-Price. (See Figure 7-4.) AT&T has used advertisements that promote its long-distance telephone service as a way for grandparents to keep in touch with their grandchildren.

Tip: As several shrewd marketers have already discovered, ads that show older persons with their grandchildren are usually warmly received by the mature market.

Opportunities exist for businesses in a wide range of product and service categories who can tie together grandparents and grandchildren in their marketing programs. In developing such programs, you should keep these three things in mind:

1. Grandparents tend to be most generous when it comes to spending for their *first* grandchild.

2. Most people today become grandparents in their early to mid-fifties.*

3. Marketing programs which build affinities between grandparents (and their grandchildren too) and a company or its products will have an excellent chance for success. Developing programs that are connected to Grandparent's Day (the first Sunday after Labor Day) is but one way this relationship could be built (such as contests, special sales, events, and so forth).

Opinion Leaders

Developing relationships with local (or national) opinion leaders can also help your business more effectively market to and serve the older consumer.

Example: One company that has successfully done this is Life Care Services (LCS) Corporation of Des Moines, Iowa. LCS is the nation's leading developer of life care communities, having been in the business for more than 25 years. The principals of LCS have been responsible for the planning, development, and management of more than 50 retirement communities. In an industry where failures and bankruptcies are commonplace, LCS' communities boast an average occupancy rate of 98 percent! Among other factors, this achievement helps explain why the organization has earned such an outstanding reputation in the marketplace.

When developing a new community, LCS tries to identify individuals

---

*The onset of grandparenthood is rising, since many couples who postponed having children until later (specifically, the baby boomers) are now deciding to start their families.

AMERICAN BABY'S

A Cahners Publication

GRANDPARENTS
TODAY

Changes in Childbirth
New Ideas in Child Rearing
Why Grandparents Matter

**WRITTEN
ESPECIALLY FOR
GRANDPARENTS
TODAY**

FIGURE 7–4

who'd help make the project successful. (On some occasions, people actually seek out LCS first.) While those selected will vary somewhat depending
on the project involved, all possess some common traits. For example, they
are older persons who've voiced strong support for the life care community
under development. In addition, they also have:

- been successful in their careers
- been active in local affairs
- gained leadership status and a certain following within their community
- attained the respect of their peers

These opinion leaders are chosen to become a part of the life care community's board. They often become its first residents. They influence others of similar stature to move in. And they help the new community grow and flourish.

Warning: Make sure that the opinion leaders you select are representative of the group of older prospects you're seeking to target. Otherwise, you may attract the wrong clientele.

Other Marketers

The intensity of interest in the mature consumer has caused a number of companies to develop marketing strategies, products, and programs to serve this market. This has created the opportunity for companies within the same industry, or in different industries, to initiate *cooperative marketing efforts.* Some businesses that market clubs or membership programs, such as Days Inn (through its September Days Club), have already benefitted from such alliances. Nevertheless, the potential for developing creative and mutually profitable linkages remains largely untapped.

Examples: The magazine, *Grandparents Today,* is the result of a collaborative relationship between two national companies: toy manufacturer, Fisher-Price, and publisher, Cahners Publishing. On the other hand, the "EverActive" network is a locally based, multi-industry mature market venture involving four Washington state corporations: Tacoma General Hospital, Puget Sound Bank, Pay Less Drug Stores, and Tacoma Community College. This group of businesses provides consumers age 55 + with a variety of health care, financial, educational, and travel services.

Reminder: Companies with an interest in products or services for the mature market may also represent a sizable business opportunity for your organization.

Marketing Approaches for Tapping into the 50+ Network

Organizations that have benefitted from networking with key groups and influencers in the mature market have utilized a number of approaches to develop these relationships. Here are a few to consider.

Develop a Good Understanding of the Network

Many public and private organizations devote most, if not all, of their time to matters that concern older adults. By knowing who these groups are, what they do, who they serve, and what their concerns are, you can magnify your understanding of the 50+ population and your ability to develop profitable product/service lines that serve them.

Key Point: Make it your business to read these organizations' publications, attend their conferences, and speak with members of their staffs.

To further your relationship *and* your knowledge, be willing to get actively involved in a group's activities by:

- writing articles for its publications
- serving on its advisory committees
- sponsoring its programs
- lecturing at its conferences and seminars

Ask Your Customers

Royal Cruise Line's experiences demonstrate how your customers can help you open the door to establishing relationships with key groups and influencers. Encourage employees to ask your older customers about groups to which they belong, their group leaders, and other persons of influence within the 50+ network. When appropriate, also ask if a customer can help you gain access to these individuals and groups. Be sure to incorporate this information into your customer or mature market data base.

Conduct Marketing Research

Both qualitative and quantitative research can help you determine key groups and influencers with whom your business may want to establish relationships. Life Care Services, for example, has used focus groups to help it identify opinion leaders within the areas it plans to build life care communities.

Important: While there is obviously a value in conducting consumer research, do not overlook the merits of business-to-business research. Through such research, you may be able to substantially increase your knowledge of the older adult network and the needs of various groups within it. More important, you may be able to develop proactive marketing strategies and new channels of promotion and distribution.

Keep Up-to-Date with Your Competitors and Colleagues

The "hotness" of the mature market can be good news or bad news for your company. On the down side, it means many companies, including your fiercest competitors, are probably trying to increase their market share of older customers. On the up side, it means there may be more opportunities than ever to establish alliances with other marketers interested in the 50+ consumer: alliances that may give you a competitive advantage.

Unfortunately, you allow yourself to be more vulnerable to "bad news" scenarios if you're not aware of what those outside your industry are doing.

Tip: To develop a more global awareness of mature market activity, read generic publications about marketing to older consumers (e.g., *Mature Market Report*) and business/marketing (e.g., *The Wall Street Journal*, *Business Week*, and *American Demographics*). Try to skim through the most important trade journals in consumer industries other than your own to see what their mature market interests and activities are. Have someone attend select conferences and trade shows where information of this type is liable to surface.

An aging work force is increasing employer/union involvement in issues concerning older adults. As a result, you should keep in contact with those in your human resources department. These individuals can make you aware of needs and opportunities that may exist among the 50+ group. They may also help you reach and communicate more easily with your company's older workers and retirees.

Assume an Active Community Presence

Opportunities to develop relationships with key groups and influencers are multiplied when your organization takes its marketing program to the grassroots level. Participation in community service programs (especially those which involve the 50+ population) can substantially increase your company's visibility and its relationship with the mass media.

On the other hand, making contact with community residents, local merchants, and town officials can help you identify important influencers and groups. As an example, Dan Dipert Tours has networked with local Chambers of Commerce to identify key groups with which it might work in running its mature market travel programs.

Nine Tips on Pursuing Your Relationships

Tony Mazur, a successful businessman and mentor, once told me that "What you yourself can do is limited, but what you can get others to do is limitless." Tony was right . . . so long as the "others" have values, capabilities, or goals that are consistent with what you seek to accomplish. For example, one company I know of doesn't go out of its way to build relationships with bank trust officers and attorneys. This is despite the fact that such individuals often work closely with older adults and can be good referral sources. Why? Because the company knows that trust officers and attorneys are not likely to recommend its product to their older clients.

Before you decide to pursue a relationship with a particular individual or group, you'll need to ask yourself a number of questions. Here are a few general ones:

1. How clear are we about what our objectives are in initiating (or strengthening) this relationship?

2. How much do we know about the corporate culture or values of the other party? (For example, are they interested only in working with nonprofit groups or on social causes?)

3. What are the other party's goals, priorities, and staffing capabilities? Do they mesh or conflict with our objectives?

4. What kind of reputation does this party have in the marketplace or with the older population? Is that in harmony with our objectives?

5. Has the party ever worked with others on similar activities? If so, what have they done and what has been the outcome?

6. How does the party view marketers or the business community? (Some seniors groups, for example, may be prohibited from working with profit-seeking enterprises regardless of the activity.)

7. How capable is the organization of delivering what it is we're asking? Can it be delivered when we need it?

8. What benefits will the other party derive by working with us? Can we clearly state those benefits? Can we deliver them?

9. How many older persons does this party serve, reach, or influence? How many of those persons would be potential purchasers and/or users of our product or service? Are these individuals the customers we're seeking?

Point: In relationship building, it's important to learn as much as you can about the other party's mature market needs, goals, and activities.

Marketing Checklist:
Six Ways to Tap into the Mature Market Network

1. Develop a good understanding of the 50+ network.
2. Ask your customers.
3. Conduct marketing research.

4. Pay attention to what's happening in other industries and job disciplines.

5. Assume an active community presence.

6. Know exactly what you want from the relationship and whether the other party can help you get it.

Chapter Wrap-up

Successful marketers know that 50 + ers come into direct contact with a variety of individuals and groups, and that many others touch the lives of this population in one way or another. These parties may have an impact on the older adult's consumer purchases, and, therefore, a company's sales.

Prosperous businesses will become aware of who these key groups and influencers are and what their relationship is to the mature consumer. They will also establish communications with them. In the process, these marketers may gain:

- customers
- distribution channels or referral sources
- assistance in developing products and in operating programs and services
- credibility or visibility
- technical expertise
- mature market data
- funding sources

Heated competition to capture market share in the older customer segment will make one group a very important one for businesses to develop relationships with, namely, other marketers. This includes those within and outside of their industry. The latter group, in particular, may offer some of the best opportunities to develop innovative products and services, product packaging, and distribution systems.

One final note: Those who successfully implement a relationship-based strategy will have to give as much as, if not more than, they receive from other parties. To do less than this may result in the *burning*, rather than the building, of mature market bridges.

---

1. "Drive-up Window Takes New Meaning with ABA," *Mature Market Report,* October 1987, p. 9.

2. Massey, Morris. *The People Puzzle*. Reston, VA: Reston Publishing Co., Inc., 1979.

3. "Religion in America, 50 Years: 1935-1985," *The Gallup Report*, Number 236, May 1985.

4. Weiss, David M., and Diane E. Mahlmann. *National Guide to Funding in Aging*. New York: Nassau County Department of Senior Citizen Affairs, The Foundation Center, and Long Island University, 1987.

5. "Corporate Public Involvement: Recommended Priorities for Insurance Companies," *Response*, February 1986, p. 4.

6. "DemoMemo," *American Demographics*, November 1986, p. 10.

7. "Reaching out: Grandparents more in touch with their grandkids, study shows," *Mature Outlook Newsletter*, February 1987, p. 12.

8. "On the Bandwagon: Grandparents Spending More Than Ever on Toys," *Mature Outlook*, November/December 1986, p. 90.

9. Lindeman, Bard, "That Special Joy—Being A Grandparent," *50 Plus*, November 1985, p. 18.

Chapter 8

Key 6: Recognize and Respond to the Diversity of the Mature Market

The Great, Gray Legion: The Impressive Success of the American Association of Retired Persons

It began in 1958 thanks to the noble vision and painstaking efforts of its founder, the late Dr. Ethel Percy Andrus. Today, this organization encompasses a central office, ten area offices, and several thousand local chapters. It employs more than 1200 staff persons and has hundreds of thousands of volunteers. And it has more than 30 million members.

Without a doubt, the growth and impact of this organization, the American Association of Retired Persons (AARP), has been impressive. A nonprofit, nonpartisan group for Americans age 50 and over, the AARP can trace its success to several factors. These include:

- the organization's ongoing commitment to utilize the collective resources and skills of its members
- its no-hype, high-quality approach to marketing membership in AARP and servicing those who become its members.

Another reason why AARP has flourished is because it understands very well the heterogeneous nature of older Americans. This remarkable ability to perceive the mature market melting pot—and act upon it—reflects another successful mature market approach. It is Key 6: *Recognize and respond to the diversity of the mature market.*

A Melting Pot within a Melting Pot

The heterogeneity of AARPs' membership shows the organization's ability to recognize and respond to the diversity of the mature market. While each of its 30 + million members is over 50, there is little else they all have in common. For example

- about 40 percent are Republicans, 40 percent are Democrats, and 20 percent are independents.
- about 38 percent are ages 50-64 and 62 percent are 65 +.
- about 53 percent are women and 47 percent are men.
- roughly two-thirds are married, and one-third are either single, separated, divorced, or widowed.

And while the majority of members are high school or college graduates, 20 percent are not.

Despite its name, AARP is open not only to retirees age 50 +, but to all Americans of that age group. Thus, there are also differences in the employment status of its members. About 30 percent still hold paying jobs. In part, this accounts for the wide range of household incomes found among AARP members.

Attracting the Members: The Benefits of Joining the AARP

To those who might choose to become members of its organization, AARP offers a whole gamut of programs and services. It's safe to say that at least one of these would be of benefit to almost anyone over 50. For those who want to be informed consumers and/or entertained about matters of interest to the mature adult, AARP provides *Modern Maturity* magazine, numerous self-help books, and a monthly newsletter. *Modern Maturity* features articles about a wide scope of topics of interest to mature adults such as finance, pensions, second careers, retirement locations, travel, and health. The self-help books cover a similar range of subjects and are provided to members at discount prices.

For those interested in taking part in social, legislative, or educational programs, AARP offers other opportunities. Members can get involved in one of AARP's 3600 chapters, most of which meet monthly. They can partake of AARP's numerous consumer education programs on such topics as traffic and driver safety, coping with widowhood, tax preparation, and housing options. They can decide to become one of the more than 300,000 AARP members who volunteer their services to do such things as (1) present its educational programs, (2) serve on its citizen representation boards and legislative committees, and (3) help fulfill some of its organizational priorities.

AARP offers another compelling reason to join its organization . . . access to its assortment of membership services. These services provide another illustration of how AARP recognizes and responds to the diversity of the mature market.

How the Product Line Addresses a Diverse Mature Market

The products offered to AARP members are primarily service-oriented. They include prescription drugs and health care items, investment products, health insurance, travel packages, auto and homeowners' policies, and a motor club plan. Aside from this product line, there is also a "purchase privilege" program that provides members with discounts at designated hotel and motel chains and car rental companies.

With the exception of the drugs and health supplies (which are handled by an AARP subsidiary), all of AARP's products are offered through carefully chosen, rigorously monitored outside "providers." Among these providers are Prudential Insurance Company of America, The Hartford Insurance Group, Olson-Travelworld, Ltd., and Scudder, Stevens & Clark, an investment firm.

AARP develops its products by conducting market research of its membership on an ongoing basis. After determining which services are most preferred by its members, AARP selects those services which it believes can be effectively provided by the organization. Products are then developed with an eye toward making them attractive to as many AARP's members as possible. To do this, different product options are offered to reflect the diversity of its potential customer base of 30+ million. (See Figure 8-1.)

Consider AARP's travel program. Says Frank Forbes, AARP's director of membership services operations, "Working with our service providers, we try to put together a fairly diverse package of travel opportunities. It's represented, at any one time, by maybe as many as 18 different brochures that contain many travel options. Some may contain as many as 30 offerings. So there are a variety of opportunities designed to interest most of the people who would be interested in traveling."

AARP's investment products provide a further illustration of the organization's efforts to serve its diverse membership. There are different investment options that appeal to the broadest spectrum of AARP members. Thus, a family of six mutual funds and one money fund is made available to those who may be interested in security of principal, income, tax-free income, and/or growth. (See Figure 8-2.)

Offering Something for Almost Everyone Over 50

By virtually any measure, AARP has become an unqualified success. Its influence on the lives of this nation's 62 million persons over 50 extends from the legislative halls, to the offices of marketing executives, to the retail establishments of thousands of American businesses.

More important has been AARP's positive and pervasive impact on the mature market itself. From a marketer's perspective, one need only look at

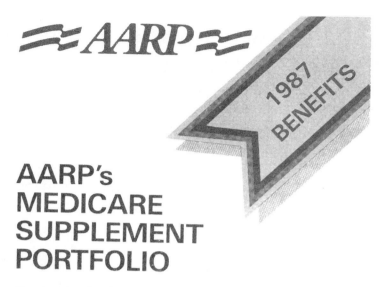

FIGURE 8–1

the organization's ability to attract members and gain their active involvement in its programs. Each day, thousands of 50+ers join its membership rolls or choose to volunteer for its programs. Moreover, nearly one-third of its members decide to participate in at least one of its membership services. In fact, when one counts AARP's purchase privilege program, the rate of participation is almost 50 percent!

With the AARP Investment Program, You Can Choose from These 7 Mutual Funds

Income Funds
AARP GNMA (GINNIE MAE) AND U.S. TREASURY FUND
AARP GENERAL BOND FUND
Seek to provide high current income from a portfolio of high quality securities

Tax Free Income Funds
AARP INSURED TAX FREE SHORT TERM FUND
AARP INSURED TAX FREE GENERAL BOND FUND
Seek to provide tax-free income

Growth Funds
AARP GROWTH AND INCOME FUND
AARP CAPITAL GROWTH FUND
Seek to provide opportunities for long-term capital growth primarily from common stocks

Money Fund
AARP MONEY FUND
Offers today's money market rates, stability of principal plus check writing.

Plus, No Other Investment Program Brings You the AARP ADVANTAGE

Professional Management by Scudder, Stevens & Clark, one of the nation's leading investment firms with over 65 years of experience. After a careful search, AARP selected Scudder as the firm most qualified to offer the Investment Program to you.
Value because the AARP Funds are pure no-load. Unlike more than 80% of the mutual funds available today, there are no sales charges or commissions. And the minimum initial investment is just $250.
Prompt, Friendly Service from a staff of professionally trained Service Representatives just a toll-free phone call away.
Convenience because it's easy to invest and make transactions on your account.
Clear and Concise consolidated monthly statements.
Up-to-Date Information through monthly newsletters and a helpful Shareholder's Handbook.
A Wide Range of Investment Choices from the 7 different funds available.
Flexibility so you can exchange from one AARP fund to another at no cost to you.
AARP's Commitment to represent your interests.

FIGURE 8–2

AARP's recognition of, and response to, the diversity of the mature market has played a key role in its success. Indeed, the trademark of the organization may be its ability to meet one or more needs of so many within its varied membership. Reflecting upon this, Frank Forbes offers these words of guidance to those marketing to the older consumer: "Don't just treat this market as a mass of people out there. Rather, determine—based on what they have to say—the varying needs of the group. And develop a line of products that hopefully is perceived by them to meet those needs."

Recognizing the Diversity: How to Segment the Mature Market

The first step toward effectively implementing this chapter's mature market strategy is to move away from defining the 50+ population as monolithic.

Not only is the concept of a homogeneous older group inaccurate, it also presents some major marketing obstacles. For example, it:

- Leads to an unfocused, mass market approach to marketing your products—something which is unlikely to yield the best return on your investment

- Precludes you from identifying untapped mature market niches

- Limits your ability to develop new or modified products for older consumers

The best way to approach the heterogeneous mature market is to *segment* it. There are several ways in which this can be done, each with its strengths and limitations. Your responsibility will be to determine which options are the most important for your business and its products.

Tip: Since any of these options can be of value, you may want to consider utilizing multiple approaches to get the best possible market definition. Obviously, this will depend on the specific circumstances involved, and the feasibility of market segmentation to your business.

Segmentation Approach 1: Use Demographic, Socioeconomic, and Health Characteristics

The simplest, most concrete way to segment the mature market is by examining various demographic, socioeconomic, and health characteristics of the 50+ population.

Of all these characteristics, *age* has been the one most frequently used to segment the mature market. The reason for this is that *many demographic, socioeconomic, and health variables seem to be closely correlated with specific age cohorts of the 50+ population.* Using age as a means of segmentation, the mature market essentially can be divided into two major groupings: those under 65 and those over 65. Members of the larger 50-64-year-old group (i.e., the prime lifers) differ from those age 65+ (i.e., the seniors) in several ways. For instance, the prime-lifer group includes . . .

- more workers, especially in full-time positions
- more persons living with spouses and other family members
- more middle and upper-income households
- more persons with high school—and college—degrees
- fewer persons with chronic health problems
- a more balanced ratio of men to women (although both groups— those 50-64 and 65+—include more women than men)

Note: Survey data show that prime lifers also possess values, attitudes, and purchase behaviors that are different from those age 65+.

A more meaningful picture of the 65+ population also requires segmentation. I prefer segmenting the group into three cohorts: ages 65-74, 75-84, and 85 +. In my opinion, this refinement of the 65 + group is more precise.

The three subsegments of seniors are differentiated by four major characteristics:

- marital status
- financial status
- educational attainment
- health status

Those 65-74, the "young old," are the most likely to be married. They possess the highest incomes, financial assets, net worths, and educational levels. They also are the least likely to have chronic disabilities.

Note: In many respects, the "young old" more closely resemble those under 65 than they do those over 75. This will become even truer over the next few decades.

At the other end of the spectrum, those 85 +, "the oldest old," are most likely to be living alone, to be below or near the poverty level, to have had the least years of formal schooling, and to be suffering from medical problems that make it impossible for them to live independently. They are also the segment with the largest majority of women. The 75-84-year-olds, meanwhile, fall in between these two age cohorts, although they are more like the 85 + group than those 65-74.

While age is the most obvious way to segment the mature market, focusing on other demographic and socioeconomic characteristics can also be useful. For example, income, household composition, education, and work status are important in their own right, regardless of age considerations. These characteristics can help determine which members of the mature market may have the time, money, or motivation necessary to purchase your product or service.

Health is also a critically important segmentation dimension. In general, health is likely to be closely related to the demographic and socioeconomic characteristics of the mature market. As noted, the older the age cohort, the more its members will have health problems. Similarly, income plays a role in how older individuals perceive their health. As Figure 8-3 illustrates, the less income a senior has, the more likely it is that he or she evaluates his (or her) health as being no better than "poor" or "fair."

Key Point: Of all demographic, socioeconomic, and health variables, *age* is the one most capable of helping you predict the other demographic, socioeconomic, and health characteristics of today's mature consumers.

Keep in Mind: The product or service your business is marketing will, to a great extent, determine which specific demographic, socioeconomic, or health characteristics are the most important ones to consider in segmenting the mature market.

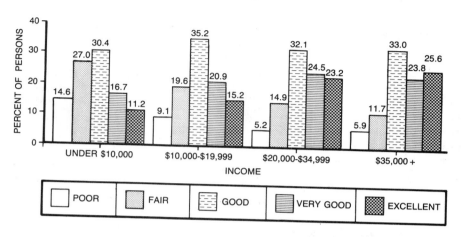

SELF-ASSESSMENT OF HEALTH BY INCOME FOR PERSONS 65 YEARS AND OLDER: 1986

FIGURE 8-3

Benefits and Drawbacks of Demographic, Socioeconomic, and Health Segmentation

Overall, the use of demographic, socioeconomic, or health-related variables to segment the mature market has its strengths. There are certain tangible characteristics that seem to fall within the various age brackets. The data acquired may be helpful in defining which older consumer groups represent your best target markets. And there are already numerous sources available that either have this information or can help you get it. There are, however, several problems for those who rely on this approach as the sole basis for segmenting the mature market:

- While the data give useful information about the composite mature market, they fail to account for individual differences among those in the same age cohort—and these differences can be huge.

- The data fail to account for the role that emotions, perceptions, and other nonstatistical factors play in older consumer behavior.

- The approach assumes that each new group that enters a specific age 50+ cohort will be like those it replaces. In reality, *the mature mar-*

ket is a moving target—thus the characteristics of its age cohorts will change somewhat over time.

Segmentation Approach 2: Consider Psychographics

The mature market can also be segmented through the use of psychographics, an approach also known as "lifestyle analysis." Rather than focusing on the cold, hard data of demographics, psychographics focuses on the mindsets and lifestyles of consumers. Thus, psychographics looks at things like consumer attitudes, beliefs, values, opinions, hopes, fears, aspirations, and behavior.

A number of individuals and firms have attempted to segment or profile the mature market by using psychographics. The behavioral categories they've created include "The Vitally Active," the "Satisfied Selves," the "Negative on Everything," and the "Survivors."

Useful Psychographic Profiles

The *best* and *most useful* psychographic profiles of the mature market integrate other information into their segmentation model . . . for example, demographic variables. Three individuals who have segmented the 50+ population along these lines are Nona Wegner of Chinn & Cassidy Associates, James O. Gollub of SRI International, and Dr. Morris Massey of Morris Massey Associates. Each of their models relates the older adult's behavior to either his age or the aging process.

Nona Wegner's "Stages in Adult Development" model focuses on the effects that various life stages or cycles can have on the older consumer's behavior. As Figure 8-4 shows, these stages—and the activities/behaviors that accompany them—are primarily driven by the process of aging.

Key Point: The timing and effects of these life stages will not be the same for all individuals. As the life cycle of mature adults becomes more cyclical (through work, travel, relaxation, education, parenthood, grandparenthood, and so forth), these stages—and their impact on the older person's life—will probably need to be refined.

Passage into new stages of life can have a definite impact on one's outlook and actions. For example, many persons become more spiritually centered when they pass middle-age. As consultant David Wolfe has observed, they begin to seek out experiences that emphasize the simpler things of life, such as interpersonal relationships, nature, arts and culture, learning, and volunteerism, rather than acquisition of material wealth.[1]

A related, though different perspective on understanding older consumer behavior, is James O. Gollub's "Life Span" concept. Rather than focusing on life stages, "Life Span" seeks to explain consumer lifestyles, perceptions, and actions by looking at the decades in which people grew up . . .

Stages in Adult Development

Stages (Age Relationships)	Work Patterns	Relationships	Buying Patterns
Transition to Adulthood 16-21	School, a job	Single living at home/Early relationships and marriages	Quantitative/self-acquisitive
Early Adulthood 21-35	Stable Employment/Career Identification and Growth	Developing relationships/ marriage/children	Environment acquisitive
Middle Adulthood 35-50	Career Achievement/ Change/Second Careers	Mature relationships/divorce/ second marriage/parent care	Family acquisitive
Mature Adulthood 50-64	Career Peak/Pre-Retirement	Stable relationships/empty-nest grandchildren/late divorce	Qualitative self-acquisitive
Older Adulthood 65-80	Career Pre-Eminence, Retirement/Jobs/Volunteerism	Grandchildren/beginning of widowhood/late second marriage	Selective acquisitive
Late Adulthood 75+	Retirement/Volunteerism	Increasingly single/social network more fragile	Maintenance acquisitive

Stages in Adult Development

Stage	Life Need (Shelter)	Lifestyle Component (Transportation)	Market Impact (Audience)
Transition	Parent's Home/School	Parents Car or First Car	Parents/Peers/Self
Early Adulthood	Apartment/Shared Home	Own Car/Own Insurance	Peers/Self
Middle Adulthood	Own House	Larger Car	Self/Spouse
Mature Adulthood	Remodel House/Build Second Home (Vacation Home)	Luxury Car	Self/Spouse/Advisors
Older Adulthood	Condo/Smaller Luxury House	Luxury Car/Smaller Car	Self/Spouse/Children
Late Adulthood	Retirement Community/Live with Children	Transportation Services	Self/Children/Peers

Source: Mature Market Report, January 1988

FIGURE 8–4

a function of one's age. Each of these decades has what Gollub calls "time signatures," or significant historical events, associated with them. These major events (such as the Great Depression and World War II) help shape the way members of each group live and perceive themselves. Figure 8-5 identifies time signatures pertaining to the mature market.

Gollub has also identified personality types within the mature market

Time Signatures

Time signatures can be seen in the cohorts emerging from each decade:

- **1900–1910**—"Children of the Century" have a time signature of struggle and achievement. Today old world immigrants and natives alike are a diverse group of older survivors, the first American generation to be entitled to retire, often surprised to have made it.

- **1910–1920**—"Those of the Dream Deferred" have a time signature of disappointment and deferred compensation. Now they are the mainstream aged, attempting, in their own way, to make up for the past. They are often caught between wanting to give and to take. They feel they have earned their retirement and will not let anyone take it away from them.

- **1920–1930**—"Children of the American Dream" who were children of the depression and parents of the baby boom have a time signature of great expectations and strong national identity. While raised in a period of governmental patriarchy, they are often cynical about big government. Today, those aged 55–65 who created America's suburbs and corporate cultures stand on the edge of retirement, uneasy, not sure how to cross the threshold, or what they will find on the other side.

- **1930–1940**—The "Eisenhower-Elvis kids" have a time signature of patiently muddling through—from the war era into the politically cautious and organization-focused 1950s. Now 45 to 55, they rode the tail of the 1960s economic boom and today they uneasily straddle the transforming U.S. economy. They are caught between the management style of the 1950s, which they were coached in, and the technological and entrepreneurial pressures of the 1980s. They are the parents of today's teen and punk cohort—and view them with more understanding than expected.

Reprinted with permission: James O. Gollub, SRI International, "Life Span"

FIGURE 8–5

based on what he calls "birthmarks"—important *personal* events in the life of an individual—college, marriage, parenthood, and so forth—which can also help shape one's consumer behavior.

Key Point: The Great Depression has had a profound impact on the attitudes that many of today's 65 + ers have about spending and managing money. These seniors are extremely concerned about their financial security and independence. As a result, they tend to behave in ways that bolster their economic well-being—such as accumulating large savings accounts and buying medical insurance policies—while avoiding behaviors that might jeopardize their financial welfare, such as purchasing extravagant or faddish products and services.

A similar but less segmented analysis of the mature market is put forth by Dr. Morris Massey. He believes that individuals are strongly influenced by the era in which they grew up and the major events that occurred during the time in which they were "value programmed."

Thus, members of the mature market primarily fall into the "Traditionalist" category of Dr. Massey's "contemporary generational clusters." (See Figure 8-6). Traditionalists were greatly influenced by such events as the Great Depression, the World Wars, and The New Deal. They also tend to hold a common set of values, such as

- An emphasis on working together in a group or team concept
- A respect for—and belief in—authority, large institutions, and those in leadership positions
- A willingness to adhere to a formalized, structured code of rules, regulations, and behavior
- A preference for stability rather than change or experimentation

These values are in stark contrast to many held by the "Challengers," a group virtually synonymous with the baby boomers. Overlapping these two groups are what Massey calls the "In-Betweeners." In-Betweeners are persons who were "programmed" from the late 1940s to the late 1950s. Massey believes the In-Betweeners are really caught in the middle between the values of the Traditionalists and the Challengers.

Key Point: The In-Betweeners are an extremely important group for marketers since they include today's younger members of the mature market (those in their early fifties) and those about to enter it (those in their forties).

How can the paradigms developed by Wegner, Gollub, and Massey help you in marketing to the 50+ group? *They can provide you with clues on what specific forces may dictate the older consumer's actions.*

Example: Massey's identification of the values often held by Traditionalists may explain why many seniors are "belongers" and why Airstream's Wally Byam Caravan Club has been so popular with older adults. It may also explain why Royal Cruise Line's strategy of working with key groups and influencers has been so effective.

The values which Massey ascribes to "In-Betweeners" may help one understand why many of today's prime lifers have adopted aspects of the baby boomers' lifestyle, such as their focus on self-fulfillment and health/fitness activities. Many prime lifers matured during the post-World War II economic boom years, rather than the Great Depression—something which Gollub's model considers too—and which may also account for this behavior.

Contemporary Generational Clusters

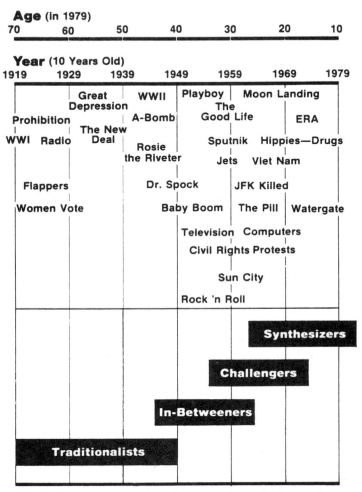

Reprinted with permission from *The People Puzzle* by Dr. Morris Massey, Reston Publishing Co., 1979

FIGURE 8–6

The three paradigms are bound to make you more aware of how a person's values, attitudes, preferences, activities, and so forth *can be shaped by the era in which he or she matured as well as the aging process. This, in turn, can play a significant role in influencing consumer behavior.*

Strengths and Weaknesses of Psychographic Segmentation

It is vitally important that you understand a mature adult's *cognitive* age as well as his *chronological* one in developing effective marketing strategies. Psychographics helps you do this by giving you information about how the older individual perceives himself in relation to others. Because it looks at feelings rather than facts, psychographics can help you better understand the emotional and psychological makeup of older consumers.

Remember: As anyone in sales knows, in many product purchases, logic comes into play only *after* the consumer's heart has already made the decision to buy.

Through exploring the mindsets and lifestyles of older adults, you can also learn more about how they feel about your company, your competitors, and the marketplace in general. This information can provide you with valuable insight into the reasons why members of the mature market may or may not be the right targets for the kinds of products or services offered by your company. Furthermore, psychographic research can provide information that can help you produce marketing communications whose words and images strike the older consumer's "hot button."

Key Point: Psychographic research can help you determine the older consumer's wants and the messages you should transmit to make the individual feel that you can satisfy those wants.

There are, however, several drawbacks associated with psychographic research.

- Costs for customized studies can be high, and perhaps, prohibitive for some organizations.
- Expert skills are necessary to collect and analyze the data.
- Individual beliefs, perceptions, and values often change depending upon one's role or life cycle, thereby hampering the long-term reliability of lifestyle segmentation findings.
- Such research usually does not provide information about consumer reactions to specific product and service options.

Caution: Such research, by its very nature, also tends to lump people into categories.

Example: About 80 percent of the older adults in SRI International's VALS (Values and Lifestyles) Program fall into its "Belonger" category. In such cases, the mature market has hardly been segmented at all. Similarly, psychographic research fails to account for individual differences among those over 50.

While demographic, socioeconomic, and health segmentation are often based on tangible, indisputable data, psychographic segmentation is largely a matter of subjective interpretation. It's no surprise, therefore, that the mature market has been segmented in so many different ways through the use of psychographic research.

Psychographic research may also be more driven by demographics than some researchers would be willing to admit. As Leo Bogart, executive vice president of the Newspaper Advertising Bureau and author of *Silent Politics: Polls and the Awareness of Public Opinion*, commented: "A lot of this seems to be just taking social and economic variables and repackaging them as psychological traits."[2] Indeed, several lifestyle-oriented approaches to segmenting the mature market give credence to Bogart's opinion.

Example: One model divides the mature market into three broad segments: the go/gos, the slow/gos, and the no/gos.[3] Upon close examination, it is apparent that this model really uses age and health-related characteristics of the mature market to create a psychographic segmentation model.

Making the Most of Psychographic Segmentation

Despite its limitations, psychographic segmentation can provide you with another good tool to use in better understanding the mature consumer. Its value will be best served if you:

1. recognize its strengths and its limitations *before using this approach*, and

2. integrate psychographic research with other segmentation techniques rather than approach it as separate and distinct

Segmentation Approach 3: Track Purchase Behavior

Tracking consumer expenditures of the mature market can be another effective way to segment the age 50+ population. This can be done by utilizing information provided by various government, trade, and marketing research organizations. For example, an analysis of the Bureau of Labor Statistics' 1985 Consumer Expenditure Survey shows that there are definite differences among the purchasing patterns of householders ages 55-64, 65-74, and 75 and over. (See Appendix A for more information.)

Information from the U.S. Travel Data Center reveals differences in purchase behavior between prime lifers and seniors. Those 50-64 tend to spend their money by using first-class air and hotel accommodations. The 65+ group, however, tends to be more budget conscious, and therefore generally uses more economical means of transportation and lodging. Despite this, the 65+ traveler allots more of his disposable income toward travel than does the younger group.[4]

The above resources can provide important data about the composite mature market. This may be useful in helping you segment this consumer base at the national level or in the localities in which your product or service is (or may be) distributed. The data do *not*, however, provide you with information about *your* older customers' purchase behavior. To do this requires primary research and/or an in-house customer information system.

Key Point: If possible, develop a system to identify your older customers and the products/services they purchase. In addition to the many other benefits this system can provide, it may also be an effective tool in helping you segment your older customer base.

Strengths/Weaknesses of Product Usage Analysis

Analyzing older consumer product/service purchases can be helpful in:

- Determining if there is a viable customer base for your mature market product or service in total or in a given geographic area (Other factors, such as competition and current market penetration, are also critically important in making such decisions.)
- Developing a profile of those age 50+ consumers who are most (or least) likely to purchase your product or service
- Increasing product consumption among users
- Developing strategies to gain new customers or increase business with existing ones

Caution: This segmentation technique has its weaknesses. For example, product usage information tends to focus on groups of older consumers rather than individuals. The interpretation of this data—as well as the recommendations and marketing strategies that such analyses lead to—may also be more subjective than scientific.

Key Point: As with psychographic research, using information about purchase behavior to segment the mature market will be most effective when used in tandem with other segmentation approaches.

Other Segmentation Approaches

Segmentation based on *media exposure* differentiates older consumers by the communication channels they use (TV, radio, newspapers, and so forth) and the media vehicles they prefer—such as the radio stations they listen to and the TV programs they watch. (See Chapter 12 for more information on the mature market's mass media preferences.)

The mature market can be segmented by considering *geographic variables* such as market scope (national, statewide, or local), population density (urban vs. rural), and climate-related factors (Sun Belt states vs. Mid-Atlantic states). These variables should not be taken lightly. For example, almost half of the nation's seniors are located in just eight states. Further, the characteristics, lifestyles, needs, interests, and purchase behaviors of older consumers are likely to be related to the areas in which they live.

Example: In a recent survey conducted in Florida, mature consumers were asked about their interest in long-term care services. The level of interest expressed was found to vary greatly from one area of the state to another.[5]

Benefit segmentation differentiates the mature market according to the needs or wants satisfied by purchasing a given product. Thus, one group of older Airstream RV buyers may buy its travel trailers primarily because their purchase gives them access to a social network (that is, the Wally Byam Caravan Club). Another group may see the RV's durability and resale value as its major benefits. By employing this segmentation technique, you can put together strategies that position your product differently to different segments of the mature market.

Another highly sophisticated, seldom-used option is *micro-segmentation*: the breaking down of a market to the individual level. By effectively using a comprehensive marketing information system, you can develop mature market profiles that provide detailed information about each of your older prospects and customers. This information can be obtained in a variety of ways such as through completed order forms, telemarketing, in-depth personal interviews, and customer service contact.

Who can benefit from this form of segmentation? One group would be those businesses who sell a product or service that has very limited appeal. For example, a bank, insurance company, or travel agency may find this a useful technique in developing customized programs for its most upscale mature market clientele.

Note: While most businesses may find micro-segmentation isn't cost effective, it is bound to become more widely used in the future. Consumers—especially those among the hotly pursued mature market—are likely to demand more customized products and services. Businesses will also enhance their capability to provide the consumer with personalized programs. Some already have.

Marketing Checklist: Ways to Segment the Mature Market

- demographic, socioeconomic, and health characteristics
- psychographics
- purchase behavior
- media exposure, geographic variables, benefit segmentation, and micro-segmentation

Six Ways to Respond to the Diversity of the Mature Market

1. Conduct Ongoing Marketing Research

Marketing research is so important that the need for *it cannot be overstated.* It is through marketing research that you will be able to:

- identify various segments within the mature market
- develop effective strategies that respond to one or more of these segments
- measure changes occurring within the mature market over a prolonged period of time
- determine new niches, strategies, and product/service opportunities

Before engaging in any marketing research project, you must have a clear idea as to what you want the research to accomplish. Then consider your available budget, staff size, time frame, and research capabilities. From this assessment, you should be able to determine what kind of research will be best for you—primary or secondary—and how it should be obtained.

Information obtained from secondary research—for example, published studies and reports—is the least expensive and most accessible type of research. In some cases, however, secondary data may be insufficient to enable you to formulate a segmented mature market strategy. You may need to conduct some form of primary research.

Keep in Mind: If you can get answers to your research questions through secondary sources, you need go no further. If you can't get your answers—or if you need additional, more up-to-date, or more company-specific information—primary research will be necessary.

Syndicated research studies may also provide you with useful information to segment the mature market. And their cost will often be less than that of a full-blown, proprietary study.

Tip: Syndicated products that provide information which cuts across more than one segmentation base (such as Information Resources, Inc.'s InfoScan™ consumer panel data base) may be particularly helpful.

2. Develop Products for a Wide Range of Older Consumers

To the extent that it is feasible, your organization can develop an array of products or services to serve the spectrum of older consumers.

Example: One organization that does this is the Baptist Medical Center in Oklahoma City, Oklahoma, through its Third Age Life Center. Its products and services include wellness and fitness programs, osteoporosis screening, a caregiver support group, aging sensitivity training, durable medical equipment, and an inpatient rehabilitation unit. Through this diversified approach, Baptist's Third Age Life Center has been able to serve a wide spectrum of older adults . . . from the healthy to the chronically ill.

Warning: While offering a wide range of products and services may be one effective way to respond to the diversity of the mature market, such an approach should be undertaken with great caution. To begin with, such a strategy may be inappropriate for a small-to-medium-sized business or for one whose product or service niche doesn't lend itself to diversity. In such cases, it may still be possible to offer diversity in other ways (such as in pricing, distributing, or servicing the product).

Another danger is the possibility of trying to be all things to everybody. By overextending your product line—particularly into areas in which your company has no prior experience—you may be stretching your resources and capabilities too far. As a result, two things may occur:

- First, your business could face a problem in positioning your product to the older consumer.
- Second, and more important, the quality of your product and/or your sales and customer staffs could decline.

If either scenario should arise, your mature market sales are likely to suffer.

What to Do: If your organization faces any of these potential hazards, your best approach may be to:

1. specialize in a product or service line in which you can excel and be profitable
2. expand your product line over a gradual period in conjunction with your growth in expertise and resources, or
3. link up with other businesses which can fill in your product "gaps" or complement your existing product line

3. Consider Clubs or Membership Programs

Another way to respond to the diversity of the 50 + population is to establish club or membership programs. A number of organizations including Days Inn ("September Days"), Sears ("Mature Outlook"), HealthWest Foundation ("Elder Med America"), and Walden Books ("60 + Club") have enrolled a large number of persons into their mature market-only programs.

Mature market clubs may be geared to a specific product line (such as air travel or books) or toward a wide range of products (such as Mature Outlook's program). They may be one-of-a-kind programs or those of the pre-packaged, syndicated genre. They can be for older adults of various ages, depending on the preferences of the marketer. The *benefits* of these programs to marketers may include

1. The ability to offer products at lower prices than competitors due to larger volume sales.
2. The ability to offer 50+ers convenience in the form of one-stop-shopping.
3. The ability to capitalize on the fact that many older Americans are comfortable with, need, and/or enjoy, group participation and socialization.
4. The ability to differentiate your product from others if you are either *first* in the market or "the only game in town."
5. The ability to build a data base of information about individual club members for future marketing purposes.

Keep in Mind: Mature market clubs make it readily apparent that your program is intended for the older adult. Thus, they stand a greater chance of attracting the older consumer's attention.

Despite the appeal of mature market clubs, they have several potential drawbacks.

• *Clubs may attract older customers, but they won't necessarily keep them.* Club programs should never be viewed as a "quick-and-dirty" approach to gaining mature customers, or as the last word in successfully marketing to them. While clubs may attract 50+ers to try what it is you have to offer, such programs won't—in and of themselves—guarantee the older person will be your customer over the long haul. To do that requires the provision of a product or service that is of outstanding value, is backed by excellent customer service, meets specialized needs, and so forth.

The vulnerability of a "club-based" focus is underscored by two factors: (1) Since more and more marketers are jumping on the club bandwagon, it is becoming very difficult for older consumers to differentiate one club from another. (2) The mature consumer, including those over 65, may not be as loyal as some marketers believe. For example, recent research shows that a good many older consumers, like younger groups, *do* switch brands and try new products.

• *Clubs may place their emphasis on the wrong things.* In the highly competitive quest to gain or retain a share of the mature market, it can be easy to pursue short-sighted or misdirected marketing strategies. A number of businesses have already done this. In some cases, for example, they have focused the mature market's attention primarily on their low or discounted prices.

Caution: This strategy can be very dangerous, since many other factors beyond price can affect an older buyer's product or brand loyalty. Even those who are very price-sensitive are likely to shift their loyalties should a competitor offer a lower price.

Remember: Marketing programs built upon low or discounted pricing are typically the easiest for competitors to match or dislodge.

• *Clubs can lead to one-dimensional thinking.* Since clubs, by their very nature, focus on a commonality of interest or purpose, there is the danger of assuming all members of a mature market club have the same needs and wants. This trap can be easy to fall into, especially for those who consider purchasing "canned" (e.g., syndicated) packages or who administer their programs in a highly centralized style.

Warning: Be careful about using generic advertising campaigns, such as those that often accompany a syndicated program for older consumers. Such advertising may fail to promote your organization's unique capabilities in the market(s) you serve. Moreover, they may also fail to reflect the special needs and preferences of mature consumers in *your* community.

How to avoid the one-dimensional trap: Communicate regularly with your members (or potential members) to determine both their shared and individualized traits and needs. The use of market research—particularly if it is conducted at the local level—is an excellent way to do this. In fact, some companies have decided against mature market clubs after finding out it wasn't what their older customer base really wanted from them.

• *Clubs may cause you to divert your customers' and your company's attention too far away from your primary product line(s).* Some businesses have diversified their club programs to such an extent that one begins to wonder what they're really marketing, and whether it's what the older customer really wants from them. A number of financial institutions and hospitals, for example, have plunged full-speed ahead into senior travel or entertainment programs. In many cases, such diversions are prompted more by "me-too" marketing strategies than by solid consumer research.

Example: Shying away from such tactics, one savings and loan marketing executive recently said, "We thought a travel package might be attractive, but we wanted a different approach. They can get travel packages from travel agencies." Instead, this S&L decided to focus on its "bread and butter" business by offering the older customer a more attractive financial product . . . something that marketing research had shown the mature market actually wanted.

Note: Diversification into new businesses may be a prudent mature market strategy if:

• marketing research suggests such a move
• the expertise and experience needed can be acquired internally or through outside collaboration
• such activity will not dilute the quality of—or resources available for—a company's primary product lines

Better Strategy: Most marketers will no doubt be better served by enhancing *the value* of the products/services in which they specialize.

• *Clubs may limit your ability to attract younger persons to use your product or service.* Restricting a program to members of the mature market may inadvertently have an adverse impact on doing business with the rest of the population. For example, promoting programs or specific products and services as "for seniors only" automatically excludes other, qualified customers from participating.

Example: A club package designed to increase a bank's deposit base may unwittingly close the door on a group of cash-rich, younger persons if it opts only to target older customers. The same might be said for a number of products or services that, while most likely to be of interest to older customers, may still appeal to—or be needed by—other individuals.

Warning: Marketers may also face the prospect of alienating younger persons by offering specific programs or clubs solely to the 50+ group. In fact, a few businesses have had to initiate special programs for younger persons due to public relations concerns which their mature market-only packages were creating.

Tip: If you decide to go with a club or membership program, give serious consideration to opening it up to *persons of all ages* who meet the entry qualifications that you establish. Several organizations, including Travel Companion Exchange and Security Savings, a financial institution in Milwaukee, have used this approach very successfully. It has enabled them to gain a large group of older members while still attracting many younger participants.

Checklist of Potential Pitfalls or Limitations of Mature Market Clubs and Membership Programs

• They may attract older customers, but they won't necessarily keep them.

• They may place their emphasis on the wrong things.

• They can lead to one-dimensional thinking.

• They may cause you to divert your customers' and your company's attention too far away from your primary product line(s).

• They may limit your ability to attract younger persons to use your product or service.

4. Include Some "A La Carte" Options within Your Product or Service Line

Another way to respond to a diverse mature market is to give the older consumer some options to choose from among the product(s) you offer.

Example: At Methodist Retirement Center in Madison, Wisconsin, new residents are able to pick their own carpeting, draperies, and wall coverings. Allowing residents to help design their own homes is one factor which has contributed to Methodist's success.

Example: Elderhostel, the organization that has successfully run educational programs for older travelers, has also benefitted from this approach. Older learners who consider attending one of its programs can choose from an expansive menu of courses in the sciences and liberal arts. Offered at one or more of Elderhostel's nearly 1,000 host educational institutions, these courses include anything from "The Archaelogical Heritage of Southern Alberta" to "The Magic of Maple-Sugaring" to "Yoga."

5. Discard the Stereotypes of Aging When Marketing Your Products and Services

Over the past 25 years or so, she has climbed Mt. Whitney more than 20 times. For those unfamiliar with this mountain, its summit stands more than 14,000 feet above sea level. She is 92-year-old Hulda Crooks. Hulda's achievement is made all-the-more spectacular when one learns that she did not begin her exercise program in earnest until she was 70!

Perhaps no one better illustrates that "it's never too late to try something new" than does Hulda Crooks. Your company needs to keep Mrs. Crooks firmly in mind when developing or marketing products and services for the mature market: by discarding stereotypical thinking about the older adult, the door to business opportunity begins to open wide.

Example: One organization that can attest to this is The Arizona Bank in Phoenix. Repudiating the common perception that older adults won't utilize new technologies, the bank embarked upon a program to increase its older customers use of automated teller machines (ATMs). The program had several elements:

- Specially trained "demonstrators" helped individual customers use the machines at all of the bank's ATMs.

- People were allowed to choose their own personal identification numbers to make them easier to remember.

- Customers who worked with the demonstrators—or who used their own cards to make withdrawals during a one-month period—were eligible to win cash prizes.

Result: The Arizona Bank was able to increase ATM usage among older people, especially in two retirement communities the bank serves. In fact, at those two locations, there was a 250 percent increase in ATM transaction volume![6] Overall, the bank had capitalized on its ability to:

- *recognize* the diversity of the mature market (that is, to realize that some older consumers may indeed respond to new technologies), and

- *respond* to it by developing an excellent marketing program . . . which itself included some highly individualized components.

6. Customize Your Service to the Individual Mature Adult

Customizing your service means one-on-one marketing, where products and services are developed for the consumer on a personalized basis.

Example: One organization that has successfully used this approach with the mature market is the Rehabilitation and Conditioning Center (RACC) in Santa Ana, California. At the RACC, many older persons (as well as younger individuals) pursue fitness and rehabilitation programs. Each participant's custom-made program is carefully set up based on the results of some initial testing. After that time, programs are modified in accordance with the individual's progress. Throughout this process, older members are closely supervised and aided by exercise physiologists trained to design programs for people over 50.

Marketing Checklist:
Six Ways to Respond to the Diversity of the Mature Market

- Conduct ongoing marketing research.
- Develop products/services for a wide range of older consumers.
- Consider the possibility of club or membership programs.
- Include some a la carte options within your product or service line.
- Discard the stereotypes of aging when marketing your products and services.
- Tailor your products or services to the individual older consumer.

Chapter Wrap-up

To maximize its mature market success, your company must recognize that the 50 + population is as diverse as it is large. This diversity is driven by the spectrum of demographic, socioeconomic, health, and psychographic characteristics of the mature market. By failing to see this, you're likely to miss out on the opportunity to:

- increase the sale of your existing products to older adults
- develop new products which capitalize on the many niches and "mini-segments"—yet to be discovered or exploited—within the 50 + population

At the core of recognizing and responding to the mature market's diversity is consumer research. Only through an understanding of the aggregrate 50 + market—and that market as it relates to *your* business and its products—can you really formulate effective marketing strategies.

Keep in Mind: The mature market is a moving target. Thus, today's segmentation approaches, and the segments they identify, will surely need to be refined over time.

———————

1. Wolfe, David B., "The Ageless Market," *American Demographics*, July 1987, p. 28.

2. "Everyone Has an Opinion of Polls," *Insight*, March 23, 1987, p. 23.

3. Stockman, Leslie Ensor, and June Fletcher, "A Maturing Market," *Builder*, June 1985, p. 73.

4. Rosenfeld, Jeffrey P., "Demographics on Vacation," *American Demographics*, January 1986, pp. 38-40.

5. Bennington, William, "You're Communicating, But Are They Responding?" A presentation at the Mature Market Institute Annual Conference, Amelia Island, Florida, April 15, 1988.

6. *Older Bank Customers: An Expanding Market.* Washington, D.C.: (c) American Bankers Association, 1985. Reprinted with permission. All Rights Reserved.

Chapter 9

Key 7: Use a Soft-Sell Approach

A Drug Store Chain with a Unique Prescription for Success

Unlike others in its industry, this drug store chain's retail units are owned by its franchisees . . . the store pharmacists. Also, this chain's pharmacies specialize in selling prescription drugs rather than beauty products, greeting cards, or other sundry items. In fact, over 90 percent of its sales come from the dispensing of prescription medications. This compares with about 30 percent for most chains.

Also different is this company's target market: the mature adult. Close to 60 percent of its customers are over 50.

What really sets this company apart, however, is its growth curve. For example, in 1968, it operated only one midwest drug store. Today, it has more than 700 stores located in all 48 mainland states—a claim none of its competitors can make. Similarly, the company's sales volume has consistently risen, averaging more than 20 percent per year. In 1987, its drug stores had over $325 million in sales, an increase of 21 percent from 1986 and more than triple that of 1982! This 21 percent sales increase was *double the industry growth rate* for traditional chain drug stores during the same 12-month period.

Medicine Shoppe International, a chain of franchised drug stores based in St. Louis, has experienced such dramatic and steady growth for several reasons:

- The stores' pharmacies offer prescription drugs at prices that can't be beat. That claim is backed by a national price guarantee and instant credit if any price exceeds what the competition charges.

- All of its pharmacies are conveniently situated in places where large concentrations of middle-aged and older people live and can easily shop.
- Medicine Shoppe thrives because of its outstanding customer service. Store pharmacists routinely take the time to explain how to use the medications they dispense. They monitor potential adverse reactions and patient compliance by keeping detailed in-house records. And, they refund $1 to any customer who waits more than 15 minutes to have a prescription filled.

There is another major factor which accounts for Medicine Shoppe's prosperity and its success with the mature market. It is the company's unswerving commitment to provide its customers and would-be customers with many important community programs and services . . . all at no cost. Offered in a personal, caring way, with "no strings attached," these programs and services illustrate Medicine Shoppe's use of another successful mature market strategy. It is Key 7: *Use a soft-sell approach.*

Reaching Out to the Community with Free Health-Screening Programs

Unlike other pharmacies, or for that matter, businesses in general, Medicine Shoppe uses little paid advertising to sell its products. Instead, the company relies heavily on other, soft-sell forms of sales promotion such as consumer education programs. For example, store pharmacists go to senior centers and high rises where they make presentations and answer questions on related medical topics. They also show health-oriented films to older adult groups and provide an inordinate supply of relevant booklets, both in and out of their stores. And, they go to the local newspapers and offer to be their advisor on health and drug-related matters.

Medicine Shoppe's free health-screening programs represent its most visible soft-sell technique. Each year, these programs are held on a regular basis at all of the chain's stores. In 1987, Medicine Shoppe conducted three national health-screening campaigns along with more than 3,200 locally run programs. These programs are hosted by the local Medicine Shoppe franchisee/pharmacist who relies upon the services of qualified health professionals to actually do the screenings.

Medicine Shoppe's health screenings are designed to prevent and detect a number of medical conditions. These include foot problems, glaucoma, colon-rectal cancer, high blood pressure, hearing and breathing problems, and diabetes. While these conditions may affect someone of any age, they are most commonly found among the older population. Thus, about three-quarters of the company's screenings are oriented to serve its primary customer prospects, that is, the mature market.

Medicine Shoppe pharmacists receive major support from corporate headquarters in publicizing the health screenings to the community-at-large. Corporate public relations personnel prepare press releases, media kits, posters, advertisements, and letters to help inform store neighbors and customers about both the screenings and the nature of the health problems being addressed. (See Figures 9-1 and 9-2.) They also obtain the services of older celebrities such as Estelle Getty, Sherman Hemsley, and Rose Marie to heighten public awareness and support of the programs.

For residents of the community, the screenings have served as a means of enouraging and promoting their well-being. More important, the programs have *saved lives*. For example, at least 2,000 life-saving, cancer surgeries

FIGURE 9–1

Our take-home test kit
can save your life

Dear Neighbor:

More than 140,000 people will contract colon-rectal cancer this year. Thousands will die--needlessly.

Our free take-home test kit can literally save your life by detecting hidden blood in stool samples, an early warning sign of colon-rectal cancer. With early detection and treatment, three-fourths of CRC victims can lead normal, productive lives.

Pick up your free test kit October 9 through 11 during our 6th National Colon-Rectal Cancer Screening. You simply complete it at home (instructions are enclosed) and mail it to our co-sponsor, AMC Cancer Research Center for free analysis.

Come in and take home our free test kit. It's an opportunity for a lifetime.

Regards,

Pharmacist
THE MEDICINE SHOPPE

FIGURE 9–2

have been performed due to results obtained from the national colon-rectal cancer screening.

For Medicine Shoppe, the screenings have elicited a tremendous amount of free advertising. In 1987, for example, free publicity generated by its screenings and community service programs resulted in nearly 4,000 separate television, radio, or newspaper items about Medicine Shoppe. This included coverage in six national magazines. All of this publicity enabled the company to receive exposure to millions of potential customers.

The screenings have also brought an enormous amount of traffic into Medicine Shoppe stores. In 1987, more than half a million potential customers visited the company's pharmacies to participate in its health screenings. Medicine Shoppe derives at least three major benefits from this flow of traffic:

- First, its prospective customers have a nonthreatening opportunity to witness firsthand Medicine Shoppe's high quality, friendly service, and low prices.

- Second, store pharmacists register the attendees, develop a mailing list, and initiate a sales recruitment effort from it; for example, each new visitor is sent a letter which cites the benefits of patronizing a Medicine Shoppe pharmacy.

- Third, the drug stores gain new customers as a result of the screenings. According to Medicine Shoppe's market research, the screenings are one of the three most important sources of new customers for its stores.

Its Marketing Approach: The Company That Cares

Medicine Shoppe's soft-sell approach to marketing reflects one of its major corporate philosophies. This philosophy is expressed in one of the company's frequently used slogans which says quite simply: "Caring . . . it's often the best medicine." Indeed, the company recognized a long time ago that prescription drugs aren't bought on impulse. As Jeff Atkinson, vice president of marketing says, "I love to say that we tried several promotions that say 'get sick' and nobody paid attention. It doesn't work that way."

Thus, Medicine Shoppe's emphasis is on keeping people well . . . making friends with them *before* they're ever sick. Adds Atkinson, "Then, when they are ill, they suddenly, hopefully, will remember there's a place that cared about me when I wasn't even sick." Without a doubt, the caring displayed by the company's consumer education programs and health screenings has been good medicine for Medicine Shoppe and those it serves, including, of course, its many older customers.

Why You Should Use a Soft-Sell Approach to Attract the Mature Market

As Medicine Shoppe's success story illustrates, there are several good reasons for using soft-sell techniques when marketing your products or services to the mature consumer. A soft-sell strategy offers the potential to gain:

- Heightened visibility (often times through significant media exposure)
- Extensive networking opportunities
- More positive public perceptions about your business and its products
- Reduced expenditures for marketing activities (such as lower advertising costs)
- Increased sales

There are at least two other reasons for using a soft-sell approach with the mature market.

The Mature Market Is Wary of "Hard-Sell" Techniques

The older consumer too often has been the prey of quacks, con-men, and high-pressure, door-to-door salespeople. Intimidated, confused, frightened, or just plain deceived, older adults have wasted money on such things as fake medical cures, unnecessary insurance policies, and phony mail-order offers. As one who once counseled seniors and their families on buying health insurance, I have learned of many individuals who paid hundreds of dollars for duplicate medical policies solely because of the bullying tactics of a few unscrupulous insurance agents.

During the past decade, concerns about the defrauding and abuse of the mature consumer have become widespread. They have also been extensively publicized. In response to this, congressional committees have met to investigate deceptive business practices affecting older adults. Congressman Claude Pepper of Florida, for example, has been very much involved in these activities. In some cases, Congress has passed laws designed to prevent such acts and to punish those who commit them.

Key Point: This problem has caused many older consumers to adopt a stronger "caveat emptor" posture in the sales arena.

Even if older persons have not been victimized personally, the odds are good that they have parents, other family members, or friends who have.

Key Point: A pushy, high-pressure sales approach will most likely meet up with resistance or rejection from older consumers. Further, anything that smacks of hype or hyperbole will almost immediately trigger a red flag.

Example: A business counselor friend of mine, Sam, who is in his seventies, lives in a high-rise apartment complex. A man selling emergency medical systems asked Sam if he could give a presentation to the older residents of the high-rise. Sam agreed to allow the man to speak so long as he didn't try to push the company's product. The salesman gave an excellent generic presentation about emergency medical systems. When he left, there was no doubt he'd made a great impression with the audience. Moreover, there was every reason to believe that a number of residents would buy his company's product.

Unfortunately, about a week later, this man and his staff began to deluge residents of the complex with telephone calls aggressively soliciting sales for the medical device. This approach angered the residents. According to Sam, not only was this selling technique ineffective, but it also destroyed whatever credibility the company salesman had earned from his earlier presentation. In fact, Sam says his neighbors will never invite this man or others from his company to speak there again!

Point: One pushy sales maneuver on a group of older consumers can instantly undo the goodwill generated by a previous positive encounter. It can also result in a number of lost sales!

Today's Mature Consumer Appreciates the Soft-Sell Approach

While many members of the mature market have been lured by hard-sell techniques in the past, several factors argue against using this type of approach today. These factors concern characteristics held by many of today's older consumers, particularly those under age 75.

Unlike their predecessors, many of these individuals possess the *education, experience,* and *time* to make prudent buying decisions. Strong educational backgrounds have enabled them to become more informed consumers. Years of experience in the work force and the marketplace have taught them to exercise a little healthy skepticism and caution before signing "the dotted line." Early retirement and more retirement years are giving many older shoppers the time to be patient and to comparison shop.

Given this information, your business should heed the words of Dennis LaBuda, formerly of the AARP, and now an executive with the Miami Jewish Home and Hospital for the Aged. Says Mr. LaBuda of the mature market:

> . . . older people want a lot of information. They want it to be fairly understandable and in layman's language. They want to be at ease and have time to review the material.[1]

Note: This is particularly true of the 50-64-year-olds and the well-to-do members of the 65+ group. Having lived through both unfavorable and prosperous times, the affluent seniors may be the *most* experienced and demanding consumers of all.

Six Soft-Sell Approaches When Serving the Mature Market

Here are six specific soft-sell strategies I recommend.

1. Mention the "Cons" as well as the "Pros" of Using Your Product or Service

Sometimes salespeople can get so caught up in selling their product or service that they fail to recognize or mention that it may not be appropriate for everyone. Even worse, some may deliberately choose not to alert potential buyers to the risks or weaknesses of their products. The older consumer frequently has been the recipient of the latter tactic.

If your business wants to establish a long-term foothold in the mature market, however, it must be able to see the older consumer's side of the sales transaction. That means providing the information he or she needs in order to make a sound purchasing decision. This will not only help prevent costly consumer and public relations problems, it will also bring new customers via the extensive word-of-mouth publicity given by satisfied older buyers.

Remember: With the seemingly endless stream of new and modified products and services being introduced to the 50+ market, (in health care, housing, financial services, insurance, and so forth), this method of selling has become a virtual necessity to help differentiate one's products and ease the burden of the overwhelmed consumer.

Example: The American Association of Retired Persons provides an excellent example of an organization that uses soft-selling techniques. AARP goes to great lengths to make sure that products or services offered to its members aren't oversold. In fact, close to 50 percent of the creative concepts presented to the organization are rejected on the basis that they are too "heavy sell" in nature.[2]

When products or services are offered, AARP tries to educate its members about them *before* they make their purchase. That way, members will know if a given product or service is appropriate for their needs. As an example, advertisements that run in AARP's *Modern Maturity* magazine about its Ginnie Mae investment product not only attempt to explain what this financial instrument is, but also the potential risks (as well as the rewards) of investing in it. (See Figure 9-3.)

I just learned that the AARP Ginnie Mae Fund *is* a good investment for me.

And I also found out why it's *not* for everyone.

This "What Is a Ginnie Mae" Information Kit showed me how the AARP Ginnie Mae Fund is an investment designed to earn me high current income each month.

It helped me understand that the AARP Ginnie Mae Fund is a longer-term investment — not a savings account — that I should consider only after I have set aside money for everyday and unexpected expenses.

I also learned that although yield does vary, this Fund has historically paid higher yields than most insured, fixed-rate CDs. However, unlike a CD, the value of my investment will change with market conditions. For example, on 5/15/86 the Fund's share price was $15.99. One year later it was $15.34.

While this example is no indication of future performance, I now know I must be able to tolerate fluctuation in principal to earn higher current income each month. And it's important to remember that no matter what the value of my principal is on any given day, I will continue to earn high income every month.

The kit went on to explain how this is a no-load mutual fund that invests principally in Ginnie Mae securities. These securities are guaranteed by the Government National Mortgage Association against default.

Want to find out how the AARP ADVANTAGE can give you even more? Return the coupon at right to receive the AARP GNMA Fund Information Kit. Or call 1-800-331-1100, ext. 687.

The Fund's underwriter is Scudder Fund Distributors, Inc.

8.41% 30-day current average annualized net yield as of 5/15/87. For today's yield call 1-800-631-4636.

☐ **Yes!** Please send me your "What Is a Ginnie Mae?" Information Kit, which includes a Prospectus containing more complete information about the Fund, its expenses, the roles of Scudder and AARP, and the fees they may receive. *Please read all materials carefully before you invest or send money.*
Please print clearly.

Name_____

Address_____

City_____ State_____ Zip_____

Please send me information on:
☐ The AARP IRA.
☐ All the funds in the Program.

Mail to: AARP Investment Program
Processing Center
P.O. Box 34935
Omaha, NE 68134-0935

AARP Investment Program from SCUDDER

8/87   2380

FIGURE 9–3

2. Provide Helpful Consumer Information

Another good soft-sell approach is to provide information that helps educate older consumers about items or issues connected to your line of business. This generic information can be communicated through several different media: seminars, newsletters, calendars, booklets, toll-free numbers, videotapes, public service announcements, and advertisements.

Tip: Sponsorship of consumer-oriented publications in very targeted geographic areas represents a low-cost way to reach, attract, and capture the mature market.

Example: A few years ago, I worked with the General Learning Corporation of Northbrook, Illinois to develop and produce newsletters for businesses and employers who serve the older population. One such newsletter is "Senior Health Report." Senior Health Report™ is used by health care providers such as hospitals and HMOs, and is distributed by the hospital or HMO to older adults in its service area.

Senior Health Report provides the reader with useful information and guidance on such topics as stress management, exercise, nutrition, and safety. The newsletter also allows the sponsoring organization to identify itself and to include customized messages relevant to those in its community. Senior Health Report has been very well received by both General Learning Corporation's customers and the older persons they serve. (See Figure 9-4.)

Several pharmaceutical companies have also provided important health care information to the mature adult in a soft-sell way. Sandoz Pharmaceuticals has been very active in supporting the dissemination of information about Alzheimer's disease, which Sandoz helps treat through its FDA-approved drug, Hydergine®.

Example: Sandoz provided a $140,000 grant to fund the production of the one-hour dramatic special, *There Were Times, Dear.* This film—which has been shown thoughout the country on public TV—has helped educate the public about Alzheimer's disease. Community presentations of the movie have raised large sums of money that have been used to assist local Alzheimer's programs, patients, and family members.[3]

Note: A byproduct of Sandoz' community/patient education programs is that they have caused many older persons (and family members) to ask their physicians about Hydergine Liquid Capsules.

Other companies outside of the pharmaceutical industry have also used this consumer information approach in reaching out to older consumers. These include:

- Grand Circle Travel, through its booklet, "101 Tips for the Mature Traveler"
- AT&T, through its "Senior Telephone Counselor" consumer education program

St. Francis-St. George

SENIOR HEALTH REPORT ™.

Keeping Your Cool in Summer Heat

Summertime, and the living is easy. Perhaps that should be a guiding phrase for these hot months.

When exposed to excessive heat, the healthy body responds by sweating. As the sweat evaporates, it acts as the body's cooling system. Also, the blood vessels near the surface of the skin automatically dilate to allow increased blood flow where surplus heat is released.

This sweating, coupled with the diversion of blood to skin vessels, can result in circulation problems. Loss of salt and water through excessive sweating reduces overall blood volume. This, along with the diversion of blood to the skin from vital organs, including the heart, brain, and kidneys, can lead to dizziness and fainting.

If the body contains enough fluid to sweat, it can withstand high temperatures. Therefore, the most important preventive step against heat disorders is maintaining proper fluid intake.

Some people are at higher risk of developing problems during hot weather, including the elderly and those with certain chronic diseases such as hardening of the arteries and diabetes.

Mark Rudemiller, M.D., emphasizes that there are less fluids in the systems of the elderly than in the younger population. "The cardiovascular abilities are not what they were, and that affects fluid retention," he notes.

Tim McCarren, M.D., cautions about being too precautious. "If you're older, don't isolate yourself. If you're healthy, you can just about do what exercise you want," Dr. McCarren says. "Follow some simple guidelines, don't overdo, and use your common sense. And talk with your doctor, especially if you have a chronic condition, such as heart problems or diabetes, or if you're taking regular medications."

(continued on p. 8)

Tim McCarren, M.D.   **Luis Quiroga, M.D.**   **Mark Rudemiller, M.D.**

Reprinted with permission of General Learning Corporation and St. Francis–St. George Health Services, Inc.

FIGURE 9–4

- Aetna Life Insurance and Annuity Company, through sponsorship of the educational program, "Choice Time: Thinking Ahead on Long-Term Care"

- Avon Products, Inc., by providing funds to help print materials for the National Council on Aging's "Facing Our Future" workshops.

● Giant Food Stores, through its booklet, "Shopping Sense for Seniors"

Remember: Behind all of these educational initiatives is the recognition that, by helping older persons become better consumers, you strengthen your affinity with them. In the competitive marketplace, that can spell the difference between mature market success and mere mediocrity.

Tip: This specific soft-sell approach is well suited for small businesses. For example, one dentist with whom I consulted was able to substantially increase the number of older patients he treated through the provision of consumer education. His approach included making presentations on dental hygiene to local groups (made up largely of older adults), and the publication of a one-page, two-sided dental education newsletter that he distributed to 50+ers in the community.

3. Develop Programs That Assist the Older Population

Numerous benefits can be realized by developing creative programs that assist mature adults and/or their families. Three companies engaging in such efforts are Ralston Purina, May Department Stores, and Puget Sound Power & Light Company.

Example: Ralston Purina's "Pets for People" program underwrites the cost of placing cats or dogs in the homes of those over 60. Pets are taken from humane shelters around the country. These shelters select the recipients from those over 60 who apply for the pets. Purina pays for any medical care provided in the first two weeks as well as any adoption costs. The company also gives the new pet owner a startup kit of products.

Feedback on the Pets for People program has been so positive that it has grown from a pilot project in St. Louis to a nationwide program.

Note: In addition to generating much goodwill, and helping older persons find companionship, Pets for People has also provided an innovative, subtle way for Purina to introduce its products to the dog or cat owner.

Example: Since 1982, May Company Department Stores has provided space, supplies, staff resources, and major financial support for the Older Adult Service and Information System (OASIS) program. OASIS is an educational, cultural, and health promotion program for adults age 60 and older. The program offers numerous free classes on such topics as nutrition, exercise, and painting. Through the use of many outside resources, such as Marylen Mann, OASIS' founder, these classes are offered at May Company stores in ten cities around the country. More than 40,000 persons belong to the program.[4]

Note: From the outset, May Company has supported the OASIS program purely as a goodwill effort—not for marketing purposes. Its gesture has proven beneficial for both OASIS members and May Company. Older adults enjoy the self-improvement classes, socialization, and comfortable surroundings of the department store environment. In some stores, they also are given price discounts during special events and holidays. May Company, on the other hand, benefits from the enormous visibility and positive feedback the program brings.

May Company may also realize another, unintended benefit. As founder Marylen Mann puts it, "These people are [consumer] traffic and they bring a lot of additional traffic into the stores. There is no doubt about the fact they increase sales."[5]

Point: The beauty of a soft-sell approach is that it can attract more older customers without directly soliciting their business.

Example: Washington state's Puget Sound Power & Light Company developed its "Gatekeeper Program" in 1983. The program is specifically designed to train meter readers, supermarket clerks, and others to watch out for the vulnerable elderly in their community. The utility company does this by teaching customer-contact employees to spot danger signals that may indicate an older person is in need of assistance. About 100 individuals per month are now referred to appropriate community services by Puget Power's staff.

Tip: While several utilities have since adopted the Gatekeeper Program, other companies—banks, restaurant chains, and supermarkets, for example—could also benefit from establishing similar programs, or working hand-in-hand with those organizations that do.

Remember: A major benefit of all of the above programs is that they bolster your company's image, credibility, and visibility with the older population.

4. Sponsor Community Events of Benefit to 50+ers

There is much to be gained by sponsoring community events that are of value to the mature adult. NCNB National Bank of North Carolina and Rancho Bernardo Convalescent Hospital offer excellent illustrations of this soft-sell approach.

Example: For the past few years, NCNB has been a major sponsor of the North Carolina Senior Games. The North Carolina Senior Games feature recreational and athletic events for the state's age 55+ adults. The games feature a statewide network of local games which culminate in an annual state final each fall.

Beyond providing financial support for the Senior Games, NCNB has assisted in developing communications' materials for and about the events. The bank has also provided various items used by Senior Games' staff and participants including medals, tote bags, golf towels, hats, and shirts. In honor of its major contributions to the success of these games, NCNB received the National Association of Area Agency on Aging's 1986 Corporate Award. In the process, NCNB has developed an even stronger image and relationship with North Carolina's older banking customers.

Keep in Mind: Another plus associated with NCNB's activities is that it lends support to the belief that Americans can remain healthy, energetic, and active citizens regardless of their age (a reflection of Key 3).

Example: Rancho Bernardo Convalescent Hospital, a southern California-based skilled nursing facility, has used an extensive community outreach program as a major part of its marketing effort. The facility has sponsored a number of holiday-related events which bring its patients and members of the community together. These activities have not only brought goodwill to this health care provider, they have also enabled it to attract an unusually high percentage of private-pay patients.[6]

5. Offer Product Samples or Coupons

Giving the older consumer the opportunity to try your product or service under low-pressure conditions can also be a good soft-sell approach. Couponing is one effective way of doing this. This technique can be particularly effective since the mature market is comprised of many coupon clippers and users. Along with the traditional forms of couponing (newspaper, magazine, and newsletter inserts), co-op programs, such as Donnelley Marketing's "New Age" direct mail co-op, offer a more targeted way of distributing your coupons to the age 50+ consumer.

Two outstanding examples of this approach are offered by Southwest Airlines and Mature Concepts, Inc.

Example: Southwest Airlines' "Home for the Holidays" program provides specially selected older adults with free tickets to any city in Southwest's system during the Christmas holidays. Qualifiers must be at least 60 years old and living on a fixed income. They are chosen by local aging organizations in each of the 27 cities served by Southwest. In 1986, Home for the Holidays received the Presidential Citation for Private Sector Initiatives.

Example: Mature Concepts disseminates retailers and manufacturers' coupons to the mature consumer via the leaders of older adult groups. These group leaders, in turn, distribute the coupons to their members. Mature Concepts encloses the coupons in envelopes known as "H.A.P.P.Y. Kits." (Note: "H.A.P.P.Y." stands for healthy, active people in their prime years.) Mature Concepts also gives away product samples and other gifts at entertaining shows it puts on for the group leaders and their club members. All of this is paid for by participating businesses in exchange for the opportunity to disseminate their wares in an upbeat, soft-sell way to the mature consumer.

Keep in Mind: What makes these programs especially good is that they involve key groups and influencers within the older adult network.

6. Use the "Open House" Technique

Inviting members of the mature market to see what it is you have to offer under low-pressure conditions is also an effective soft-sell approach your business can use. One way this can be done is through open-house programs.

Example: Fallon Community Health Plan, the Worcester, Massachusetts-based HMO, uses the open-house concept to attract older persons to its program. During their visits, seniors have an opportunity to meet Fallon's staff and learn more about the HMO's facilities and services. Similarly, Freedom Village, a retirement community in Bradenton, Florida, encourages prospective residents to visit its site, use the pool, and get to know the residents before moving there. As Diane Sampson, director of marketing for Freedom Village, puts it, "It's a soft sell. Traditional real estate salesmen don't make it here."[7]

Note: A high content, low-pressure sales strategy is particularly important in marketing senior housing.

The Methodist Medical Center of Illinois has used another kind of open house technique. The hospital has taken representatives from older adult groups on tours of its facilities. While not directly tied to any sales campaign, this educational marketing effort has enabled these individuals to better understand the hospital environment. It has also allowed them to become acquainted with Methodist's special skills and equipment under comfortable conditions. This and other soft-sell techniques have enabled Methodist to attract more 50+ers to use its services.

Keep in Mind: Giving members of the mature market access to your organization's facilities (conference rooms, stores, malls, offices, pavilions, and so forth) represents a good soft-sell strategy . . . regardless of whether or not it's for the purpose of lending space, conducting tours, or familiarizing older consumers with your staff and operations.

Marketing Checklist: Six Soft-Sell Approaches

1. Advise prospective older customers up front of the risks (as well as the rewards) of using your product or service.
2. Provide the older shopper with helpful consumer information.
3. Develop programs which assist the older population.
4. Sponsor community events of benefit to the mature market.
5. Use coupons, product samples, or other promotional techniques which enable mature consumers to try your products or services.
6. Use open house events to give the older consumer an opportunity to experience what it is you have to offer under low-pressure conditions.

Chapter Wrap-up

To achieve maximum success with the mature market, your organization should use a soft-sell, rather than a hard-sell, marketing strategy. Along with its inherent benefits, the soft-sell approach is ideal for the 50+ group because it:

- satisfies the increasing informational needs and demands of the mature market
- realizes the value of developing (1) long-range mature market strategies and (2) long-term relationships with older customers
- recognizes the healthy degree of skepticism which has been engendered in many mature shoppers by . . .

   —a lifetime of consumer experiences

   —the deceptive sales tactics sometimes perpetrated against the older population

   —the increasing number of laws, programs, organizations, and communications dedicated to educating and/or protecting the mature consumer

The soft-sell approach is also more likely to appeal to the most desired older customers, namely, those with the greatest income and assets.

Keep in Mind: Astute marketers will realize that America's mass of upcoming age 50+ consumers—the baby boomers—will bring a level of education and sophistication to the mature market that should make this approach even more important in the future.

---

1. "Panelists shed light on diverse elderly market," *Marketing News*, November 22, 1985, p. 35.

2. Personal telephone conversation with Frank S. Forbes, director of membership services operations, AARP, June 1987.

3. Personal telephone conversation with William Connelly, director, scientific affairs/external affairs, Sandoz Pharmaceuticals Corporation, September 1987.

4. "May Department Stores Co. Offers Goodwill through OASIS," *Selling to Seniors*, June 1987, p. 4.

5. Sahagun, Louis, "As America ages, advertisers bow to 'maturity'," *Los Angeles Times*, reprinted in *Wilmington News Journal*, February 3, 1985, p. B5.

6. Midgett, Matthew, "Skilled Nursing Facility Marketing: A Better Piece of the Pie," excerpted from *Marketing Long-Term Care and Senior Care Services*. William J. Winston, Editor. New York: Haworth Press, 1984.

7. Edmondson, Brad, "Is Florida Our Future?" American Demographics, June 1987, p. 69.

Chapter **10**

Key 8: Develop Marketing Programs That Reflect the Closeness of the Older Parent/ Adult Child Relationship

Serving the Family: A Pathway to Success for One Nursing Home Chain

It began two decades ago as a small chain of eight nursing homes. Today, this organization operates more than 140 facilities housing more than 18,000 beds. These facilities are located in 23 states and are serviced by the company's 18,000+ employees.

Manor HealthCare Corporation has experienced steady and spectacular growth since its inception in 1968 as a subsidiary of the newly formed holding company, Manor Care, Inc. The nation's fourth largest investor-owned nursing home system, Manor HealthCare would make any stockholder proud. Between fiscal years 1982 and 1987, for example, the company's revenues rose by 146 percent and operating profits by 183 percent. During the same period, its operating margin averaged higher than 18 percent, a figure which almost anyone in the nursing home industry would admire.

The company's nursing center occupancy rate and percentage of private-pay patients are equally impressive. In an industry where occupancy rates run about 80 percent, Manor HealthCare's hover around 90 percent. And, while the percentage of private-pay nursing home residents (that is, those paying for services out-of-pocket rather than through programs like Medicare or Medicaid) averages 30 to 40 percent nationally, at Manor Healthcare, it is over 60 percent.

Why has Manor HealthCare been so successful? For one thing, the company has paid a great deal of attention to delivering a high quality level of health care services. It does this in several ways, including: operating effective employee recruitment, training, and promotion programs, and conducting detailed quality assurance audits annually at each of its facilities.

Manor HealthCare also displays superb marketing skills. Its nursing facilities excel at developing relationships with referral groups within the communities they serve. Moreover, the organization has a knack for initiating innovative programs and services for its residents that have helped the company differentiate itself from other nursing home operators and, in the process, helped to attract a large private-pay clientele.

There is another factor which has contributed to Manor HealthCare's success. It is the organization's recognition of the importance of the older parent/adult child relationship—and its ability to incorporate that knowledge into the company's day-to-day marketing and operational activities. This directly relates to Key 8: *Develop marketing programs and services that reflect the closeness of the older parent/adult child relationship.*

Long-Term Care and the
Older Parent/Adult Child Relationship

The long-term care industry provides an outstanding example of the significance of the older parent/adult child relationship. For example, about 60 percent of America's nursing home residents are admitted by a family member or other relative, *not including the spouse*. Quite often, it is *a child* of the older person who makes the nursing home placement.

At Manor HealthCare, in more than half of the admissions, a child (or children) is involved in placing someone into one of its facilities. These individuals also become their loved one's guarantor, that is, the person legally responsible for paying the bills. In many instances, they will remain so for the balance of their parent's life since fewer than half of Manor HealthCare's residents return home once they've been admitted to one of its centers. Recognizing this, Manor HealthCare has developed a marketing program with components that address the older parent/adult child relationship. As you'll see, this program begins long before people enter its facilities and continues even after they are no longer its residents.

The Importance of Demographics in Selecting a Site

In determining where it will build a new facility (or whether it will acquire an existing one), Manor HealthCare gives primary consideration to the demographics of an area. Areas that include a sizable number of persons age 55 + are sought even though the average age of the company's nursing center residents is about 80. This is because those areas represent both a large number of potential residents . . . *and* their adult children. Indeed, most of the "children" who help make placements to Manor HealthCare are in their fifties and sixties. Locating facilities in these areas also makes sense, since, as Manor HealthCare has learned, many children are likely to favor a nursing facility that they can conveniently visit.

How Manor HealthCare Builds Awareness and Trust

Manor HealthCare expends a great deal of energy building an awareness of its facilities and trust in the minds of the adult child. According to Kit Carlson, a director of marketing services at Manor HealthCare, it is important to do this long before the need for nursing home placement arises. Said Carlson: "This is especially true since you are dealing with a product where there is such an investment of money, time, love, and care. We are essentially doing for these older people what their children should or would like to be doing but can't. And you have to build that awareness and sense of trust over a long period of time. It's not like you're buying a toothbrush. You're buying a much more important service."

To build awareness and gain trust, Manor HealthCare employs a number of strategies. As an example, the company uses creative advertising aimed at family members facing the difficult decision of placing a loved one in a nursing facility. In one ad, targeted directly at the adult child, the reader is asked the question: "Who can take care of Mom as well as I can? We can."

Like other messages that the company uses to reach family members, this ad is intended to achieve at least two important goals:

- First, it seeks to make people feel OK, rather than guilty, about the decision to placed a loved one in a nursing facility.
- Second, it seeks to reassure the caregiver that his or her loved one will be cared for at Manor HealthCare in the same dedicated, competent, and compassionate way as he (or she) was treated at home.

Manor HealthCare also uses the "We can" ad to invite caregivers to the open houses it stages for new nursing centers. Anywhere from 500 to 1200 people show up for these open houses. There, family members (again, frequently the children) can see the center and meet its staff. All visitors are given a copy of the brochure "How to Select a Nursing Center." This consumer guide is another approach which the organization uses to educate nursing home shoppers and help them gain confidence in Manor HealthCare and its capabilities.

Manor HealthCare also develops creative programs to reach family members in need. One of these, Care Givers at Home, is a program of free seminars designed to assist those who are taking care of a family member at home. (See Figure 10-1.) At these seminars, community health care professionals provide attendees with helpful information on performing the daily tasks of caregiving and dealing with its accompanying stresses. By sponsor-

CARE
GIVERS
AT
HOME

A program to aid, instruct, and
support those providing care for
a disabled family member.

November 15 and 22, 1986
1:00 - 3:00 p.m.
at Penn State/York
York, Pennsylvania

*Presented by
Manor HealthCare Corp.*

FIGURE   10–1

ing Care Givers at Home, Manor HealthCare strengthens its relationship and reputation with those adult children who may later need to place a parent in one of its facilities.

Keeping Family Members "In Touch"

Manor HealthCare maintains a close relationship with an adult child once a parent is admitted to one of its facilities. At the outset, family members may be invited to attend the "In Touch" program held at several of the organization's centers. During this hour and a half meeting, individuals receive assistance in dealing with the psychological effects of placing a loved one in a nursing facility. They also learn how to make the transition to nursing home living easier for themselves and their family member. Finally, they discuss their loved one's plan of treatment with the nursing center's health care professionals.

Every Manor HealthCare facility has a designated social service department representative who acts as a liaison between the family and the center. On a daily basis, this individual communicates to families any special social, emotional, or personal needs of their loved ones. Each nursing center also produces its own monthly newsletter, which is distributed to residents and important others, including the responsible family member.

Another way in which Manor HealthCare stays close to its residents' families is by routinely soliciting feedback from them through its guarantor satisfaction survey. (See Figure 10-2.) This survey allows Manor HealthCare to assess the quality of its services from the customer's perspective.

Manor HealthCare also does its best to share with guarantors the happy times experienced by a loved one. Thus, the centers regularly hold special events for residents which family members are invited—and encouraged—to attend. On the other hand, the organization is present in times of over-whelming sadness, too. In addition to providing bereavement counseling, nursing centers typically arrange for one key member of the staff to visit the family after a death.

Satisfying the "Other Customer"—the Adult Child

Knowing the significance of the older parent/adult child relationship, Manor HealthCare has effectively developed and implemented numerous programs to reach, assist, involve, and satisfy its "other customer" . . . the adult child. How much of a factor has this been in the organization's ongoing success? Kit Carlson put it this way:

> I think it's been crucial. If you don't keep your customers—who are not only our residents but their children—if you don't keep them all happy, there is no way you can succeed. If you don't communicate with the chil-dren, consistently offer them a quality product, make them feel like they are important in their parents' lives, then you lose them and you lose the business. I think the success of our business is based on that kind of rela-tionship which we have developed with our clients.

Why Marketers Should Pay Attention to the Parent/Adult Child Relationship

Why is it so important for marketers to be aware of the parent/adult child relationship? Here are two good reasons.

Adult Children Can Influence Their Parents' Decisions

Most older persons have living children, including 80 percent of those over 65. Many of these children live near their parents and have regular contact with them. Among the 65+ group, for example,

Dear Guarantor,

I wish to thank you for selecting our nursing center to care for your loved one. I recognize the importance of your decision, and I am also aware of our responsibility to provide the highest quality health care services available.

I am sending you this evaluation form so that we can measure our performance by your standards. I hope that you will take the time to express your opinion so that we are able to correct problems and give credit to those who have performed to your satisfaction.

The comment form is prepared so that you can remain anonymous or disclose your name and address if a response is appropriate. The decision is yours.

Thank you for taking the time to assist us with this quality measure. The comments you provide ensure that our residents receive the finest care possible.

Sincerely,

Karen Caldwell

Karen Caldwell
Vice President, Professional Services

- Detach Here -

- Return Lower Portion

Please <u>check</u> the box that best describes the quality of care or services received:

	Very Good	Good	Fair	Poor	Very Poor	Did Not Use
CARE						
Quality of nursing care	☐	☐	☐	☐	☐	☐
Courtesy and attitude of licensed nursing staff	☐	☐	☐	☐	☐	☐
Courtesy and attitude of nursing assistants	☐	☐	☐	☐	☐	☐
Attention to personal care and grooming needs	☐	☐	☐	☐	☐	☐
Respect for resident's privacy and dignity	☐	☐	☐	☐	☐	☐
FOOD						
Promptness of food delivery	☐	☐	☐	☐	☐	☐
Quality of food	☐	☐	☐	☐	☐	☐
ACTIVITIES						
Opportunities for meaningful social interaction	☐	☐	☐	☐	☐	☐
Variety of activities and outings	☐	☐	☐	☐	☐	☐
THERAPY						
Quality of therapy program	☐	☐	☐	☐	☐	☐
Courtesy and attitude of therapy staff	☐	☐	☐	☐	☐	☐
FACILITY						
Cleanliness of center	☐	☐	☐	☐	☐	☐
Center's odor	☐	☐	☐	☐	☐	☐
Upkeep and safety of facility	☐	☐	☐	☐	☐	☐
Care and safekeeping of personal laundry and belongings	☐	☐	☐	☐	☐	☐
ADMINISTRATION						
Experience with Administrator	☐	☐	☐	☐	☐	☐
Experience with Admissions Director	☐	☐	☐	☐	☐	☐
Courtesy and attitude of office staff	☐	☐	☐	☐	☐	☐
Overall satisfaction with stay	☐	☐	☐	☐	☐	☐

Would you use this center again?   ☐ Yes   ☐ Not Sure   ☐ No
Would you recommend this center to others?   ☐ Yes   ☐ Not Sure   ☐ No

Please indicate your reason(s) for selecting this center:

☐ Hospital Recommendation   ☐ Center Reputation   ☐ Physician Recommendation
☐ Convenient Location   ☐ Therapy Program   ☐ Bed Availability
☐ Attractiveness of Center   ☐ Friend Recommendation   ☐ Other: _____

COMMENTS: _____
_____
_____
_____
_____
_____

NAME AND ADDRESS (Optional): _____
_____

FIGURE 10–2

- more than half live within 30 minutes of a child
- 62 percent see their children at least weekly
- more than three-fourths talk to their children on the phone at least once a week[1]

It should come as no surprise, then, that adult children can play a role in determining their parents' consumer purchases for such things as appliances, food products, automobiles, insurance, hotels, restaurants, financial services, hospitals, and life care communities.

Key Point: The older a person gets, the more likely it is that a child will influence his or her major purchasing behavior. For example, according to SRI International's "Lifestyles and Values of Older Adults" (LAVOA) study, 65 percent of those over 75 who were surveyed said they relied on their children's advice when making important decisions.[2] This finding should not be taken lightly. Those over 75 already account for more than 4 in 10 of the 65+ population. In about ten years, they'll represent *half* of that group.

Keep in Mind: During the next several decades, many of those entering or among the 75+ group will be the parents of the baby boomers. And a large majority of the baby boomers believe that adult children should have at least some responsibility for the well-being of their parents.[3]

Why can adult children be a factor in determining what their parents will or will not buy? There are at least four reasons:

Children Often Have Implicit Credibility. Older consumers rely heavily on word-of-mouth testimonials when making important buying decisions. Generally speaking, no one has more credibility and trust than members of the immediate family.

Keep in Mind: Word-of-mouth information and/or approval supplied by a child is more likely to be believed by the parent than comments made by almost any other source.

Children May Be More Familiar with the Offering. In some cases, parents may be influenced by their children because they are more conversant with a given product or service.

Example: I consulted with a company that was developing an HMO for those over 65. During the subsequent marketing of the product, I was not surprised to learn that the HMO was receiving a significant number of enrollment forms from *children* who had filed applications in behalf of their parents. These children were, no doubt, much more familiar with the HMO concept than were their parents.

Children May Have More Experience or Confidence in Making Specific Purchasing Decisions. Some older adults, especially those over 75, may lack confidence in their ability to make certain consumer purchases. This may because they are unaccustomed to making such decisions or they lack the necessary education to do so. Some older women living alone, for example, may lack confidence in choosing "big-ticket" items. Often, this is because those decisions had always been made by their husbands. In such cases, they tend to rely upon their children's help.

Example: At one seminar, Peter Francese, President of American Demographics, Inc., explained how he spent hours counseling his 79-year-old mother on how to buy a new refrigerator because she lacked the confidence to do this herself.[4]

Older Parents May Have Health Problems. Children may, of necessity, be compelled to influence the purchasing decisions of their parents. A parent's physical and/or mental health may make it difficult, if not impossible, to make important consumer purchases. In these situations, decisions may be informally delegated to the child or he or she may become the legally responsible party.

There Is Great Potential for Developing Successful Intergenerational Marketing Programs

Adult children and their parents frequently do things with, or for, each other. For example, they may shop, travel, or attend cultural activities together. Or, they may purchase gifts for one another.

Tip: All of these situations present opportunities for your business to sell products and services which older parents can buy for their children or vice-versa. They may also allow you to serve both of these consumers at the same time. Furthermore, with the aging of America, *more and more adult children are members of the mature market themselves.* Thus, you may also have the chance to serve two generations of 50+ers simultaneously!

Keep in Mind: There may also be an opportunity to include grandchildren and greatgrandchildren in these marketing programs.

I would be remiss if I didn't make one more point before leaving this section: *"Mature" parents can also influence their adult children's consumer behavior.* Younger persons, for instance, frequently make major purchases with the advice or financial assistance of their parents. This is often the case the first time someone buys a new home. For example, a 1985 *Money* magazine survey about "Americans and Their Money" found that 36 percent of those over 50 expected to give their children financial help in purchasing their first homes.[5]

Keep in Mind: The influence of a parent may continue even after the child passes middle age. In his book, *Talking Straight,* Lee Iacocca, the 64-year-old chief executive officer of the Chrysler Corporation, notes that he still seeks advice from his mother.[6]

The impact that older parents can have is often more subtle.

Example: A few years ago, a New York-based health plan discovered that satisfied members of its Medicare HMO (that is, for those age 65+) had actually helped cause the number of enrollees in the plan's HMO for under-65 persons to increase. In this case, some of the older members had influenced their children to join the HMO.

Key Point: Older parents and adult children often influence each other's consumer behavior. Recognition of this can help you improve your effectiveness in marketing to consumers who are either *over* or *under* the age of 50.

Marketing and the Older Parent/Adult Child Relationship

Obviously, it's not enough to be aware of the significance of the older parent/adult child relationship. Like Manor HealthCare, you must also develop marketing programs and services that reflect the nature of this familial bond. Your efforts should be based primarily on the state of the parent's health. Generally, this results in two different stages of marketing activity: Stage 1, when the older parent is still healthy, and Stage 2, when his or her health begins to decline.

Three Marketing Approaches to Pursue When the Older Parent Is Healthy

The majority of 50 + ers will stay healthy throughout most of their retirement years. Therefore, the opportunity to develop successful older parent/adult child marketing programs during this stage is particularly good. Most of these intergenerational business opportunities have hardly been tapped!

Here are three marketing strategies you should pursue in Stage 1. One of them is specifically intended to help you maximize your potential for success in Stage 2. In fact, while reading the first two recommended strategies, you should also keep this in mind: *By successfully implementing the first two strategies outlined, you'll also be building the foundation for a strong Stage 2 marketing program.*

1. Identify Older Parent/Adult Child Relationships

If you seek to develop marketing programs that target older parents and their adult children, you must have methods to identify these relationships.

Customer contacts represent the best sources of information in uncovering parent/child relationships. The approach you take in requesting this information will vary depending upon your industry and products. Probably the simplest way to do this is to tell your customers about special programs or services that may be of benefit or interest to other members of their family.

Then ask if you can have some basic information (name, address, age bracket, and so forth) about their relatives so that they, too, can be alerted to your services when it's appropriate.

The precise methods you use to obtain the information—and the nature of the information you request—will depend upon your industry and company. Here are a few examples of *when* your customers can be asked to give you the details you need.

Business	Information requested
Financial institution	When account opened, credit card obtained or monthly statement mailed
Packaged goods manufacturer	When rebate form sent in or coupon redeemed
Group tour operator	When tour evaluation sheet completed
Appliance/auto manufacturer	When warranty registration card mailed in
Hospital	When admitted or discharged, or when family members visit
Airline or hotel	When frequent flyer (or frequent traveler) notices mailed

Note: As with any information-gathering or solicitation program, the more creative, user-friendly, and benefit-oriented your specific approach is, the greater the chances will be for its success.

Promotional programs may be a very good way to identify older parent/ adult child relationships, particularly for those businesses with little or no direct contact with the customer.

Example: If your company markets food products or personal care items, it can sponsor a contest in which entrants and their parents (or children) become eligible to win prizes if they submit an entry form that provides specific requested information.

Tip: The contest itself could be built upon a theme that ties into the older parent/adult child relationship.

Direct marketing (for example, co-op programs) can also be used to elicit information about specific adult child/older parent relationships. Since many of those over 50 have either adult children and/or a surviving parent(s), *mailing lists* that contain the names of persons age 50 + might be helpful too, not only in identifying relationships but in implementing intergenerational marketing programs. At least one of the companies offering these mailing lists, Senior Citizens Marketing Group, Inc. in Dallas, also has lists that contain the names of seniors who *live* with their middle-aged children.

Note: The latter information may be more useful during Stage 2 marketing activities since seniors who live with their children are more likely to have health problems.

Internal communications can generate information about specific older parent/adult child relationships too. For example, many of your employees and retirees are likely to have relationships of this kind.

Note: Companies with older work forces and/or large retiree populations may find this to be a very good resource.

2. Develop Marketing Campaigns, Programs, and Products Which Integrate the Two Generations

Close family relationships between older parents and their adult children pave the way for creative advertising campaigns, marketing programs, and new products . . . all of which can increase your company's business.

Example: IDI-Maryland, Inc. has used a clever print ad to promote The Greens at Leisure World, its successful adult resort community for those over 50. (See Figure 10-3.) Kodak, Fleischmann's, and AT&T have also used advertising that portrays this special bond.

Occasions like Christmas, Thanksgiving, Mother's Day, and Father's Day provide obvious opportunities to link together these two generations with your product line. (See Figure 10-4.) However, other events may offer equally promising possibilities. These include birthdays, anniversaries, retirement parties, and second honeymoons.

Tip: Your company can promote and develop products or services that are ideal for parents (or adult children) to give in celebrating special moments.

Keep in Mind: Comfortably Yours was started by a middle-aged woman, Elaine Adler, who wanted to purchase a birthday gift for her mother. Today, many of Comfortably Yours' customers are adult children who buy products for their parent(s).

For those in the travel/leisure industry, there are exceptional opportunities for intergenerational marketing.

Example: Not long ago, the middle-aged president of one of my client companies told me how he purchased a vacation for his widowed mother. He said that his mother had a "Depression" era mentality, meaning that she wouldn't spend money to indulge herself. Buying the vacation was his way of helping her "live it up" without feeling guilty. Conversely, in 1983, my wife and I were part of a group tour to Italy. Among the group was an older couple whose daughter joined them. This woman's trip had been purchased by her parents to celebrate her fortieth birthday!

Tip: The older parent-adult child connection also presents a great opportunity to market gift certificates that address this special relationship.

IT'S 10 P.M.
DO YOU KNOW WHERE YOUR PARENTS ARE?

What a switch. After years of your parents looking out for you, now you're looking out for them.

Well, when your parents live at The Greens at Leisure World, you'll not only know *where* they are, you'll know *how* they are.

You'll know they're secure, in a private country club community with attended gatehouses, where taking a walk before dawn or a stroll past midnight is common, and uncommonly safe.

You'll know they're comfortable, in a condominium home with all the luxury appointments of a single family home, plus a spectacular golf course view from every window.

You'll know they're never bored, with more than 65 social, recreational and cultural activities in the community center each month, plus golf, tennis, and year-round swimming. And they're never lonely, with more than 4,000 neighbors to share it all with.

But best of all, you'll know they're

never far away—just off Georgia Avenue in Silver Spring. So they'll always be near when you need them . . . or when they need you.

The Greens at Leisure World, from the $70's to the $170's. To visit, take the Beltway, north on Connecticut Ave. to Georgia Ave., left to Leisure World and The Greens. Open 7 days, 10-6, or by appointment. *Phone* 598-2500.

A better environment for people . . . developed by IDI:

FIGURE 10–3

FIGURE 10-4

Example: The Family Backed Mortgage Association (FBMA) illustrates how the older parent/adult child relationship can create new product offerings. FBMA developed its Grannie Mae and SMILE programs to help older homeowners unlock the equity in their homes. Under the Grannie Mae plan, 50+ers sell their home to their children and lease it back from them. Under the SMILE program, older adults sell their home, and their children buy a new smaller home for them. The parents then rent the new home from their children.

Keep in Mind: In both instances, FBMA winds up serving *two* customers . . . the adult child and the parent(s).

3. Make Families Aware of Your Special Products/Services for Caregivers and Parents in Need

Up to 80 percent of the older population is assisted by their children in times of crisis. At such times, children often are compelled to make decisions in their parents' behalf in rapid-fire fashion.

What this means, of course, is that if you offer products or services for older adults with major health problems—or for children who assist them—you should try to make people aware of that long before the need ever arises.

Caution: If you wait until a crisis develops, it may be too late.

Marketing Checklist: Three Marketing Approaches to Pursue While the Parents Are Still Healthy (Stage 1)

1. Identify specific older parent/adult child relationships.
2. Develop marketing campaigns, programs, and products that integrate the two generations.
3. Make families aware of products/services you offer for caregivers and older parents in need.

Six Marketing Approaches for When the Parent's Health Declines

Many opportunities exist for businesses to serve the adult child when a parent's health deteriorates. Potential products or services that may be needed include:

- asset management
- medical supplies, drugs, and medication guidance
- legal, psychological, and nutritional counseling
- food shopping
- housing and transportation services
- insurance
- inpatient and outpatient health services

Along with some of the activities suggested in Stage 1, there are other approaches you can use during Stage 2 that will maximize your company's potential to fill these needs. Here are six of them.

1. Target Your Marketing Activities to the Women

Unquestionably, when older adults need assistance from the family, it is the *women*, not the men, who provide most of it. Wives, daughters, daughters-in-law, and other female relatives comprise nearly 75 percent of all such caregivers.[7] According to Elaine Brody, a director at the Philadelphia Geriatric Center and an expert on caregiver problems, about 5 million women find themselves in the position of caring for an older parent.[8]

Not only are most caregivers female, *they also tend to be middle-aged or older.* For instance, a study by the National Center for Health Services Research (NCHSR) found that the average age of caregivers was 57 and that about a third of the group was over 65.[9]

Tip: Your primary target for Stage 2 (and for many of your Stage 1) marketing activities should be middle-aged and older women.

Note: This also reinforces another key point: As many of these caregivers are themselves age 50+, by serving their parents' needs, you open yourself up to supplying products and services which meet their needs as well.

2. Learn About Caregiver Problems

Having a keen understanding of caregiver needs and concerns increases your ability to develop and market products for this group and their parents. This knowledge can be gathered in a number of ways, including the following:

Primary research studies. Conducting qualitative and/or quantitative research studies involving either actual and/or potential caregivers (e.g., women ages 40+) can provide you with helpful primary research data.

Warning: One potential barrier to conducting this kind of research may be the cost, especially if you're looking for individuals actually engaged in caregiving activities. That's because the incidence rate in recruiting participants for such a study is very low.

Money-Saving Alternative: Conduct a survey of your own employees' and/or retirees' caregiving activities. A few companies including The Travelers, Remington Products, Pitney Bowes, and People's Bank have already done this. The Travelers developed a special benefits program for its employee caregivers after the survey disclosed the difficulties some of them were experiencing in taking care of an older relative.

Tip: While "elder care" surveys of employees and retirees have, thus far, been conducted for human resource purposes, there is no reason why they can't be used to serve corporate marketing functions. In fact, in some organizations, such studies can be undertaken to meet the needs of *both* departments.

Remember: The marketing and human resources departments can work *collaboratively* to better serve members of the older population ... whether they are your older workers, your retirees, or your customers.

Publications, published studies, and other media. More and more information is available on family caregiving and its accompanying problems and implications. This includes a number of published studies such as those undertaken by the New York Business Group on Health, the National Center for Health Services Research, and the Philadelphia Geriatric Center. The information gleaned from these studies and reports will enhance your ability to relate and respond to caregiver and care receiver concerns.

Organizations. Many organizations engage in caregiver-related activities or programs. Among these are university gerontological departments, disease-related groups (such as the Alzheimer's Disease and Related Disorders Association), government agencies, and organizations for older adults. There are also groups like the Children of Aging Parents, whose primary purpose is to serve family caregivers.

Tip: A helpful source in identifying and reaching the caregiver groups is The National Council on Aging's *Ideabook on Caregiver Support Groups.*

Conferences. With the heightened interest in the family caregiver problem has come the introduction of conferences and seminars on this topic. Recently, the Conference Board and the American Society on Aging sponsored programs dealing with this issue. These conferences can provide up-to-date information about caregiver studies and the impact of this problem on society, the workplace, and the business community.

Keep in Mind: Of almost equal significance, they allow marketers the ability to interface with key figures in the older adult and caregiver networks.

3. Communicate with Those Who Are—or May Become—Caregivers for Their Parents

Earlier, I referred to the importance of making family members aware of your services for caregivers and their parents while the latter are still healthy. Now, let's talk about how you can actually build or strengthen such relationships. Regardless of whether your marketing activities are directed to potential caregivers during Stage 1 or actual caregivers in Stage 2, the same fundamental principles apply:

- Direct the majority of your efforts at middle-aged and older women.
- Make your communications informational in nature.

Targeting the women. Since the likelihood of experiencing chronic, debilitating health problems increases after age 65, particularly after age 75, it follows that those women ages 40+ face the greatest potential for assuming the child caregiver role.

There are many distribution channels to reach these women. For example, some may already be your customers, or, as The Travelers, Southwestern Bell, PepsiCo, and Florida Power & Light Company have discovered via in-house activities, they may be your employees. These two groups—customers and employees—are within easy access. Where else can you reach these women with your communications?

- Through business, social, and civic groups, especially those with large numbers of female members (such as the League of Women Voters, the Junior League, and chapters of Business & Professional Women)
- Through established caregiver groups
- Through newspaper sections, magazines, and TV/radio programs that reach large numbers of middle-aged women (such as food/ entertainment/ health columns; *McCalls*, *Ladies Home Journal*, and *Family Circle* magazines; news and talk shows, and so forth)
- Through the human resource departments of other companies

Keep in Mind: Recent corporate studies indicate that 20 to 30 percent of all full-time employees are caring for an elderly parent or relative.[10]

Tip: *Lear's*, a magazine targeted to women ages 40+, and *McCall's* "Silver Edition," a bimonthly insert sent to women in the 50-to-64 age group, may also be good communications' vehicles for you to use.

There are also many places you can turn to for information about the various distribution channels. For example, government agencies and Chambers of Commerce should be able to help you track down women's groups. The state of Delaware's Department of Community Affairs, for instance, annually publishes a "Delaware Directory of Women's Organizations." Chambers of Commerce may also help you gain access to a network of human resource professionals as can organizations like the American Society for Personnel Administration (and its local chapters). Resources like Mediamark Research Inc. (MRI), the Newspaper Advertising Bureau, and *American Demographics* magazine can provide useful data on the media habits and preferences of the age 40+ woman.

Building relationships through informative communications. By providing an adult child with practical information to help her (or him) deal with the difficulties of caregiving, you can help generate awareness of—and goodwill/credibility for—your organization and the products or services you offer.

Publications that assist the family caregiver represent one effective communications tool. A resource directory for families of Alzheimer's victims has been published by the Administration on Aging's Dallas Regional Office. In this case, Sandoz Pharmaceuticals was one of a few organizations that helped fund the project.

Keep in Mind: Sandoz's role dovetails with its marketing of Hydergine®, a prescription drug used to treat the symptoms of Alzheimer's disease.

Example: One creative publication that serves to help marketers and caregivers is *Advice.* Developed by Helpful Publications, Inc. of Glenside, Pennsylvania, *Advice* is an eight-page, bimonthly newsletter for adults with aging parents or a dependent spouse. (See Figure 10-5.) Written by professionals, the newsletter offers information and guidance on a variety of issues that concern caregivers, such as how to cope with the specific health problems of a loved one or where to turn for financial help.

Helpful Publications sells *Advice* to hospitals and other health care facilities. They, in turn, distribute it to family caregivers or others who influence health care decision making (such as physicians). Bethany Methodist in Chicago has used the newsletter to promote its image as a "geriatric center of excellence in Chicago."

Note: According to Alan Reiman, vice president of marketing and planning for Bethany, *Advice* helped his organization generate about $125,000 in business during the first year it was used. These revenues came from caregivers and care receivers who obtained medical services from Bethany.[11]

Remember: Informative, company-sponsored newsletters, magazines, calendars, and so forth can be a very cost effective way to reach and attract mature adults and their families.

Training programs and *seminars* are another excellent way of disseminating needed information to caregivers and building relationships with them. Along with Manor HealthCare and its "Care Givers at Home" series, a few other organizations have also developed these programs.

Example: Southwestern Bell has produced "Caregiving: The Challenge of Elder Care." This educational package includes a video documentary, a training manual, and an audiotape. Southwestern Bell created the program to meet the needs of the many caregivers who are its customers and employees.

Recently, a number of organizations including The Travelers, Florida Power & Light, and Ciba-Geigy have held fairs for family caregivers. At these events, caregivers can attend seminars and meet with representatives of organizations that offer related services.

Tip: While many of these fairs have been put together by employers for their employees, marketers can also help to sponsor these programs.

As an example, a local chapter of a national social service organization I came into contact with was specifically looking for someone to sponsor its caregiver event. The limited cost of underwriting the program versus the enormous potential for positive visibility from sponsorship made this an excellent opportunity for one of my clients, who went on to become the program's major underwriter.

ADVICE
for Adults with™ Aging Parents
or a dependent spouse

Volume 1, Number 2

April/May 1986

Parent Care and Women's Competing Roles

At no time in history have so many women had the responsibility of helping an elderly parent or parent-in-law. The need to provide such help may compete with responsibilities to other family members, to their house-holds, and to a job or volunteer work. As a result, millions of women all over the country and in all walks of life are finding themselves pulled by the demands of the many different roles they play.
2

Talking with your Parent's Doctor

Older people are more likely to turn first to family when physically sick; if they are no longer living independently, they may turn to family to provide most health-related care.
5

FIGURE 10–5

Keep in Mind: Even if you don't sponsor a caregivers' fair, your company may still benefit from participating in these programs as exhibitors or presenters.

There are, of course, dozens of others ways in which your business can communicate with adult child caregivers. They are limited only by your organization's knowledge of the problem and your employees' imagination. Indeed, creativity can play a vital factor in developing a relationship with caregivers. For example, Pottstown Memorial Medical Center in Pennsylvania held a professionally staged play on coping with older parent/adult child relationships. Attendees of the performance then helped the center form caregiver support groups and develop a series of community programs dealing with the needs of aged parents.

Tip: Community-service programs can help you identify and build relationships with caregivers.

4. Use Sensitive, Compassionate Advertising

Many children experience feelings of stress and/or guilt in serving as caregivers for their parents. If your organization plans to advertise to this group, you must be acutely aware of this. For example, if your ads either dwell upon—or ignore—the difficulties of caregiving, they are unlikely to be effective. Much the same can be said about advertising which, in one way or another, shows disrespect for the ill parent.

Example: One organization that recognized this, and as a result, developed a successful marketing campaign, is ARA Living Centers of Houston, Texas. A few years ago, ARA—the second largest investor-owned nursing home system in America—created a successful advertising program geared to the emotional concerns of its customers. ARA defined the long-term health care customer as the "55-year-old daughter or son" who selects a nursing center for the ultimate *consumer:* the child's parent.[12]

ARA developed a series of ads for this highly targeted group of customers. Each of these "Is This Someone You Know?" ads told the story of a family very much concerned about the health and well-being of an aged parent. (See Figure 10-6.) Displaying a profound degree of sensitivity and empathy, the ads invited readers to contact ARA to learn more about the services its facilities could offer to those seniors in need. Along with these ads, ARA created a direct-response mechanism by offering a free copy of a helpful, caregiver-oriented publication.

Result: In the 48 markets where ARA used the advertisements over a two-year period, its admissions increased 11 percent. In contrast, in the 35 markets where it did not use the advertisements in either of the two years, its admissions went down 9 percent.[13]

The Clear Message: Sensitivity, honesty, compassion, humanity, simplicity, empathy, and helpfulness—using any or all of these appeals in your advertising can have a dramatic effect on your organization's ability to influence both the decision-making adult child and your bottom line.

Is this someone you know?

Life has changed for the Klein family since Grandma moved in. At first it was fun because she could baby-sit and tell ghost stories. But lately having Grandma around has become a strain on everybody.

Mom and Dad are arguing more. The children's grades in school have slipped. And Grandma never seems happy.

Recently the family wanted to go on vacation. Everybody was afraid to leave Grandma in the house alone, and Grandma didn't want to go along.

We've known lots of families like the Kleins over the years. The stress that accompanies caring for an elderly parent is not new. Especially the stress on the parent. We've created a special living environment for important people like Grandma, who need:

• special attention,
• the warmth of companionship,
• a sense of security,
• nutritious meals
• and someone to rely on in emergencies.

If your family is like the Klein family, call us today, for more information and a free copy of the book, "When Love Gets Tough." We offer the things that make life worth living.

 LIVING CENTERS

Reprinted from *Building Marketing Effectiveness in Health Care: A Proceedings.* Chicago: Academy for Health Services Marketing, American Marketing Association, D. Terry Paul, 1985

FIGURE 10–6

5. Develop Products and Services Specifically Designed to Assist Children Whose Parents Have Health Problems

Opportunities abound for those who develop new products and services to meet the needs of adult children and/or their ailing parents. Helpful Publication's introduction of the *Advice* newsletter offers one example of this. While *Advice* represents a *product* that can be introduced to serve this market, the vast majority of opportunities probably lie in the service area.

Example: In 1984, Brenda Shimmel, a social worker in Sarasota, realized that many middle-aged children who lived "up North" needed someone to monitor their parents in Florida. Shimmel and her husband started Family Partner, Inc. For a monthly fee, they will visit a client's home twice, call two times a week, arrange for needed services, take care of emergencies, and write monthly reports to the family.

Some hospitals, retirement communities, and nursing facilities are offering a similar service for children whose aging parents live with them. This service, sometimes known as a "weekend guest" program, enables the children to place their parent at the facility so they can travel or have some time to themselves. The service offers peace of mind to those who are afraid to leave their loved one alone.

Note: In the future, the most successful travel/leisure companies will probably make arrangements for such services. Some may even offer them directly.

Keep in Mind: There may also be situations in which your company may be able to provide products or services to both older persons with health problems and their healthy adult children. For instance, Sophisticated Seniors, the business that sells attractive clothing and jewelry to nursing home residents, has sold some of its wares to the children of these individuals, too! This is an excellent illustration of another way that older parent/adult child marketing activities can be integrated during Stage 2.

Remember: The opportunity to provide these and other products/services will boom as the eldercare crisis escalates over the next several years.

To create innovative products and services for caregivers/care receivers, you need to

- have a good general understanding of the difficulties caregivers/care receivers face
- draw upon information gleaned from primary and secondary research studies to identify actual or anticipated caregiver needs
- determine how much, if anything, the adult child (or older parent) would be willing to *pay* for your product or service

Note: The third item is particularly important. While many older adults and family members might say a specific service is needed, this often does *not* mean they would be willing to pay the price you'll have to charge to make it profitable. This should be less of a factor as the demand for caregiver services explodes and public/private means of financing these services (via long-term care insurance, for example) becomes widespread.

6. Recognize the Proximity Factor as an Important Marketing Consideration

Where an adult child lives in relation to his or her parent can be an important factor in determining your success. For example, many persons who choose to move into retirement housing prefer to be near their children. As a result, some developers have used that as a basis for selecting areas to establish their communities.

On the other hand, "long-distance" caregivers also present opportunities. This is true not only for the providers of health and social services but also for other businesses as well: telephone companies, banks, supermarkets, direct mail merchandisers, and so forth.

Keep in Mind: *Distances between adult children and their parents may determine whether your product or service is needed and profitable.* Therefore, learn as much as you can about the demographic and socioeconomic characteristics of those areas in which you are planning to target your marketing efforts.

Marketing Checklist: Six Marketing Approaches for When the Older Parent's Health Declines (Stage 2)

1. Recognize who most family caregivers are.
2. Learn as much as you can about caregiver problems.
3. Communicate with those who are—or who may become—caregivers.
4. Use sensitive, compassionate advertising.
5. Develop products and services that assist caregivers and their ailing parents.
6. Consider the proximity of adult children to their parents when developing, distributing, or promoting your products and services.

Chapter Wrap-up

Successful businesses will both understand and act upon the close relationship that exists between most "mature" parents and their adult children. As you develop marketing programs in response to this phenomenon, keep these three important points in mind:

1. The potential to develop and sell products/services which link *healthy* 50+ers and their adult children is still largely untapped.
2. Because America is aging, your company will often be serving *two* segments of the mature market at the same time if your programs link older adults with their adult children.
3. The focus of your Stage 2 marketing activities should be on *middle-aged and older women*; it's the latter group which represents the majority of America's seniors (the persons most likely to

need caregiver support), and the former one which usually comes to the rescue when aging parents need help.

One other piece of advice: learn as much as you can about older parent/adult child relationships; such as how often the groups see one another, what factors influence the nature of their relationships, what each group expects of these relationships, and so forth. By broadening your understanding of the dynamics of this important kinship, you'll improve your chances of prospering in an aging America.

---

1. *Statistical Abstract of the United States:* 1988 (108th Edition.) Washington, D.C.: U.S. Bureau of the Census, Tables 41 and 42, p. 36.

2. "LAVOA Study Finds Independence Primary," *Mature Market Report,* September 1987, p. 3.

3. Price, Barbara, "What the Baby Boom Believes," *American Demographics,* May 1984, pp. 32-33.

4. Francese, Peter K. "How to Target the 55 + Market," a presentation made at the *American Demographics* magazine conference, "Managing Consumer Change," Febraury 12, 1987.

5. Hodge, Marie, "Gifts that Join the Generations," *50 Plus,* December 1986, p. 67.

6. Iacocca, Lee, with Sonny Kleinfield. *Talking Straight.* New York, Toronto: Bantam Books, 1988.

7. Select Committee on Aging, U.S. House of Representatives. *Exploding the Myth: Caregiving in America.* January 1987.

8. Gallagher, Geraldine, "Caught in the Middle," *Mature Outlook,* July/August 1986, p. 36.

9. Wood, John, "Labors of Love," Modern Maturity, August-September 1987, p. 29.

10. Loyd, Linda, "Firms, workers face new problem: Caring for elderly," *The Philadelphia Inquirer,* April 25, 1988, p. 1-D.

11. Personal telephone conversation with Alan Reiman, vice president for marketing and planning, Bethany Methodist, October 1987.

12. King, Harley, "Creating Successful Customer-Oriented Advertising," excerpted from D. Terry Paul, *Building Marketing Effectiveness in Healthcare: A Proceedings.* Chicago: Academy for Health Services Marketing, American Marketing Association, 1985.

13. Ibid.

Marketing Checklist:
Eight Keys to Successfully Marketing
to/or Serving the Mature Consumer

KEY 1: Emphasize and demonstrate the value of your product or service.

KEY 2: Address the needs and concerns of the mature consumer.

KEY 3: Promote the positive attributes of older adults and aging.

KEY 4: Involve the older consumer in your mature market programs.

KEY 5: Establish relationships with key groups and influencers.

KEY 6: Recognize and respond to the diversity of the mature market.

KEY 7: Use a soft-sell approach.

KEY 8: Develop marketing programs that reflect the closeness of the older parent/adult child relationship.

3

Effective Mature Market Communications

Chapter **11**

Six Fundamental Principles of Successful Mature Market Advertising and Promotion

Little more than two decades ago, few businesses were interested in directing their advertisements to the over-50 population. Today, that situation has changed dramatically. Recognizing the size and spending power of the mature market, a myriad of marketers now plunk down enormous sums of money to design and place ads they want to reach the older consumer.

In some cases, advertisers have badly misjudged or misunderstood the mature market. This has led to the creation of advertising campaigns which at best, failed to realize their intended objectives, and at worst, elicited a public outcry from representatives of the older adult community. The pioneers of advertising to the mature market would have a legitimate claim if they attributed at least some of their mistakes to the lack of information available about the over-50 consumers of their day. This explanation would be harder to swallow today, however. Research studies, increased media coverage, and the results of mature market sales campaigns all offer an ever-mounting supply of information about mature consumers and their reactions to advertising.

In the pages that follow, I will present six fundamental principles that you should keep in mind concerning advertising and promotion to the mature market.

Remember: While these principles can serve as guideposts in developing and implementing advertising and promotional campaigns for the older consumer, they should *not* be followed blindly. The dynamic and diverse nature of the 50 + population dictates that you regularly test the validity of these principles through consumer research and continual tracking of the mature market.

Principle 1: Include the Older Consumer in Your Advertising

In the summer of 1987, I received a letter from a 56-year-old woman living in Virginia. She was responding to some comments of mine which had just appeared in an article in The Washington Times' *Insight* magazine. The article concerned business opportunities for those marketing to the older consumer. One line in the woman's letter was especially meaningful. It concerned her displeasure with the fact that certain businesses failed to include older adults in their ads. Here's what she said:

> It is difficult visualizing using a product that is featured with people the ages of your children and/or grandchildren.

Key Point: If older adults don't see themselves as part of the group that might use a product or service, they are less likely to purchase it. By including older adults in your ads, you've developed an effective way of getting mature consumers to relate your product to their needs and wants.

Choose Older Adults with Whom Others Can— or Would Like to—Identify

Including those over 50 in your ads isn't enough. It's also important to know *which* older adults you should use. For example, not too long ago, I had the pleasure of working with the National Tour Association (NTA), the organization that represents the group travel industry. While participating in one of NTA's seminars, I heard one of the panelists discuss the results of a marketing research study done with older consumers. The research was conducted for a large retirement community in Florida who wanted to differentiate itself from its competitors. One of the most important findings of this survey was the respondents' desire to "see *themselves*" in this marketer's ads, that is, to see people they could relate to . . . people who actually *lived* at the community.

What this and other research indicates is that it's important for advertisers to use older persons with whom other mature adults can—or would like to—identify. These will be individuals who reflect a positive image of the 50+ years.

Caution: Even though the use of 50+ers can enhance your product's credibility and relevance to the mature market, the sight or portrayal of an atypical or stereotypical older person in your ads (for example, the crotchety, old lady or man) can negate those benefits.

Example: One company that has successfully utilized "real" people in its mature market advertising is Jockey International. One ad features 55-year-old Catherine Councell Moll, who is identified as a grandmother and banker from Sheybogan, Wisconsin. (See Figure 11-1). The graphic also

FIGURE 11–1

shows Ms. Moll with her grandchildren. This ad has been so popular that Jockey is recruiting other mature women for future promotions.

Note: Another outstanding quality of this ad is its use of an intergenerational marketing appeal. As you'll see, the copy makes it clear that both grandmothers and their grandchildren can wear Jockey underwear.

The Celebrity Approach

In deciding upon which "real" 50+ers to include in ads, marketers should be careful about using older celebrities. While a number of companies have launched successful campaigns using media stars, there is some risk to adopting this approach. For example, some older buyers believe (rightly or wrongly) that the use of well-known personalities can add to the cost of a product or service. Others question whether the individual really needs, uses, understands, or "fits" the product promoted. Because of this, marketers thinking about using famous 50+ers should be sure their use is warranted. It is quite possible that the words and/or sight of an "ordinary" older adult may project more sincerity and believability than those presented by the gray-haired matinee idol.

Key Point: If you decide to use an older celebrity, be sure it is someone the mature market relates to, respects, trusts, and believes is likely to need (and/or use) your product or service.

Suggestion: Including mature adults in your advertising campaign shouldn't be limited to the advertisements themselves; rather, members of the mature market should be called upon to help develop and evaluate your advertising as well. Some astute advertising agencies have utilized members of the Gray Panthers Media Watch project as consultants in tailoring their ad campaigns. Other organizations, like Busch Gardens® in Tampa, Florida and Retirement Community Developers in Silver Spring, Maryland, have used focus groups of older persons to design and modify their ads. The feedback received from these activities is invaluable.

Principle 2: Present Your Message in an Upbeat Tone

A few years ago, there was a brief announcement in the community events section of a Philadelphia newspaper. A local hospital invited older adults in the area to attend a special wellness workshop the facility was sponsoring. The title of the workshop: Staying Alive. I don't know if that program was well attended, but I'd be shocked if it was, given the morbid title attached to it.

Fact: Most older persons don't identify with, or respond to, messages that cast a dark shadow over either aging or the aging process. Mature adults like to see or hear communications that reflect the good feelings they have about themselves and their lives. Thus, advertising campaigns that recognize such things as the mature adult's experience, sense of humor, accomplishments, contributions to society, willingness to take on new challenges, active lifestyles, and so forth will be well received by this group.

Examples: Two companies whose advertising has done this well are McDonald's and Archway Cookies, Inc. A popular McDonald's commercial features an older man who goes back to work by taking a job at a McDonald's restaurant. During his first day, the "new kid" charms the customers and performs superbly alongside employees young enough to be his grandchildren. Using his years of experience, he even teaches his teenaged co-workers a few tricks to improve their job performance. When he returns home that evening, the man mentions to his wife that he wonders how the restaurant ever got along without him! In a delightful way, McDonald's demonstrates that seniors are able to learn new skills, share their wisdom, and be productive, enthusiastic employees.

Archway Cookies presents one of the other rewards that comes with maturity . . . grandparenting. Recognizing the warm feelings that most older adults have for their grandchildren, Archway has used ads that build upon the closeness of this special relationship. (See Figure 11-2.)

Keep in Mind: Archway's "kids of all ages" theme is also uplifting because it depicts the fact that, even as we age, there remains within us someone whose youthful passions are still aglow. In this case, it's the love for cookies.

Be Careful How You Advertise Products That Treat the Problems of Older Adults

For some products or services, it may be very difficult to create an upbeat advertising campaign. This is particularly the case when dealing with health problems that may affect members of the mature market: problems like arthritis, incontinence, cancer, and so forth.

Tip: Marketers should advertise these products in as honest, straightforward, and sensitive a fashion as possible. But they should still strive to deliver a positive message.

One way this can be done is by demonstrating how, through the use of the advertised product, the problem becomes either more manageable or less bothersome. One company whose advertising has done this well is Kimberly-Clark. In one ad, Kimberly-Clark uses actress June Allyson to show how the company's "Depend"® undergarment can help those with bladder control problems "get back into life." (See Figure 11-3).

Be Careful about Descriptive Words and Images

In striving to keep your message on the positive side, be careful about the words and images you use to describe the 50+ group. A number of surveys and focus groups have found that some words, such as "elderly" and "senior citizen," are unappealing to most older consumers. Apparently, it is the *connotation* of these words, rather than their actual meaning, which causes the problem. For example, "elderly" and "senior citizen" seem to be associated with images more befitting a needy, frail, or isolated older person.

FIGURE 11-2

Warning: For some people over 50, *any* label—including such terms as "mature," "senior," "retiree," and "prime lifer," is unappealing simply because it differentiates them from the mainstream of society.

Just as beauty is in the eye of the beholder, an older consumer's reaction to a specific word or group of words or images may vary depending

FIGURE 11-3

upon the individual. In some situations, use of one of these "off-limits" terms may be appropriate. For example, in one of my recent marketing research projects, half of those age 65+ who were surveyed *preferred* to be referred to as "senior citizens." It should be noted that the survey participants were all located in a very conservative, traditional New England community where, at least in the eyes of the respondents, the term "senior citizens" conveyed a readily identifiable, acceptable, and respectful message.

Key Point: The demographic, socioeconomic, geographic, and psychographic composition of your target audience should be the primary determinant of the actual words and images you use when advertising to 50+ers.

One final caveat: In your efforts to present an upbeat advertising message, be careful not to glorify the life of the mature adult. While aging does have its rewards, it is, like the rest of the life cycle, not without its emotional and physical pains. By going overboard with your portrayal of the "50+ years," you are likely to see the credibility and impact of your message suffer.

Principle 3: Create Credible, Benefit-Oriented Ads

Sadly, too many older Americans have been "conned" by ads, commercials, and other promotional literature that promised them the world but gave them much less.

While some unscrupulous businesses continue to engage in such practices, there is little chance they will achieve any measure of long-term success. That's because their bait is unlikely to lure many of today's (and tomorrow's) older shoppers. This is particularly the case with the older consumers most desired by marketers: the affluent, the well-educated, and those ages 50-64 . . . the prime lifers. (Often, of course, these groups overlap.)

Key Point: These consumers are not motivated by gimmicks, fads, puffery, frills, hype, and competitor-bashing. They prefer advertising that is truthful, relevant, and substantive.

How to Make Your Advertising More Believable and More Appealing

Here are a few suggestions on how you can make your ads more credible and more interesting to the older consumer.

Provide Testimonials and Endorsements

Including statements of support from individuals or organizations can enhance your ad's credibility with the mature market. Ideally, those cited should already be familiar to those over 50 and be held in high esteem by them (such as prominent local or national figures, the AARP, medical associations, government agencies, and so forth).

Example: Figure 11-4 shows Eddie Albert, a popular older celebrity, speaking on behalf of Beltone® Electronics Corporation. The effectiveness of this ad is enhanced by Albert's revelation that he wears Beltone PETITE hearing aids.

EDDIE ALBERT FOR BELTONE

"My Beltone PETITE hearing aids are helping me enjoy life more. Find out if Beltone can help you too!"

©1988, Beltone Electronics Corporation

Do you hear but not understand all the words said to you? Do people seem to mumble more than they used to? Do you often ask people to repeat themselves?

If so, you may be one of over 20 million Americans suffering from a gradual hearing loss, or "nerve deafness."

Chances are, Beltone can help...just as we've been helping people to hear better for nearly 50 years. With professional care and quality hearing instruments like the tiny Beltone PETITE hearing aids Eddie Albert wears!

For a free copy of "The Beltone Guide to Better Hearing," mail the attached postage-paid card. Or send your name, address, and phone number to: Dept. 14502, Beltone Electronics Corporation, 4201 W. Victoria, Chicago, IL 60646. Or call the toll-free number below. (In California, your local authorized Beltone dealer may call.) And take the first step toward enjoying life to its fullest again!

Call today for your free booklet!

1-800-922-8700

The Beltone Guide to Better Hearing

FIGURE 11–4

Keep in Mind: Testimony from relatively obscure, "everyday" people can also generate believability . . . especially if they are perceived as peers or role models by the group the ad is targeting (such as if they are employed by a similar company or are members of the same organization).

Tip: Whenever possible, use testifiers whom the older adult can contact to verify your ad's validity.

Make Claims and Promises You Can Fulfill

In a highly competitive marketplace, it's easy to see why businesses want to entice the older consumer with eye-catching phrases like "our lowest prices ever," "a medical breakthrough," "highest rates available," "satisfaction guaranteed," and "recommended by more doctors than any other brand." Unless you are able to *substantiate* or *follow through* on these and similar claims, avoid using this kind of language in your ads.

Important: You'll be better off if you skip the hype and the fine print, and focus on presenting an honest and candid ad whose promises you can deliver.

Focus on What Your Product Can Do, Not on Whom It Does It for

As several advertisers have learned, most mature consumers don't respond well to products that are promoted as being specifically for "older persons." Mature adults object to these ads not only because they are stereotypical, but because they separate the group from the rest of society. *To avoid this pitfall and strengthen the appeal of your advertising:* Focus on your product or service's *benefits* rather than the *age group* it is likely to serve.

Examples: In the ad in Figure 11-5, Weight Watchers International, Inc. points out the benefits of its Frozen Dessert: It has 90 percent less fat than ice cream yet is still just as rich in calcium. While the need for low-fat, high calcium foods may be greatest among mature adults, you'll notice this ad skillfully avoids reference to any specific age group. Similarly, the ad for Procter & Gamble's Puritan® brand vegetable oil emphasizes the product's lower content of saturated fat, not the fact that it is those over 50 who are most likely to benefit from Puritan. (See Figure 11-6.) It is marketing efforts like these which have helped both Weight Watchers and Procter & Gamble successfully serve the mature market.

Keep in Mind: Most 50+ers do *not* mind being segregated from the rest of society if it is in a *positive* context. Therefore, ads that tastefully promote such privileges as membership programs or special benefits for those who've reached the age of 50 will likely meet with the mature market's approval.

There are a few other important advantages gained by thinking of your mature market advertising as benefit-oriented, not age-oriented.

There's something missing from all these delicious desserts.

90% of the fat is missing. But the great taste is all there! Weight Watchers Frozen Dessert contains 90% less fat than ice cream, yet is just as rich in the calcium you need. It tastes so good, the only thing you're missing is the fat.

Mature Outlook, July/August 1986

FIGURE 11–5

Proof:
Puritan® has less saturated fat than safflower or sunflower oil. Read the label.

PURITAN®

NUTRITIONAL INFORMATION PER PORTION:

PORTION SIZE 1 TABLESPOON . (14g)   PROTEIN, g 0
CALORIES 120   CARBOHYDRATE, g 0
FAT, g (100% of calories from fat) . 14   SODIUM 0
POLYUNSATURATED, g 4   SATURATED, g 1
CHOLESTEROL, mg (0mg/100g) .. 0

ON AVERAGE, PURITAN HAS 30% LESS SATURATED FAT THAN SAFFLOWER AND SUNFLOWER OILS.

PURITAN OIL 6%
SAFFLOWER 9%
SUNFLOWER 11%

INFORMATION ON FAT AND CHOLESTEROL IS PROVIDED FOR INDIVIDUALS WHO, ON ADVICE OF A PHYSICIAN, ARE MODIFYING THEIR TOTAL DIETARY INTAKE OF FAT AND CHOLESTEROL.
CONTENTS: 100% PURE VEGETABLE OIL: (CANOLA OIL).

Make Puritan® Your Oil For Life

PURITAN

FIGURE 11–6

1. *It allows you to see the 50+ crowd as having some of the same product/service needs and desires as younger consumer markets.* This allows the opportunity to advertise what appear to be "youth-oriented" products to the mature market. This kind of thinking has helped Busch Gardens, Archway Cookies, McDonald's, and General Foods, among others, develop successful ads for the older consumer. (See Figure 11-7.)

summer cooler.

**Chilled Filled
Cantaloupe**

2 medium cantaloupes
1 package (3 oz.)
   JELL-O® Brand
   Gelatin, any flavor
   or Sugar Free
   Jell-O® Gelatin
³/₄ cup boiling water
¹/₂ cup cold water
   ice cubes
1 banana, sliced

Cut the melons into halves lengthwise. Scoop out seeds and drain well. Dissolve gelatin in boiling water. Combine water and ice cubes to make 1¹/₄ cups. Add to gelatin. Stir until slightly thickened. Remove any unmelted ice. Add banana. Place melon halves in small bowls. Spoon in gelatin mixture. Chill until firm. Cut into wedges. Garnish. 6 servings. If you're counting calories, try making this recipe with Sugar Free Jell-O® Gelatin. Jell-O® is a registered trademark of the General Foods Corporation.

orange
ARTIFICIAL FLAVOR

JELL-O®
gelatin dessert ᴮᴿᴬᴺᴰ

Pet-Ritz
DEEP DISH
Pie Crust Shells

We're up to something good.

FIGURE 11–7

2. *It allows you the see the 50+ group as a part of the mainstream of society.* In some instances, this may obviate the need to create special ads for the mature market. General Foods, for example, has found its advertising for the broad population is popular with older consumers too.

Tip: To maximize the impact of your ads, include both younger and older adults in them.

3. *It increases your ability to influence the older consumer to use new products and services.* Years of shopping experiences, some of them bad, have made many older adults understandably cautious about trying new things. But they will ... if it can be shown how something different will benefit them. Videocasette recorders, for example, have been very popular with the prime life generation because they enhance that group's ability to enjoy their home and their leisure activity. They also give prime lifers greater control over their time. Other products and services (automated teller machines, credit cards, special telephone services, home shopping, computers, and so forth) also offer the older adult special benefits. By recognizing the need to focus on these benefits in your advertising, you'll enhance the potential for gaining new mature market customers.

Remember: Benefit-oriented ads can also help differentiate your organization from its competitors.

Learn from Mature Market Publications

Magazines and other literature produced for the mature market by organizations, government agencies, and publishers often contain some helpful hints on advertising to the older consumer.

Tip: While this information is typically provided for the benefit of over-50 shoppers, it can be especially valuable for those who market to this group. A great example of this is the American Association of Retired Persons' booklet, *A Consumer Guide to Advertising*. This booklet, primarily written for those over 50, should be required reading for every advertiser in the country... regardless of what consumer groups he's targeting!

Marketing Checklist: Four Ways to Create Credible, Benefit-Oriented Ads

- Provide testimonials and endorsements.
- Make claims and promises you can deliver.
- Focus on what your product does, not on whom it does it for.
- Learn from mature market publications.

Principle 4: Use Evocative, "Call-to-Action" Ads

While most older consumers tend to prefer a "heavy content, low-fluff" approach to advertising, you could be making a serious mistake if you carry that principle to an extreme. Although perhaps to a lesser degree than other groups, the mature market's consumer behavior can also be influenced by emotional factors.

Tip: Ads that pique the mature consumer's curiosity, and/or make it easy for him to respond to your message, will maximize the effectiveness of your advertising budget.

Example 1: In the Busch Gardens, Tampa ad (Figure 11-8), the older adult is exhorted to "Take a ride to the exotic side of Florida." This ad exudes excitement. Evidently, readers thought so, too, as Busch Gardens was deluged with requests for information after the ad first appeared in *Modern Maturity* magazine.

Example 2: Virginia Home Medical is a supplier of medical equipment. In 1986, it introduced a creative program in which, under certain circumstances, Medicare enrollees can rent its equipment without cost. The retailer calls this program SURE (Secure Use of Rental Equipment) CARE.™ To promote the program, Virginia Home Medical has used an ad with the eye-catching headline, "SURE + CARE makes cents in your pocket!" To reinforce this interest-triggering message, the ad includes a graphic of two pennies (see Figure 11-9). Since the campaign was introduced, many seniors have enrolled in SURE + CARE.

Key Point: The more you know about the *needs* and *wants* of the mature market segments you seek to target, the more likely it is you will be able to create emotionally appealing, action-triggering advertising copy and graphics.

TAKE A RIDE TO THE EXOTIC SIDE OF FLORIDA.

The wonders of Florida's west coast begin at Busch Gardens, Tampa. There, you'll experience all the romance and adventure of an African safari. From the Serengeti Plain to the Congo River. From the bazaars of Morocco, all the way to Timbuktu. It's a day filled with exotic animals, exciting rides, exhilarating shows and excellent foods.

For valuable discount coupons and information (including area hotels), clip this coupon and send it to: Busch Gardens, Marketing Department, P.O. Box 9158, Tampa, FL 33674.

NAME

ADDRESS

CITY

STATE   ZIP

BUSCH GARDENS
THE DARK CONTINENT
TAMPA, FL.

FIGURE 11–8

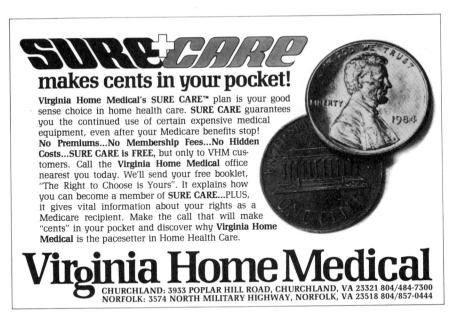

FIGURE 11–9

Make Your Message Attractive and Easy to Respond to

The Busch Gardens and Virginia Home Medical ads are good not only because they arouse the older adult's interest, but also because they make it attractive and easy for him to respond to them. In the former case, the reader is asked to clip the ad's coupon and send it to Busch Gardens' marketing department. In so doing, he will receive information about the theme park and "valuable discount coupons." Virginia Home Medical's ad, on the other hand, asks readers to call the number of one of its local offices to receive a booklet on SURE CARE and information about Medicare's new guidelines on reimbursement for medical equipment. The other benefits realized by such direct response ads are that they:

- enable you to track your advertising's effectiveness, and
- help you develop a mailing list of 50+ers

Note: A few words about "cents-off" coupons and the mature market. Older consumers are heavy users of cents-off coupons. For example, Donnelley Marketing's survey of a sampling of members in its New Age ℠ (a co-op program involving the 50+ group) database indicated that 84 percent use coupons at least once a month.[1] Similarly, a Simmons Market Research Bureau survey of *Modern Maturity* magazine readers found that more than 90 percent of those polled use cents-off coupons when shopping.[2]

Offer Free Special Incentives

Along with using coupons and informational booklets, consider using any or all of these other techniques to stimulate the older consumer into action:

- Free trial periods
- Toll-free telephone numbers (put them in bold type)
- Money-back guarantees
- Free product samples
- Bonus gifts and prizes

Key Point: Cents-off coupons, free-trial periods, money-back guarantees, and free product samples are particularly effective in encouraging older consumers to try new products and services.

Offer an Opportunity to Purchase with a Credit Card

Another technique to elicit the older consumer's response is allowing him the opportunity to purchase by credit card. This suggestion may seem unwarranted since older consumers tend to use credit less than other groups. Part of this may be due to the fact that some marketers have not actively promoted their credit cards to the mature market, or they've made it difficult for older adults to qualify. Nevertheless, some astute businesses, such as American Express®, Sears, and May Company, have a large number of older credit cardholders.

Remember: Most of today's prime lifers are more comfortable and familiar with credit card use than are older members of the mature market. Undoubtedly, this will be even more true of those who enter the 50+ group in the years ahead.

Warning: All of the above techniques assume your ability to deliver, in a courteous and responsible way, what is promised in your advertising. Obviously, the use of deception, high-pressure sales tactics, and so forth nullifies any potential benefit offered by pursuing these approaches.

Principle 5: Consider the Changes That May Occur with Aging When Developing Your Promotional Message

Common Physiological Changes That Occur During the Aging Process

As we age, many of us experience a reduction in our ability to see. For example, more than 90 percent of those over 60 require some correction of vision.[3] In some instances, this decline can be severe. Indeed, 60 percent of the visually impaired are people over 55, with those over 80 having the most problems.[4]

There are also physiological changes which take place in the older eye. For example, the lens of the eye becomes thicker, yellow, and more opaque. As a result, less violet light gets through. This can make it difficult to differentiate between colors in the blue, green, and purple end of the spectrum.

The incidence of hearing loss is greater in the mature adult as well. Overall, about 25 percent of those over 65 have experienced some hearing loss.[5] The chances for hearing problems are greatest among the oldest members of this group: about 65 percent of those over 80 will have some type of hearing deficit.[6]

The most common form of hearing loss involves one's ability to pick up sounds in the high frequency range. As a result, high-pitched voices and certain consonants (such as "f," "c," "g," and "s") may be difficult to hear. Other hearing problems such as distortion of sounds and an increased sensitivity to loud and extraneous noises may also occur.

The ability to process information also undergoes some change as we get older. Research has shown that these changes become more apparent after the age of 60. What are these changes?

- New information may be absorbed, and integrated with prior knowledge, *at a slower rate* than before.
- The specific names of persons and objects (not the details about them) may be more difficult to remember.
- The ability to divide one's attention between concurrent activities may decrease.
- The ability to organize information quickly to make it meaningful and retrievable may decline.
- The ability to distinguish between relevant and extraneous information may become a problem and result in confusion.
- Short-term memory capabilities may be somewhat diminished.[7,8,9]

As you consider all of the above changes, *remember this: Any declines or difficulties which may occur in aging are selective. They may affect some people, but not all, and some abilities, but not all.*

Seven Ways Your Advertising Can Accommodate the Aging Process

How can your advertising allow for these age-related changes? Here are some suggestions.

Keep in Mind: Whether or not you need to implement *any* of these suggestions will depend upon the specific characteristics of the 50+ group you are targeting. In general, the older your target market is, the more important it will be for you to put these tips into practice.

1. *Use a high level of contrast to make your ads easier to see and understand.* Problems in reception and perception can occur when dark colors are used on dark backgrounds or light colors on white ones. To avoid these potential obstacles to effective advertising, maximize the contrast between the color of your ad's background and the copy/images used in it. Black ink on white paper would be preferable to black ink on brown paper. Be sure your pictures are clear, bright, and sharp.

Be careful about using blues, greens, and violets. While these colors have been found to be appealing to older adults and they tend to have positive associations, it is more difficult to see them clearly. Therefore, avoid mixing these colors together, especially if your message requires the reader to distinguish between them (especially if you are using charts or graphs).

2. *Use appropriate type size and spacing to make your copy more readable.* To help the older adult read your ad's copy, close attention should be paid to the type size used. No less than 10-point size type should be used for an older reader. However, 12-point size type is highly suggested, especially if your audience includes a large number of those over 65.[10] Figure 11-10 illustrates the difference between 4, 10, 11, 12 and 14-point type.

Warning: Be careful about using too-large type unless you're doing it to create a special effect or to reach a group primarily comprised of the visually impaired. Otherwise, you run the risk of offending your audience.

To facilitate reading, the white space between individual letters should be kept constant. In addition, the white space between the lines (or "leading") should be large enough to make copy easily discernible. In general, the larger the type size, the smaller the leading needs to be. Figure 11-11 shows the difference between copy with one point in leading, one-half point in leading, and no leading.

Keep in Mind: When considering the style of type used, recognize that ornate faces, italics, or anything unusual will be more difficult for an older

This is 14 point type.
This is 12 point type.
This is 11 point type.
This is 10 point type.
This is 4 point type.

FIGURE 11–10

Copy in small type set closely together is difficult to read.
(8 point Paladium boldface, no leading)

Same type, same size. The only difference is the leading or white space between the lines. Leading increases readability.
(8 point Paladium boldface, 1 point leading)

Type size itself is a critical factor. You can see the difference two type sizes larger (with just ½ point in leading) makes in legibility.
(10 point Paladium boldface, ½ point leading)

Reprinted with permission from the booklet, "Truth About Aging: Guidelines for Accurate Communications," © 1984, American Association of Retired Persons.

FIGURE 11–11 Leading

person to read and understand. A serif typeface tends to be easiest to read and is also the one those over 50 have grown up with.

3. *Deliver a comfortably paced, clearly articulated advertising message.* To allow for hearing deficits or declines in information processing capabilities of some members of the mature market, you'll need to pay special attention to the spoken word. This is particularly true with radio advertisements since the listener will not have the benefit of any accompanying visual stimuli.

Advertising copy should be written so that it can be spoken at a comfortable pace allowing the words to be carefully enunciated. Furthermore, effort should be made to reduce the number of words requiring sounds in the higher frequency range. If other noises are to be heard during the commercial, they should be coordinated so as not to interfere with the listener's ability to hear the speaker.

Important: The narrator should speak clearly and try to deliver the message in as low-pitched a tone of voice as possible.

If the commercial is to be shown on TV, there are other ways to maximize the effectiveness of the communication. For example, the set can be designed so that the narrator (if used) or actors can speak while facing the viewer some or all of the time. Captions, product samples, and demonstrations can be used to supplement or reinforce the spoken words. And the visual message can be presented so that it is easy to follow.

4. *Present your message in a simple, concise, relevant, and organized way.* To maximize your advertising's impact on the older consumer, don't clutter your copy with highly technical terms, esoteric phrases, or industry jargon. Be direct—get right to the heart of your message. Avoid big words

Only one leading coffee is naturally decaffeinated with pure mountain water and nature's sparkling effervescence. Sanka. Of course.

SANKA INSTANT, FREEZE-DRIED AND GROUND—ALL NATURALLY DECAFFEINATED.

FIGURE 11–12

when small ones will do. Use down-to-earth language. Keep your sentences and paragraphs as short as possible.

Example: In the ad in Figure 11-12, readers succinctly are told that General Foods' Sanka® is the only leading coffee that uses pure mountain water to decaffeinate its product. A graphic showing Sanka immersed in sparkling, natural water is used to support the copy's message.

To further enhance the older consumer's ability to grasp your commercial message, present your material in a well-structured, organized fashion. Be careful not to include extraneous details or to make your offer too complicated by discussing too many options in too little space or time.

Warning: While it's important to keep your copy simple, do not oversimplify it, or your ad could insult the older adult's intelligence.

5. *Integrate copy and audio-visuals to help your advertising be understood and remembered.* As the Sanka ad demonstrates, the combination of a few choice words and a clear, crisp picture can produce a good piece of communication. Pictures, captions, product samples, labels on charts, logos, product demonstrations, and so forth all can help the mature consumer more accurately receive and recall your advertising message.

Warning: Be careful to use only those audio-visuals that enhance the clarity and retention of your message. By overloading your ads with audio-visuals, you may distract the older consumer and therefore, diminish the effectiveness of your communications.

6. *Restate your message for better recall.* Along with audio-visuals, repetition of your advertising message can help to make it more memorable to the older adult. If possible, state the central theme of the ad more than once in the copy. To avoid unnecessary repetition, present the message using slightly different words but conveying the same concept.

Tip: Don't expect to be successful with any "blitz" or "one-shot" advertising campaigns. Run your advertisements often and for a reasonable length of time before dropping or changing them. Consider using more than one medium to maximize the reinforcement and retention of your message.

Be careful about changing your ads. Certainly, there will be times when new ads and new campaigns will be appropriate. If at all possible, however, *keep the major theme of your ads the same.*

Key Point: Consistent use of a theme will serve as another cue to help the mature consumer associate your company with a specific image or product. Repeated use of the same actors, slogans, or key words are ways in which this consistency can be maintained. As an example, for several years, Block Drugs has used Martha Raye to promote its Polident denture cleanser; International Games has repeatedly touted its Skip-Bo card game as "not for the retiring type"; and Levi Strauss has constantly emphasized the *comfort* of its Action Slacks.

7. *Consider having your ads relate something to the mature adult's frame of reference.* If your product or service is new, different, or unfamiliar

to the older consumer, create ads that connect it to something within his or her realm of experience. This can be particularly effective if you're promoting a high-tech item such as automated teller machines or computers. However, the technique is equally appropriate when the concept is applied to other, more common services.

Example: In the ad in Figure 11-13, on page 238, the culture of Toronto, perhaps unfamiliar to many, is related to the more widely known cultures of Greece, Italy, and China. The graphics cleverly and creatively tie these countries to specific streets within Toronto.

Marketing Checklist: Seven Ways Your Advertising Can Address Changes That Accompany the Aging Process

1. Use a high level of contrast.
2. Use appropriate type size and spacing.
3. Deliver a comfortably paced, well-articulated message.
4. Present your message in a simple, concise, relevant, and organized way.
5. Integrate copy with audio-visuals whenever possible.
6. Restate your message for better recall.
7. Relate your ads to the mature consumer's frame of reference.

Principle 6: Realize That Some of the Most Effective Forms of Mature Market Promotion Often Are the Least Expensive

For virtually all businesses, advertising should be an essential component in marketing to the older consumer. But don't rely too much on this form of promotion. When advertising isn't meeting the return-on-investment criteria you've set, it can be quite expensive. Furthermore, by depending on advertising, you may overlook the importance and effectiveness of other, less costly forms of promotion.

Word-of-Mouth Communication

One of the most successful motorcoach tour operators in America is Dan Dipert Tours of Arlington, Texas. An important part of Dipert's business is group tours, most of which serve the mature market. For well over a decade, Dipert has attracted older travelers to its tours. And how do the majority of

Visit Athens, Rome & Beijing The Same Day.
Now That's Incredible!

Shop Toronto's neighbourhoods.

The arts are in our blood.

All roads lead to Toronto, and beyond.

The world's cultures meet in Ontario.

Ontario offers a unique blend of the world's cultures, each of which has brought something to enrich our province.

A visit to Toronto, Ontario, is like taking a world tour, only a lot closer. And, because the U.S. dollar is strong in Canada, a holiday in Ontario is a lot more affordable.

Come on up to Ontario, Canada and experience the world at your doorstep.

For more information about Ontario vacations, call us TOLL FREE at 1-800-268-3735. One of our travel counsellors will be happy to help you plan your trip.

LITTLE ITALY
COLLEGE ST.

DANFORTH AV.
ΟΔΟΣ ΝΤΑΝΦΟΡΘ

HURON ST.
曉倫街

Ontario *Incredible!*

FIGURE 11–13

these individuals hear about Dipert? Through words of praise spoken by their friends and relatives.

The experience of Dan Dipert Tours is quite common. Surveys and "case studies" consistently show that word-of-mouth information plays a major role in:

- helping the mature market learn about products and services, and
- influencing the mature consumer's purchase behavior

What all this reinforces, of course, is this:

1. There's no better form of mature market advertising than satisfied customers.
2. The best way to spread word-of-mouth communication is to involve the mature consumer in your marketing activities.

Keep in Mind: Word-of-mouth information may be an even more important promotional vehicle for those over 60. Many of these individuals are retired, and therefore likely to spend more of their weekday activities in the company of others their age than are those under the age of 60. Word-of-mouth testimonials also can be extremely helpful in influencing this group to try new products and services.

Referrals

Another powerful form of promotion which helps attract mature market business is referrals. Asking an existing customer to identify other potential users of your product or service can be an easy and cost-effective way of building mailing lists and customers. In fact, this can become an important part of your marketing strategy.

Example: The Lakes Club of Sun City, Arizona is one organization which has done this. An affiliate of the Club Corporation of America, The Lakes Club membership is made up almost entirely of retirees. To attract new customers, the club rewards existing members who recommend their friends for membership. This approach has been very effective.

Media Publicity

In July of 1983, an article appeared in Prevention magazine about Travel Companion Exchange (TCE), the service which matches up travelers who don't want to vacation alone. The article, written for the middle-aged and older adult, was less than 200 words.[11] Despite this, TCE received more than 5,000 letters after the article appeared. To this day, TCE still receives some mail from persons who heard about or saw the *Prevention* story. TCE has seen its clientele grow by receiving similar coverage in Sears' *Mature Outlook* magazine and AARP's *Modern Maturity*.

Point: TCE's experience illustrates how valuable media coverage can be to your mature market promotional efforts. This coverage may take the form of television and radio appearances, public service announcements, press releases, feature articles, and so forth. It can also be in the form of a consumer-oriented weekly newspaper column or TV/radio program.

Tip: The value of the publicity will be enhanced significantly if it appears in media reaching and/or targeting large numbers of older adults.

Community Programs and Presentations

Active participation in community programs, presentations, or other forms of educational marketing can be a highly effective, credibility-enhancing form of promotion. Along with the important services that these programs provide, they also enable their sponsor to network with key persons and groups involved in the mature market network. And, they offer a business the opportunity to meet existing and prospective older customers on a face-to-face basis . . . fostering the "high touch" atmosphere desired by most 50 + ers.

Marketing Checklist: Four Powerful, Low-Cost Ways to Sell Your Products and Services to the Mature Market

1. Word-of-mouth communication
2. Referrals
3. Media publicity
4. Community programs and presentations

Chapter Wrap-up

To successfully advertise and promote your products and services to the mature market, you should keep these six principles in mind:

1. Include the older consumer in your advertising campaign.
2. Present your advertising message in an upbeat tone.
3. Create credible, benefit-oriented ads.
4. Use evocative, "call-to-action" ads.
5. Consider the changes that may occur with aging when developing your promotional message.
6. Realize that some of the most effective forms of mature market promotion often are the least expensive.

Also, keep these three points in mind:

- The changing, heterogenous nature of the mature market means that advertising campaigns used to reach this group should be evaluated and fine-tuned on a regular basis.

- There is no better or more powerful form of advertising to the mature market than the word-of-mouth tributes of family, friends, and opinion leaders.

- Through understanding the older adult's self-perceptions, needs, and desires, you maximize your ability to create successful mature market advertising.

---

1. "Mature Americans Aren't Risk-Takers When It Comes to Purchasing, Marketer Advises," *Selling to Seniors*, July 1987, p. 1.

2. "A Reader Profile Study: *Modern Maturity*," Simmons Market Research Bureau, Inc., 1985, p. 18.

3. Jinks, Martin and Daniel Baker, "Addressing Senior Audiences," *American Pharmacy*, Vol. NS26, No. 4, April 1986, p. 29.

4. *Truth about Aging: Guidelines for Accurate Communications*. Washington, D.C.: American Association of Retired Persons, 1984.

5. Fallon, Robert D., "From the Executive Editor," *Mature Outlook Newsletter*, April 1987, p. 2.

6. Jinks, Martin and Daniel Baker, *op. cit.* hearing loss.

7. Ibid.

8. "Business Issues in an Aging America," a report from The Travelers Insurance Companies, 1982, pp. 6-9.

9. "Savvy Marketers Distinguish Between Subdivisions of Elderly Population," *Selling to Seniors*, September 1987, p. 5.

10. Ralph, Jack, "Visual Booby Traps for Our Aging Population," *Aging*, November/December 1982, p. 3.

11. "Finding a Travel Companion," *Prevention*, July 1983, p. 72.

Chapter 12

Channels of Communication to the Mature Market: Guidelines for Success

Successful advertising, sales, and promotional activities directed to the mature market require you to know *where* and *how* to reach the older consumer. In this chapter, we'll look at various communications channels to the 50+ group and what the implications are for your marketing programs.

Mass Media and the Mature Market

Television: Number One in Reach

Without question, TV reaches more members of the mature market than all other mass media. (See Figure 12-1.) In fact, according to research by A.C. Nielsen and Company, the 55+ population watches TV more frequently than any other age group.[1] One factor which accounts for the greater number of hours of TV watched by 50+ers is that more older persons are at home during the day. Thus, it's not surprising that a sizable proportion of those adults who watch TV during weekday morning and afternoon hours are persons over 55. (See Figure 12-2.)

Key Point: The large percentage of older TV viewers during the day makes this a very good time to advertise or place public service announcements (PSAs) on this medium . . . especially if you want to reach older women and retired men.

The mature market tunes in to the "tube" strongly at other times, too. According to Mediamark Research, Inc. (MRI), well over half of the 55+ group watches TV during weeknight prime time hours. Viewership is also high between 11 to 11:30 P.M. on weeknights and 6 to 11 P.M. on weekends.[2] However, the larger number of younger persons who also watch TV during

MEDIA TARGETING FOR THE 90's
A NATIONAL STUDY OF CONSUMER MEDIA HABITS

CONSUMER PROFILE
ADULTS 50+

Media Use—Average Weekday

	Percentage Reached by Combined Media	Time Spent (Hrs.: Min.)	Share of Time Spent With Each Medium			
			Radio	Television	Newspapers	Magazines
6 AM-12 Noon	88%	2:04	44%	36%	15%	5%
12 Noon-6 PM	86	1:58	35	48	12	5
6 PM-12 Mid.	91	2:56	9	80	7	4
6 AM-6 PM	98	4:02	39	42	14	5
6 AM-12 Mid.	100	6:58	26	58	11	5
24 Hours	100	7:08	27	57	11	5

Media Reach—Average Weekday

	Percent Reached			
	Radio	Television	Newspapers	Magazines
6 AM-6 PM	64%	72%	70%	34%
6 AM-12 Mid.	67	93	79	42
24 Hours	68	94	79	42

Competitive Weekly Reach

	Percent Exposed To Medium	Percent Not Exposed To Medium
Radio	78%	22%
Television	96	4
Daily Newspaper	76	24
Weekly Newspaper (Not Sunday)	37	63
Sunday Newspaper	68	32
Shopper Newspaper	37	63
Magazines	65	35

Sources: © Radio Advertising Bureau, Inc., and R. H. Bruskin Associates.

FIGURE 12–1

these hours makes the overall percentage of older viewers less than during earlier parts of the day. This is particularly the case between 8 and 11 P.M.[3]

Tip: Advertising before 8 P.M. and between 11 and 11:30 P.M. may be the most cost-effective evening hours to target messages to the mature market.

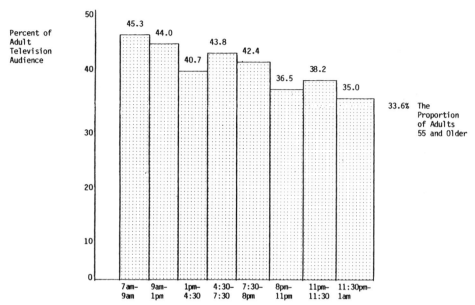

PERCENT OF ADULT TELEVISION AUDIENCE
COMPRISED OF PEOPLE 55 AND OLDER
(BY DAY PART)

Source: "Channels of Communication for Reaching Older Americans," The National Council on Aging, Inc., 1985; and Simmons Market Research Bureau.

FIGURE 12-2

When directing advertisements or PSAs to the mature market, you also need to know which programs the group most likes to watch. In general, news and news/talk shows such as "60 Minutes" and "20/20" are heavy favorites with the 50+ audience. In addition, specials, soap operas, feature films, and sports programming (particularly golf and bowling) draw a good number of older viewers. Game shows are popular, especially among those over 65.[4]

The selectivity of the mature market's TV preferences is most in evidence during the prime time hours. Among the most popular shows have been "The Golden Girls," "Murder She Wrote," and "Falconcrest."[5] Interestingly, these shows star one or more persons who are over 50. Conversely, other successful programs which have younger stars are *not* especially popular with the mature market.

Key Point: In general, shows that feature persons or situations to which the mature adult can best relate tend to attract the largest older audiences. This also reinforces the rationale for including 50+ers in your advertisements whenever possible.

Many older adults enjoy the cultural and educational programming on

Public Broadcasting System (PBS) stations. In fact, according to Sue Bomzer, a spokesperson for the Public Broadcasting Service, as many as 75 percent of the viewers of several PBS how-to and educational programs are older than 50.[6] Entertainment, news, and informational programming also attract viewers to such cable networks as the Financial News Network, the Learning Channel, C-Span, Cable News Network, the Weather Channel, The Nashville Network, Country Music Television, and Arts & Entertainment.[7]

Message: *Don't ignore the potential exposure to be gained from underwriting specific public TV programs or advertising on select cable stations and shows.*

Radio: More Selective, but Highly Targeted

The mature market listens to the radio less than younger groups. As Figure 12-1 illustrates, the largest number of persons 50+ listen to the radio in the morning between 6 and 10 A.M. The older audience drops off steadily from then on, reaching its low point in the evening, when most older adults watch TV.

Older radio listeners display strong preferences for certain kinds of radio programming. These include all news and news/talk programs as well as easy listening, nostalgia (such as big band or "golden oldies"), or middle-of the-road music formats. The youngest members of the mature market (those under 55) also listen more frequently to religious programming and classical and country music stations than does the rest of the population.

Keep in Mind: Because it tends to offer programming more suited to their personal tastes, AM radio reaches more mature adults than it does those under 50.

While radio won't reach as many 50+ers as TV, there may be times when radio advertising or PSAs *should* be used as an alternative (or supplement) to TV.

Tip: The clear-cut nature of the mature market's radio programming preferences makes this an attractive medium for highly targeted messages. Thus, advertising on one of the more than 150 stations that broadcast a "Music of Your Life" format (big band/nostalgia-type music) may be an excellent approach to reaching a select group of 50+ers. Similarly, if you're seeking to reach an affluent group of 50+ adults, one good strategy may be to advertise on specific classical music stations.

Key Point: The most effective radio advertising will focus on those stations/programs which reach older audiences who match your customer profile.

Generally, radio advertising is much less expensive than TV advertising. This is particularly true if you plan to advertise in major metropolitan areas. And the advantage may not just be an economic one.

Tip: Lower costs provide the opportunity for repeated "airing" of your advertisement, thereby enhancing the frequency and reach of your message, and the older listener's ability to understand and remember it.

Reminder: The 50+ group can also be reached through their children. In some cases, such as if you're marketing retirement housing, estate planning, or health care services, it may make sense to place radio ads on stations that are popular with *younger* adults.

Example: Drexel Square—an apartment complex in Oklahoma City, Oklahoma—found this approach successful in securing older renters. By advertising on a rock-and-roll station, Drexel Square attracted adult children who wanted to help their parents find apartments.

The Print Media: A Good Choice for Offering Information About Your Product

Mature Americans are large newspaper readers—about 70 percent of older adults read the daily and Sunday papers.[8,9] In addition, a significant number of 50+ers read two or more papers each day. Most people over 50 also read Sunday magazine supplements like *Parade* and *USA Weekend*, more so than younger persons. Within the mature market, newspaper readership is highest among the 55-64-year-old group.[10]

Magazines are less often read by the mature market than by the under-50 population. And, they're read by fewer older persons than are newspapers. Nevertheless, several mainstream magazines reach a sizable number of older adults, including *Reader's Digest, National Geographic, TV Guide, Better Homes & Gardens, McCalls,* and *Family Circle.*[11] Other magazines that are also very popular with the older reader include *New Choices, Modern Maturity, Prevention, Mature Outlook, Changing Times, Sunset, Travel Holiday,* and *Country Journal.*[12]

Key Point: Although TV reaches more older adults, *the print media may actually represent a more effective channel to reaching the mature consumer . . .* if communicating specific product information is your primary goal. This was borne out clearly in Goldring & Company's 1987 "Geromarket" study. As you'll see in Figure 12-3, while TV was found to be the preferred source for news and relaxation among the mature market, newspapers and magazines were actually considered to be better sources for *information* about products and services.[13]

There are several possible explanations for this. For one thing, certain print media such as brochures and booklets enable you to explain your product's features and benefits in more detail—and with greater clarity—than other modes of mass communication. The print media also maximize the older person's ability to

- control his/her intake of the information
- control the pace at which the material is digested
- retain and retrieve information for later use

THE GEROMARKET® STUDY DATA SHOWS:

While the mature adult market is a heavy television viewing group......

They report that print and radio are more important media for news and information and relaxation than have been reported for the under 50 market, in other sources......

	Total	Men	Women
Best Source for News			
Television	63.8%	58.2%	68.1%
Newspapers	31.9	36.5	28.3
Radio	9.4	8.7	9.9
Best Source for Relaxing			
Television	50.8%	51.1%	50.7%
Newspapers	7.5	9.0	6.4
Radio	26.8	26.6	27.0
Magazines	16.7	14.6	18.3
Best Source of Information about Products and Services			
Television	26.2%	24.6%	27.5%
Newspapers	38.9	39.5	38.4
Radio	4.3	4.4	4.3
Magazines	32.2	33.8	31.0

Source: The Geromarket® Study; 1987

FIGURE 12–3

Note: The third factor is very important since the print medium allows for the placement and storage of coupons. The 50+ group are heavy coupon users.

Four Tips on Using the Print Media

Here are four tips on using print when advertising to the older consumer:

1. *Use the print media for what they do best.* In general, if the mature

consumer's attention, comprehension, and retention are of maximum importance to you, print advertising may be a better investment than either TV or radio. This is not the case, however, if movement, sound, and/or a series of visual images is required to help the older adult either understand, or respond to, your message.

2. *Use localized publications whenever possible.* Several publications reach large numbers of mature adults who live in specific geographic areas. These publications may be regional (such as *Yankee Magazine, New England Senior Citizen, Southern Living,* and regional editions of *Modern Maturity*), statewide (such as *Indiana Horizons*), or local (such as Springfield, Massachusetts' *Senior Spirit,* Seattle, Washington's *55-And-Over,* Kansas City, Missouri's *New Years,* and so forth). In addition, there are often local newsletters or newspapers that reach large concentrations of 50+ers living within specific neighborhoods or housing developments (such as retirement communities).

Keep in Mind: If your product or service is aimed at 50+ers living within precise localities, advertising in these kinds of publications may be more cost-effective than using others that have a much broader reach.

3. *Take advantage of specialty publications.* One of the most successful companies I know that serves the mature market shuns advertising its products in publications that reach a diverse group of older Americans. Instead, the company prefers to advertise in lesser-known magazines whose readers share a common interest or background. More important, these readers match the demographic and lifestyle profile of this company's customers. This organization has discovered that, by employing such highly targeted advertising, it gets more "bang for the buck."

For some marketers, specialty magazines provide an excellent opportunity to efficiently reach a group of "blue chip" prospects. Some of these publications are read by a substantial number of 50+ers. Here are some examples:

- *Hobbies*
- *Prevention*
- *Workbench*
- *Gardening*
- *Retirement Life*
- *Gourmet*
- *Workbasket*
- *Smithsonian*

Example: Electric Mobility, a New-Jersey based manufacturer of electric motor scooters, is one marketer who has found advertising in specialty magazines to be effective. The company's ads in *American Legion* magazine, for example, have generated a flurry of consumer inquiries. *American Legion* has a circulation of 2.7 million and its average reader is 60 years old.[14]

4. *Use directories and brochures to supplement your advertising efforts.* Although older persons tend to use the *Yellow Pages* less than younger adults, this is still an important resource for those seeking to identify providers of specific kinds of services. It can also lend an element of credibility to a business . . . something very important to the older consumer. Another major benefit of Yellow Pages advertising is that it allows you the opportunity of coupon insertion.

The Yellow Pages' value as an advertising medium is further enhanced by (1) its long shelf life and (2) its ability to target specific communities of 50 + ers.

Note: In some areas, there are also consumer directories exclusively produced for—and distributed to—older adults.

Remember: Consumer directories may also be used by adult children when seeking out services for their parents or grandparents.

Brochures represent an excellent complement to your advertising program. The detailed information they provide can play a significant role in influencing a mature consumer's purchasing decision. This is particularly true when selling such products as financial instruments, health insurance, retirement housing, or travel packages . . . each of which is likely to be bought only after the 50 + er has taken the time to analyze and evaluate your offer.

Keep in Mind: Highly targeted, informational newsletters also are an excellent vehicle for communicating to the 50 + group.

Marketing Checklist: Four Tips on Using the Print Media

1. Use print media for what they do best.
2. Use localized publications whenever possible.
3. Take advantage of specialty publications.
4. Use directories and brochures to supplement your advertising.

Other Communication Channels to Reach the Mature Market

Direct Response Programs

Direct response programs (such as direct mail, co-op coupon programs, and telemarketing) reach more members of the mature market than most people might realize. For example, about one-third of all direct mail shoppers are over 55.[15] And, according to the U.S. Department of Commerce, 85 percent of the 50 + population make mail-order purchases.

Benefits of Direct Marketing

What's behind the mature market's participation in mail-order solicitations? Primarily, it has to do with the benefits offered:

- convenience
- reduced travel expenses
- less danger of impulse or high-pressure buying
- exposure to new or unusual products
- better selection of merchandise

The first advantage—convenience—cannot be overstated. For many prime lifers, work schedules often make it difficult to shop at retail locations. Then, too, as a Donnelley Marketing survey showed, waiting in long lines is perceived as a nuisance by many older shoppers.[16] There are also older adults who may be unable to visit local stores because of physical problems or lack of available transportation.

Despite all this, the impact of direct mail advertising on the mature consumer must be put in perspective. According to research conducted by Dr. James Lumpkin at the University of Mississippi, while the majority of 50+ers may make at least one purchase per year by mail, most of their money is actually spent in a retail setting.[17]

Key Point: By and large, the mature market is a "high touch" rather than a "high tech" group; that is, they prefer face-to-face contact with a salesperson or customer service representative to the impersonal nature of many direct mail transactions.

Possible Concerns That Mature Adults Have About Direct Mail

Older persons have also expressed other concerns about direct mail. Many say they've had a bad experience when making a direct mail purchase. In addition, there are other potential drawbacks cited by 50+ers regarding direct mail purchases:

- delays in the delivery of merchandise
- uncertainty about what the product ordered will actually turn out to be
- hassles with having to return orders

Note: Two of these disadvantages—delays and hassles—make direct mail seem like an *inconvenience*, rather than a convenience, for some older shoppers.

How to Determine if a Direct Response Program to Mature Consumers is Right for Your Company

A number of businesses in the health care, publishing, consumer products, and insurance industries have been able to attract older customers successfully through the use of mail-order and other direct response programs. These include AARP, AMEX, Burpee, Comfortably Yours, GEICO, and Rodale Press. Are such programs right for your company? Here are eight questions you can ask to help you determine the answer:

1. Does your product require face-to-face contact? If so, can you use direct response programs to generate prospect leads? (They can then be followed up by in-person sales presentations.)
2. Is your company and/or its product already known to the older consumer?
3. Can you provide a clear and accurate written explanation of what your product is and what its benefits are? -
4. Can you make it easy for the older consumer to respond to your offer?
5. Can you deliver your product satisfactorily and promptly?
6. Can you clearly communicate your refund policy?
7. Can you process refund requests quickly and courteously?
8. How does direct response fit in with your other modes of advertising; that is, does it replace, complement, or duplicate them?

Techniques That Can Enhance Your Direct Response Program's Effectiveness

Using any or all of the following techniques should help improve the impact of your mature market direct response program:

- Supplying higher-than-average, easy-to-redeem, cents-off coupons and refund offers
- Including toll-free telephone numbers
- Using colors, copy, layout, and type size suitable for the older shopper
- Using relevant mailing lists such as those of mail-order buyers and 50 + ers by exact age
- Timing your offers with significant events (65th birthdays, Christmas, and so forth)

- Providing free samples, catalogs, booklets, and so forth
- Including gifts and premiums with purchase orders
- Offering free trials and money-back guarantees
- Providing relevant, verifiable testimonials
- Personalizing the program as much as possible
- Training and monitoring telephone personnel to ensure they ...
  —understand your product's features and benefits well
  —communicate effectively with the older customer
  —identify, seek out, and report the concerns, needs, complaints, and ideas of older callers

Remember: One advantage of direct reponse marketing is that its effectiveness can be fairly easy to measure.

Outdoor Advertising

Outdoor advertising (such as billboards and posters), has less of an impact on the mature market than younger age groups. Figure 12-4 shows this as well as the percentage of older adults who are heavy users of TV, radio, magazines, and newspapers.

Outdoor advertising can be effective when used in conjunction with a promotional campaign. This is particularly true when marketing activities are heavily concentrated within a localized setting. Thus, for retail stores, hospitals, banks, and supermarkets, among others, this is an advertising vehicle worth considering. The strategic placement of posters, for example, (something which local Medicine Shoppe pharmacies have successfully done) can be an effective means of alerting 50+ers to a special program or activity your organization is sponsoring. Or, it can be a good way to help build or strengthen a perception you want the mature market to have about your business.

Personal Selling

For several years, a relative of mine talked about the need to obtain a burial plot. Yet, this woman, a widow in her late sixties, made no effort to purchase the plot. Recently she was contacted by a representative from a local cemetery who asked to meet with her to discuss the purchase of a burial site. The salesperson met with her, presented information about his offering and, without the twist of an arm, sold her a plot.

This story illustrates something which, though seemingly obvious, must still be emphasized: *While a variety of communication channels can be used to reach the mature market, there is often nothing more effective*

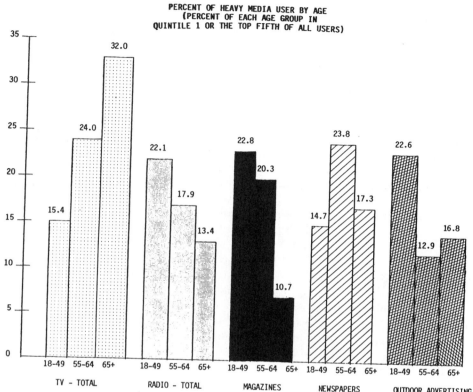

PERCENT OF HEAVY MEDIA USER BY AGE
(PERCENT OF EACH AGE GROUP IN
QUINTILE 1 OR THE TOP FIFTH OF ALL USERS)

Percent of each age category classified as heavy users (Quintile 1 or top fifth of all uses)

Source: "Channels of Communication for Reaching Older Americans," The National Council on Aging, Inc., 1985; and Simmons Market Research Bureau.

FIGURE 12–4

than face-to-face contact. In the situation just described, the woman involved had previously received much information and seen several ads about cemeteries offering burial plots. *The organization that made the sale, however, was the one that sent someone out to meet her personally.*

Here's the Point: As good as brochures, commercials, and advertisements may be, the real "closer" is often a salesperson who comes into direct contact with the older consumer. This is particularly true with products that require careful evaluation (such as long-term care insurance) or products that are sold in retail outlets. Indeed, older persons enjoy and prefer the contact of retail salespersons. Therefore, train those who sell your products and services to

- take the initiative and reach out to older prospects and customers rather than waiting for them to seek you out

- treat the older customer with courtesy and respect
- provide as much product information and assistance as possible
- avoid the use of high-pressure sales tactics

Mature Market Programming

A growing number of radio and TV stations, particularly those on public and cable networks, have developed program segments or entire shows specifically for older audiences. Most of these programs are very localized and, in many instances, produced and hosted by people over 50.

Tip: Because of their reach and popularity, some of these shows may be good places to earmark your advertising or underwriting dollars. By being associated with such programming, your organization may also strengthen its image or link with the older population. One organization that helped underwrite the cost of a "seniors" program is the Prudential Foundation. Prudential sponsored the original "Late Bloomer" series that was broadcast over 300 public radio stations. "Late Bloomer" is an upbeat program that focuses on the lives of vital, active older adults.

A similar opportunity exists with newspaper columns written especially for mature readers. A number of these columns are syndicated and appear in dozens of publications throughout the country.

Tip: You should also consider the possibility of providing financial support for such columns or of placing advertisements alongside them.

Expos and Conventions

Another way to reach the mature market is through fairs or exhibitions dedicated to those over 50. More and more of these extravaganzas are being held around the country. Some, like the "Time of Your Life Expo"® in southern California and AARP's biennial conventions, attract thousands of older Americans.

A number of companies have found that expos offer them a low-cost way to communicate with a large group of mature consumers, and in some cases, to gain new customers. Trade-show booths, for example, allow company salespeople to meet with older adults on a face-to-face basis. Through this low-pressure exchange, businesses can learn more about these consumers' needs. They also can display and discuss their company's products and services.

On the other hand, all of the following activities allow businesses to "mass market" themselves to expo attendees:

- event sponsorship
- contests

- advertising in the expo program booklet
- educational presentations

Caution: There are some potential limitations with expos. For example, as with the Seniors' World Fair in Atlantic City, some of these extravaganzas don't attract large audiences. This is especially true of first-time expos. Also, the typical expo is more likely to draw the retiree crowd than those who are in their early to mid-fifties. Keep these points in mind when deciding whether or not your company should participate in this kind of event.

Marketing Checklist: Other Communication Channels to the Mature Market

- direct response programs
- outdoor advertising
- personal selling
- mature market programming
- expos and conventions

Using Multiple Channels of Communication

Reaching the mature consumer with your advertising message generally should involve the use of more than one communication channel. Those over 50 use a variety of media, and presentation of your advertising message in more than one medium will help the older consumer better understand and remember the information you wish to convey. This is particularly important if you're seeking to market a new product or service to the 50+ segment, or to strengthen the group's awareness of your company and what it has to offer.

Warning: Using multiple channels does *not*, of course, suggest that the media be used inappropriately or to an excess; they should be engaged only insofar as they can have a positive return on the dollars you invest.

Telemarketing as a Supplementary Promotional Vehicle

In most cases, using only cold calls to sell products and services to the mature market will be ineffective, if not alienating. This may be due to a number of factors, including:

- an older consumer's "knee-jerk" skepticism about, or discomfort with, such forms of solicitation

- his or her lack of familiarity with your company or its products
- a hearing impairment an older prospect might have

Telemarketing may be very appropriate, however, as a means of *following up* on any previous contact you may have had with the older consumer. For example, it may be highly advisable to phone shortly after the individual has

- been sent a brochure or other information about your product or service
- requested information about your product
- purchased some of your products

Tip: The latter occasion can be particularly opportune since it gives you the ability to (1) determine the level of satisfaction with your product, and (2) suggest other products or offers that the older customer or his family and friends might find of interest.

Key Point: Telemarketing, when used in conjunction with other forms of advertising and promotion, can be very effective.

This is true in other instances as well. For example, while it is highly unlikely that the Yellow Pages will suffice as your sole means of mature market advertising, this directory can work very well when used in tandem with person-to-person selling and other print and broadcast media. Similarly, as some companies have found, the use of specialty, *as well as* mainstream publications, may generate the most rewarding mature market advertising.

Remember: Test and monitor your mature market advertising and promotional programs regularly to keep them as targeted and productive as possible.

Demographic and Psychographic Factors

As is true of every aspect of mature America, there is no uniformity in media preferences among older adults. Rather, use of the media varies according to the many demographic and psychographic characteristics which depict the individual members of the mature market.

For example, most younger members of the mature market (namely, those 50-54) are still working. Among this group, many individuals occupy high-ranking professional positions in American business and government organizations. This is much less likely to be characteristic of the 65+ population, however, where many persons are retired and thus removed from the day-to-day developments on Wall Street and Madison Avenue. In this case, differences in age, education, and lifestyle may explain why those 50 to 54 are larger-than-average readers of business magazines like *Barrons, Business Week*, and *Forbes*, while those over 65 read these publications much less, on average, than do other age groups.[18]

A look at some other characteristics also illustrates this point. For instance, while most older men and women like to read the newspaper, the sexes do vary on which sections of the paper they find of greatest interest. According to a survey by the Newspaper Advertising Bureau, men over 65 show a much stronger interest in sports, financial/business news, and political stories than do women of the same age. Women over 65 show a much greater interest in columns and stories concerning food, health, nutrition, entertainment, religion, and personal advice. Both groups find sections about local, national, and foreign news appealing.[19]

Rural and black readers display somewhat different media use from other mature adults, with a tendency to read magazines less frequently and to watch TV more often than other older persons . . . especially during daytime hours.[20]

Point: The need to understand the demographic and psychographic makeup of your current and potential older customers is vitally important in determining:

- which communication channels you use
- how you will mix the various media
- where and when, within a given medium, you will place your advertising or promotional message

Remember: The copy and images used to transmit your message should be a reflection of the demographic, geographic, psychographic, consumer and health characteristics of the mature adults you seek to reach.

Chapter Wrap-up

When it comes to media preferences and uses, the mature market displays some distinctive characteristics. The group prefers TV to radio, and newspapers to magazines. Nevertheless, marketers will find a large number of older adults with loyalties to specific kinds of radio programming and specialty publications. Most 50+ers also participate in direct response programs, though amounts purchased appear to represent only a small percentage of the overall dollars spent by older persons on consumer goods and services.

When considering communication channels to the mature adult, marketers should keep these points in mind:

1. For maximum exposure and impact, place your advertising message on TV, especially during the most cost-effective times for reaching 50+ers (that is, during weekday/weekend daytime and early evening hours—especially during selected news programs, talk shows, soap operas, and game shows).

2. While TV reaches the largest number of 50+ers, the print media are often the best to use in maximizing the older adult's understanding of your message and your product . . . and his ability to retrieve it for some later action (such as coupon redemption).

3. Effective use of communication channels to the older consumer requires a solid understanding of your actual/potential product purchasers and the most cost-effective media needed to reach those individuals. In some cases, the use of narrowly targeted communication channels (for example, specific radio stations or programming) may be your best approach.

4. To enhance the effectiveness of your mature market advertising, sales, and promotional campaigns, use two or more communication channels in combination with one another.

5. If it is feasible and cost effective for your business, face-to-face contact with the mature consumer is often the best communication channel to use. This assumes, of course, that the salesperson treats the older customer in a professional, courteous, and respectful manner.

6. If adult children are likely to play an influential role in the mature market's decision to purchase your product or service, *their* media preferences and use should be an important consideration in developing your marketing communications strategy.

7. Several factors, including the aging of America, the increasing popularity of "in-home" entertainment, and the baby boom generation's acceptance of and comfort with high technology, will all combine to make other communication channels to the mature consumer more attractive in the future. These include overnight or same-day message delivery, videocassettes, audiocassettes, videotex, and televised home-shopping networks.

---

1. "Table 2- Estimates of Television Usage By Daypart," from the *NTI National Audience Demographics Report*, A.C. Nielsen Company, May 1987.

2. MRI, Spring 1987.

3. Ibid.

4. Ibid.

5. Ibid.

6. Gallagher, Geraldine, "TV Teachers: How-To Shows Take Over the Tube," *Mature Outlook*, September/October 1987, p. 101.

7. MRI, Fall 1987 Cable Table

8. "The Average Weekday Audience Of The Daily Newspaper: 1986 Demographic Tables For Total United States, Top 100 Metros And Top ADIs," a survey conducted by Simmons Market Research Bureau for the Newspaper Advertising Bureau, Inc., p. 2.

9. "The Average Weekend Audience Of The Sunday/Weekend Newspaper: 1986 Demographic Tables For Total United States, Top 100 Metros And Top ADIs," a survey conducted by Simmons Market Research Bureau for the Newspaper Advertising Bureau, Inc., p. 2.

10. MRI, Spring 1987.

11. Ibid.

12. Ibid.

13. "The Geromarket 1987 Omnibus Study," Goldring & Company, Inc., July 1987.

14. "Promoting Devices For The Elderly Disabled," *Selling to Seniors*, February 1987, p. 8.

15. Duggleby, John, "Mail to Order," *Mature Outlook*, November/December 1985, p. 49.

16. "Mature Americans Aren't Risk-Takers When it Comes to Purchasing, Marketer Advises," *Selling to Seniors*, July 1987, p. 2.

17. "Likes and Dislikes of the Older Consumer," *Mature Market Report*, August 1987, p. 12.

18. MRI, Spring 1987.

19. *Senior Citizens and Newspapers*. A research report by the Newspaper Advertising Bureau, Inc., March, 1981.

20. *Channels of Communication For Reaching Older Americans*. Washington, D.C.: The National Council on the Aging, Inc., May 1985, pp. 15-17, and 19-21.

4

Marketing to the 50+ Consumer in the Future

Chapter **13**

Marketing to the Mature Consumer in the Twenty-First Century

In the preceding chapters, you've been provided with information to help you successfully understand, attract, and serve the mature consumer. In addition, you've seen six important trends that will have a profound impact on your mature market strategies and opportunities in the years ahead. But what about those "years ahead"? More specifically, what about the mature consumer of the future?

There is enough information available to make some reasonable assumptions about how your business might prosperously serve the mature market in the first few years of the next century. With that in mind, let's take a look at tomorrow's 50+ population and the opportunities they may present for your business.

What to Expect from Tomorrow's Mature Market

Growth in the 50+ Population

As America turns the corner and enters the twenty-first century, this nation will be grayer than ever before. In the year 2000, the median age of our population will be 36, older than at any point in our history. The driving force behind this phenomenon will be the growth in this country's over-50 population. According to the U.S. Census Bureau, while the under-50 group will increase by 3.5 percent between 1990 and 2000, the mature market will grow by 18.5 percent and number some 76 million people.

The number 76 million is an ironic one. That's because the major force responsible for the graying of America in the twenty-first century will be the

76 million baby boomers. By the year 2000, the first of the boomers will have entered the 50+ population. They will make their presence felt immediately as the number of 50-54-year-olds reaches over 17 million in 2000, *about 55 percent more than there are today.*[1] As Figure 13-1 illustrates, the baby boomers will cause the age 50-64 prime life market to explode during the first two decades of the twenty-first century.

Growth within the various cohorts of the 50+ group will not be equal. The prime lifer group will grow by more than 25 percent between 1990 and the year 2000, but the age 65-74 segment will actually decrease by 2 percent.[2] In fact, this group won't really "take off" until after 2010, when the baby boomers begin entering its ranks.

Note: The 75+ population will experience a 26 percent increase between 1990 and 2000, primarily due to a 50% rise in the age 85+, "oldest old" segment.[3]

Key Point: The first decade of the twenty-first century will be marked by expanding opportunities to serve 50+ers at the youngest and oldest ends of the mature market spectrum.

By the year 2000, the majority of 50+ers will continue to be those within the 50-64-year-old segment. Representing about 41 million people, this group will equal about 54 percent of the mature market. The remaining members of the 50+ population will be divided almost equally between those 65-74 and 75+.[4]

A Better Educated Group

Tomorrow's 50+ population will also be more educated than today's. To a great extent, this will be caused by a dramatic change in the composition of the group. By the year 2000, we'll have seen the passing of many of today's oldest and less schooled seniors and the entry of a large number of younger, better educated persons into this market.

Fact: Nearly 90 percent of the baby boomers will have high school diplomas and 25 percent will have college degrees by the time they enter their golden years.[5]

Increased Purchasing Power Through Employment

The mature market at the beginning of the next century is likely to have more spending power. A significant number of those over 65 will be collecting Social Security checks and pensions. Many 65+ers will still be earning money by working, principally in part-time jobs. The majority of those under 65 will be employed, including a substantial number of women in their fifties. The latter group will include the first wave of baby boomer women to enter the mature market. Unlike the seniors, however, most prime lifers will be

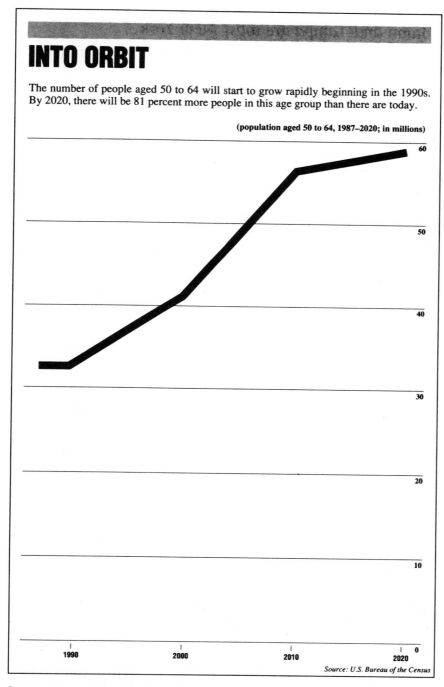

INTO ORBIT

The number of people aged 50 to 64 will start to grow rapidly beginning in the 1990s. By 2020, there will be 81 percent more people in this age group than there are today.

(population aged 50 to 64, 1987–2020; in millions)

Source: U.S. Bureau of the Census

Source: *American Demographics,* November 1987

FIGURE 13–1

working full-time. (Some will even hold down two jobs at the same time.) Many will have reached the height of their working careers.

Key Point: At the turn of the century, the majority of 50+ers will be in their peak earning years.

More Single-Person Households

While many 50+ers will be living with spouses and/or other family members, more mature adults than ever before will be living alone by the year 2000. Furthermore, their numbers are likely to keep on growing in the first two decades of the twenty-first century. Once again, it will be the youngest and oldest segments of the mature market that will be largely responsible for this phenomenon. The former group will include many baby boomers, some single, but most divorced. There are at least four factors that will create a large number of single-person households among the aging baby boomers:

1. the enormous number of baby boomers in total
2. the higher divorce rate among baby boomer couples
3. the large number of self-sufficient boomers—male and female—who will be able to afford living alone
4. the large number of childless baby boomers

While the youngest segment of the mature market is likely to experience the largest growth in single-person households, the largest number of persons living alone will be those 75 and over. It is estimated that this group will include nearly 7 million persons by the year 2000, over 70 percent more than there were in 1985. Within this group, the biggest surge will be seen in the number of single-person homeowners.[6] That segment should double in size with the overwhelming majority of its members being women, most of them widows.

Key Point: In the years 2000 and beyond, the demand for products and services that cater to 50+ers who live alone and in homes they own—whether by choice or by circumstance—will be enormous . . . especially among older women.

Seven Outstanding Business Opportunities in Serving Tomorrow's Mature Market

What products and services will be most popular or most in demand by the mature market of tomorrow? No one knows for sure. But I'm willing to make some predictions, despite the admonition I once heard about fortune-telling.

It went something like this: "People who live by the crystal ball must learn to eat broken glass."

As you'll see, my predictions are really educated guesses based on various sources of information. Here are what I believe will be some of the most successful mature market products/services in the late 1990s and the early twenty-first century. They have been grouped into seven categories, each of which represents a specific niche.

1. Home-Based Products and Services

Businesses offering products or services used in or around the home will find a bountiful supply of consumers among the 50+ population. *The demand for these products and services will be driven primarily by lifestyle preferences or changes in health or marital status.* For those at the younger end of the spectrum, particularly dual-earning married couples, the challenges of managing families and careers will have imbued them with a reverence for anything that can

- manage time more efficiently
- provide a more controlled or comfortable living environment
- increase leisure time

For this group, many of whom will be still be working, *convenience* will have solidly established its preeminent stature as one of the "hottest buttons" in marketing. Virtually nothing is more convenient than purchasing products or services that can be used in or around the house, or brought to the home. As a result, a variety of offerings, some already available in the marketplace, and others yet to be introduced, will be immensely popular, including:

- TVs, VCRs, pre-recorded videocassettes, personal computers and accessories, telephone answering machines, and compact disk players
- Microwave ovens, electric knives, food processors, recliners, firm cushioned-mattresses, and whirlpools
- Housekeeping, home remodeling, and home decorating services
- Take-out and home-delivery services
- Snack foods and precooked/single-serving meals
- Mail-order, telephone, home computer, and TV shopping/banking services
- Lawn care and landscaping services, garden supplies, and snowblowers
- Computer and remote-controlled appliances and utilities

Note: The home-centered lifestyle will make computer and videocassette advertising commonplace.

For older 50+ers, especially those 65-74, the demand for many of the above products and services will also be great. In some cases, however, the factors influencing the product purchase will be quite different, particularly for those over 75. For this group, far more so than the others, *declines in health and/or the loss of a spouse will create the need for products and services used in and around the house.* Further, the major impetus behind the demand for these services will be the desire to remain in one's own home as long as it is physically, financially, and psychologically possible. *The fact is, most older persons will not want to move.*

Key Point: While the desire for leisure time and a less hectic daily regimen will be the major factors generating prime lifer demand for home-based products/services, the desire to remain independent and in one's home will be the major forces behind a similar demand by older members of the mature market.

In the early part of the next century, a whole array of other products and services that meet the needs of less healthy older adults and/or those who live alone will be in great demand. These include:

- Transportation services and mobile units
- Home repair, home redesign, and home maintenance products and services
- Home companion and monitoring services (such as via the telephone, computer, or personal robot)
- Home security and emergency medical systems
- Physician house calls
- Adaptive products (such as specially designed, safety-oriented, and easy-to-use appliances, utilities, furniture, household products, and clothing)
- Reverse mortgages, sale leaseback programs, and other creative financial instruments that tap into the older person's home equity

Most of these products and services are already being offered in the marketplace. Some, however, are available only in selected areas or on a limited basis. Moreover, they are largely being run as "Mom and Pop," not-for-profit and/or government-sponsored programs.

By the early years of the twenty-first century, much will have changed from now. Increased market demand will have spurred the introduction of new, more technologically advanced products and services that will be widely available through highly sophisticated distribution systems. Some of these enterprises will be led by today's innovative, aggressive, and visionary entrepreneurs who, by then, may be running companies the size of McDonald's, Century 21, or Apple Computer. For the most part, however, satisfying the demand to keep the older population in their homes will probably be the domain of today's well-established, forward-thinking, for-profit businesses.

Key Point: The aging of America will spawn some of Wall Street's most glamorous and profitable stocks. Those who buy them over the next five to ten years will realize the greatest potential return on their investment.

Warning: The aging of our population "at home" should cause some companies to reassess their businesses *now*.

This is particularly true of those whose businesses have been rigidly defined. For example, real estate agencies traditionally have generated most of their revenues through the listing and selling of homes. Real estate agencies that do the most business with tomorrow's mature market, however, are likely to be those that see their role differently. Rather than seeing themselves as only in business to list and sell homes, these agencies will also see themselves as providing services that help mature adults *enjoy* and *stay* in their homes as long as possible (such as home repair, home sharing, creative home financing, home maintenance, housekeeping, and home redesign). By successfully performing or arranging for these services, an agency may earn additional revenues. More important, the agency is likely to later obtain the much-desired home listing and, perhaps, a buyer for the home!

Note: The important role that the home will play in the lives of tomorrow's mature market will also have an impact on the labor force. By the year 2010, many 50 + ers will be working at home, either as corporate America's telecommuters or in self-employed occupations. Several forces will create the work-at-home boom, including:

- health/travel limitations of some older adults
- second careers
- a more computer literate older population
- employer desires to contain costs, maintain productivity, and utilize older workers
- an increased demand for information/service-oriented skills

2. Long-Term Health Care and Related Services

An older America will mean a rise in long-term health problems. It is in the later years that chronic conditions like diabetes, hearing and visual impairment, hypertension, arthritis, and heart disease are likely to surface. In no instance will this be truer than among tomorrow's 85 + population, which is projected to *triple in size* by the year 2020. Today, roughly half of this group report having difficulty with one or more activities of daily living (bathing, dressing, walking, and so forth).

By the beginning of the twenty-first century, the need to treat and man-

age chronic or degenerative health problems will be enormous . . . and growing. So will the need to pay for such care. This, in turn, will create a huge
demand for a wide variety of products and services. The following list
identifies those that will have the greatest market potential:

- Nursing home care (especially if provided in a luxury, hotel-like at-
  mosphere)
- Adult day care centers
- Home health care
- Respite care (that which provides relief for family caregivers)
- Prescription and over-the-counter drugs
- Medical supplies/corrective devices (such as eyeglasses, contact
  lenses, hearing aids, canes, crutches, bandages, skin patches, and in-
  continence products)
- Special foods (low-cholesterol, low-sugar, low-salt, low-calorie,
  high-fiber, and so forth)
- High-tech medicine (such as prosthetic devices, pacemakers, im-
  planted pouches that release drugs, and mini-computers that monitor drug intake)
- Long-term care insurance
- Managed health care systems and case management services (such as
  social HMOs—HMOs that offer social and medical services for the
  older adult)
- Retirement centers (such as continuing care and life care retirement
  communities)

Tip: A key to prosperity in serving tomorrow's mature market will be
knowing which chronic conditions are likely to afflict older Americans and
providing products/services that help them better manage these problems.

The business potential of some of these products and services will be
stimulated as much, if not more, by the available sources of payment rather
than by the number of chronically ill 50+ers. Medicare, Medicaid, private
insurance, employers, unions, older persons, and adult children will be
among those who might help foot the bills. Of particular importance will be
Medicare and long-term care insurance (LTCI). Medicare, the major payor of
medical expenses for the 65+ population, has already begun to liberalize its
reimbursement policy for some long-term care related expenses . . . espe-
cially those incurred outside of the nursing home environment. Pressure is
being exerted by many organizations and a number of Congressmen to expe-
dite this activity. Surveys show that the bulk of the younger population also
support these efforts.

Recognition of the need for private LTCI is becoming widespread. This,
improvements in all aspects of marketing the policies (that is, products,

pricing, distribution, and promotion), and prime life generation fears of asset depletion will result in a substantial number of LTCI policyholders.

Point: By the early 21st century, Medicare and other government programs' support for long-term care related expenses should be substantially greater than it is today. This will be bolstered by an increasing number of 50+ers who will have LTCI coverage.

Tip: Marketers should monitor Medicare and national/state long-term care legislation very closely in the next few years. To a great extent, it will foretell where some of the best mature market opportunities will be in the twenty-first century.

Perhaps nowhere will business opportunities in long-term health care be greater than they will be for adult day care. The aging of the baby boomers' parents coupled with public and private sector financial support for community-based, long-term care services will create an adult day care boom by the beginning of the twenty-first century. This boom will far surpass anything ever realized in the child day care market. A baby bust and a senior boom will combine to make many of today's elementary and secondary schools the adult day care centers of tomorrow.

Increase in the need, the demand, and the payment sources for long-term care products and services provided within the home and community will make the home-based market described in business opportunity 1 even greater.

Opportunity: For many organizations, especially those in the fiercely competitive hospital industry, this is already creating an urgent need to develop or expand one's product and service lines (such as to open outpatient clinics or build medical "malls"). And rightly so! Most health-related services provided to the 50+ population as the twenty-first century begins *won't* be delivered in an institutional setting.

Nevertheless, hospitals that survive the industry fallout of the 1990s probably won't need to canvass for inpatients. Continued growth in the 50+ population will sharply increase the need for all health-related services, including inpatient hospital care. (Some experts believe that by the year 2000, the 65+ population *alone* will account for 50 percent of all health care expenses in the United States.)[7] For most patients, however, the hospital stay will be brief, as the majority of care will be given after they've been discharged.

3. Travel/Leisure Activities

While they will enjoy the comforts and conveniences of home, mature Americans will also display a zest for getting out . . . at least when getting out is to pursue leisure-oriented activity. A number of demographic, socioeconomic, and psychographic factors will help the travel/leisure industry swell with opportunities to serve the mature market.

To begin with, the number of 50+ers will be greater than ever before.

On average, they will have more income, better health, and a higher level of education than their predecessors. And, they will live longer.

Opportunity: All of this will make the 50 + ers a huge market for a variety of businesses including restaurants, hotels, airlines, theme parks, cruise liners, recreational vehicle and luxury car/van manufacturers, resorts, tour organizers, and those that interface with these groups (such as food and beverage suppliers, cultural attractions, and the entertainment industry).

Demographic trends, in particular, will result in some outstanding marketing possibilities. For example, the large number of older "singles" (whether divorced, widowed, or never married) will create an enormous market for

- singles-oriented events, vacations, and dining programs
- companionship programs and services (e.g., businesses that match up solo travelers)
- singles clubs

There will also be a market for singles who choose to stay at home or who are physically unable to go out. For these individuals, businesses will produce videocassette travelogues which allow them to "visit" places without ever leaving their front door.

Tip: The videocassette's ability to help people preview or vicariously experience other places and events will make it an extremely hot commodity among mature travelers. It will also present an outstanding opportunity for advertisers offering complementary or noncompeting products/services (manufacturers of cameras and luggage, those who offer foreign language courses, and so forth).

With Americans living longer, the typical family in the year 2000 will include four generations of people.[8] As a result, opportunities will exist to develop multigenerational travel programs. Some innovative marketers have already started doing this.

Example: Grandtravel of Chevy Chase, Maryland is packaging vacations for grandparents and grandchildren. The Chicago theme park, Six Flags-Great America, has successfully used an advertising campaign to attract three generations: grandparent, parent, and grandchild.

Tip: Savvy businesses outside the travel/leisure industry will also develop multigenerational and singles-oriented marketing strategies for the mature market (for example, greeting card manufacturers).

Lifestyle characteristics and preferences of the mature market in the early twenty-first century will create exceptional business opportunities for the travel/leisure industry. For example, a large group of 50 + ers will have more time available for leisure activities due to

- accumulation of vacation time
- onset of "empty nesthood"
- retirement

This will increase the demand for spur-of-the-moment, off-season, off-peak, and extended weekend activities. It will also make lengthier vacations, such as cruises and exotic foreign journeys, more popular.

Reminder: While some older persons, especially those over 75, will have a large supply of available leisure time, health or economic concerns may prevent them from fully enjoying it. For this group, one-to-three day outings will probably be of prime interest.

Some 50 + ers will find their supply of free time still limited by work or family responsibilities. This will include older workers in senior executive positions, "workaholics," working couples with financially dependent children, those taking care of one or more aging parents, and sandwich generation couples (those living with and/or responsible for both children and parents). Like the less healthy group, these individuals will represent an excellent market for activities and vacations of shorter duration. Weekend vacations, popularized in the 1980s and 1990s, will be particularly suited to their needs.

Keep in Mind: Travel/leisure businesses which provide or arrange for services that assist caregiving 50 + ers (or sandwich generation couples) will substantially increase their market appeal.

At the beginning of the twenty-first century, the mature market will be especially drawn to leisure activities which

1. enhance their well-being, or
2. provide them with new or meaningful experiences.

The demand for such pursuits will be highest among those under 75. Having a higher level of education and worldly experience than their predecessors, this group will want to know the "why" and "how" behind what they learn or see along with the "what", "where," and "when." Living at the height of the fitness boom, they'll be looking for activities which are renewing and invigorating as well as entertaining. And, realizing more than ever the value of life's finest pleasures, they'll display a strong interest in activities that provide spiritual, educational, and social fulfillment. All of this is likely to trigger a booming market for:

- adventure or fitness-oriented travel (examples: visits to offbeat locations, mystery tours, scientific expeditions, and tennis and spa vacations)

- special interest tours and courses (examples: golfing, wildlife, gardening, current events, and ethnic studies)

- group-oriented entertainment (examples: reunions, packaged tours, dinner theaters, and social clubs)

- activities which provide "hands-on" participation or offer "inside" information (examples: winemaking, filmmaking, and farm and factory tours)

- travel/education programs (such as Elderhostel)
- the arts (plays, concerts, dancing, and so forth)

Note: The rising number of older travelers will include a large number of persons who have at least one health problem, however minor. These individuals will require such things as special diets, better sound systems and lighting, large-type communications, readily available first-aid and medical help, and safe, comfortable, easily accessible surroundings.

Key Point: The most successful marketers of tomorrow will be those who consistently satisfy these special needs. By the turn of the century, they'll already have established a track record and reputation for doing so!

4. Personal and Business Counseling

Along with the joys of aging come the emotional bumps, bruises, and traumas. Never will this be truer than at the beginning of the next century, when 76 million persons will be in their second fifty years of life. The youngest members of this group will face several formidable challenges. Maturing baby boomers will be confronted with the realities of aging and their own mortality. Some will also be working through such difficulties as divorce, death of a parent, career plateauing, and job burnout.

Those in their fifties and sixties will likely wrestle with another major source of stress: providing assistance to a chronically ill parent. For some, this task will be even more difficult because it will be performed at the same time that teenagers or young adult children live at home (the sandwich generation phenomenon).

Opportunity: The emotional hurdles of the fifties and sixties will create a boom in the demand for individual counseling and psychotherapy.

As is true today, some seniors (namely, those over 70) will find it hard to cope with events that often occur in later life: retirement, declining health, or the loss of a spouse or other loved one. Unlike today, however, by the year 2000, the emotional woes that afflict these people will less often be attributed to "old age" or senility; rather, most will be accurately diagnosed and treated as mental health problems such as depression.

Key Point: An increase in the number of older Americans, the crises of the "golden years," and a better understanding of the aging process, will all cause a surge in mental health services for the age 65 + population. Fueling this activity will be government's quest to keep older people productive, independent, and in the community.

By 2000, American's 50 + population will have moved more fully into a cyclical lifestyle of working, traveling, volunteering, learning, and relaxing. This will increase the demand for the services of retirement planners who'll help both pre-retirees and retirees better map out their "second 50" agenda. It will also create a market for small business counselors who'll advise those interested in pursuing entrepreneurial ventures. And, it will spark a huge demand for employment counselors and placement agencies whose need will be driven as much by the effects of the "baby bust" as by those of the mature market boom.

Cyclical lifestyles, the mature market boom, and the baby bust will also generate a myriad of counseling opportunities for those who work with *business and industry.* Employers trying to maximize productivity, avoid labor shortages, control fringe benefit costs, and enhance older employee/retiree well-being will, more than ever before, be in need of:

- employee assistance and "eldercare" programs
- pre-retiree/retiree communications programs
- health care cost management strategies
- older worker recruitment services
- competent trainers and training/retraining programs

Key Point: In an aging America, those with expertise in the acquisition, development, training, and management of older workers and retirees will thrive.

Along with employers, businesses, too, will need more help in tapping or serving the mature market. Among those most sought will be:

- gerontologists
- geriatric physicians
- nurses
- geriatric nurse practitioners
- social workers
- home health aides
- retirement planners
- marketing consultants with mature market expertise

Opportunity: In the years 2000+, expertise of any kind related to the 50+ population will be one of the most valued commodities in the marketplace.

Note: By the year 2000, the most aggressive, capitalized, and competent consulting firms, personnel agencies, market research companies, and advertising agencies will have positioned themselves solidly as "mature market" specialists. They'll also capture the most business.

5. Educational and Informational Services

By the year 2000, America's economy and society will be more information-driven than ever before. Amidst this environment, the mature market will eagerly seek to further its knowledge. In part, this will be due to the compelling need to keep up with developments in a superpaced, interdependent world. However, at least two other forces will be behind this phenomenon:

- First, the 50 + group of tomorrow will be more capable of expanding its scope of knowledge than any previous older population. They'll be more educated, more computer literate, and, through the influence of mass communications, more informed.

- Second, by 2000, many 50 + ers will be loyal adherents to the maxim established in the 1980s and 1990s . . . that learning is a lifelong activity—not something which ends in early adulthood.

What educational and informational products/services will the mature market desire the most? Specifically, those that help them do the following:

1. *Understand themselves and the aging process.* The second 50 years of life will find older adults searching to find answers to philosophical questions like: What is the meaning of life? What is my purpose in life? What is my relationship with my family and with God? What is death? How shall I live out the rest of my years? In addition, they'll seek to better understand the aging process and how they can age successfully. The process of self-examination and self-understanding will be widespread among the mature market.

Opportunity: Mature adults will represent a sizable market for self-help and "how to" books, tapes, and courses.

2. *Keep abreast of local, national, and international developments.* The older population will hold most of the power seats in business, industry, and government. They'll be the largest and most influential voting lobby in America. In such an environment, older adults will seek to stay on top of the important issues and news stories of the day. Thus, the mature market will be prime prospects for those providing in-depth information about political, social, historical, and economic events.

3. *Be more effective consumers.* A more educated older population will thirst for information in order to function well in a rapidly changing marketplace. This will increase the desirability and marketability of those with specialized expertise in the areas of greatest interest to older consumers—particularly health care, financial services, and travel/leisure. It will also expand the opportunities for specialized publications (such as newsletters) and programming (such as cable and pay-TV networks), some of which might be sponsored or produced by those outside the publishing or broadcasting industries (hospitals, banks, insurance companies, and so forth).

Note: By the early years of the next century, sophisticated segmentation of the mature market will result in a variety of customized media products/services for older consumers.

4. *Improve their ability to perform in both avocational and vocational pursuits.* The majority of tomorrow's mature adults will stay active as long as possible. Many will take up new hobbies or return to old ones. This group will look for information and guidance to help them pursue their extracurricular pastimes.

Many of those over 50 will also work. Some will need to receive refresher training on the latest developments in their field. Others starting new jobs, careers, or businesses will need training or courses to help them gain the necessary skills and qualifications.

Note: An aging work force, cyclical lifestyles, and the baby bust will all drive this demand. Employers, along with older consumers, will pay to have it met.

Who has the best opportunity to satisfy the mature market's thirst for knowledge?

- Colleges, universities, vo-tech schools, and those offering home study programs
- Newspaper, newsletter, magazine, book, and audio/videocassette publishers
- Computer software and database manufacturers
- The broadcasting media
- Companies in the travel/leisure, health care, and financial services industries

A number of factors will determine who reaps the most from this opportunity. But those organizations that do will likely satisfy at least one of the four needs just described.

6. Financial Services

By the year 2000, older Americans will represent a major market for those who can help them accumulate, save, or manage their money. The 41 million prime lifers will offer the greatest business potential.

The Prime Lifers

Many of today's prime lifers worry about being financially secure in retirement. Few, however, have done anything about it. Tomorrow's prime lifers are likely to be much different. The group will be more informed about the need to plan for retirement. They'll know, for example, that retirement could last 30 or more years and that a long-term illness could wipe out all their savings. Tomorrow's prime lifers will be unlikely to rest comfortably at night knowing they can depend on Social Security or Medicare in their later years. Tax increases, benefit cuts or freezes, and a growing inbalance between the ratio of workers to retirees may all fuel these doubts.

To allay their fears, many prime lifers will look for answers to a variety of important short- and long-range questions. These include:

1. Can I afford to retire?
2. How much can I expect to receive from Social Security or my pension in the future?
3. Is it feasible to begin a second career?
4. Do we (or I) have enough life and health insurance coverage for now and in the future?
5. Will it make economic sense to move to that retirement community in Florida?
6. What are our best short- and long-term investment options?

Many prime lifers will seek out specific services and products to help them and their families remain financially independent throughout the later years of life. Among the most popular of these will probably be long-term care insurance, life insurance, products that combine long-term care insurance with life insurance, and conservative savings/investment programs (blue-chip stocks, CDs, government securities, and so forth). Others which may also do well are

- Pre-need trusts
- Prepaid legal plans and paralegal services
- Investment newsletters and clubs
- Private pension plans
- Cash-flow analyses (of projected retirement assets)
- Payroll deduction plans

Key Point: The aging of America will bring major opportunities to those in the fields of financial and retirement planning and income tax preparation. The most successful of these will offer their services through employers and unions. They'll also have "one-stop shop" capabilities.

Like today, the prime life generation will not be homogenous. Some members will be dual-working empty nesters in their peak earning years. This group will probably have significant discretionary funds to spend on such nonessentials as speculative investments and vacation homes. Others are likely to be financially strapped, such as caught between the simultaneous need to provide financial support to a chronically ill parent and one or more children still in college.

Important: Futurist David Pearce Snyder has noted that the *impact of this "sandwich generation" phenomenon could substantially undermine the rosy predictions about the affluence of tomorrow's prime lifers.*[9]

The Seniors

Tomorrow's seniors will have some of the same needs as the younger, prime life generation. For this group, however, the predominant concern will be the *management* of its money. Many older adults are likely to need the services of those who can help them oversee their assets, pay their bills, and protect their estates. Need for these services will be buoyed by the growth of the over-75 population, some of whom will be unable to handle these matters themselves but who will have the money to pay for help. Others, similarly unable, will have children willing to pay for assistance.

Opportunity: The large number of widows over 75 who live alone will increase the demand for financial management services.

Among the senior population, a number of products/services are likely to be particularly in demand:

- Low-risk, income-producing stocks and bonds
- CDs, saving accounts, money market mutual funds, and government-backed securities
- Medicare-supplemental and long-term care insurance policies
- Estate planning
- Income tax guidance and preparation
- Trust fund/portfolio management

One other note. A variety of housing options will be more widely available and acceptable to older Americans by the year 2000. These will include reverse equity mortgages, home sharing, home renovation, continuing care retirement communities, senior high rises, life care communities, and mobile homes. Many older adults will also need an advisor to help them determine which of these alternatives will best meet their financial and lifestyle needs and objectives.

7. Fitness-Oriented Products and Services

Spanish explorer Ponce de Leon would have felt right at home if he lived in the United States at the beginning of the twenty-first century. For never before in this country's history will so many Americans over 50 be striving to regain or retain a youthful appearance and attitude.

At least three things will be responsible for mature America's obsession with trying to look and feel young.

(1) There will be an overwhelming supply of evidence to support the notion that *older adults can indeed retard or even reverse some of the de-*

clines typically associated with aging. Perhaps the greatest testament of this will be the giant army of older role models. These youthful 50 + ers will irrefutably bear witness to the remarkable possibilities offered by healthy lifestyles, breakthroughs in aging research, and improved medical products, treatments, and technologies.

(2) *America's major health care purchasers will also stimulate the move to keep a graying America young.* Faced with the enormous burden of paying medical costs to support the older population, government programs, large and mid-size employers, and union trust fund managers will do everything possible to continue the wellness movement of the 1980s and 1990s. All kinds of incentives (financial and other) will be offered to encourage the practice of preventive medicine. By 2000, most health care payers will have created a major market for health insurance policies that reward (or penalize) individual enrollees for their good (or bad) behavior. In fact, like the auto insurance industry, such policies may be the market norm.

Key Point: By the turn of the century, most major purchasers of medical care for the mature market won't just encourage health promotion services, they'll pay for them—and they'll reward those who incur little or no medical expenses.

(3) *No force will have a greater impact on the quest for the fountain of youth than the aging of the baby boomers.* As Cheryl Russell has observed in her book, *100 Predictions for the Baby Boom: The Next 50 Years:* "The baby boom will not grow old gracefully."[10] Having built their identity as America's youth generation, the boomers will not enter the second 50 years of life with a whimper. Instead, they'll do everything they can to delay or counteract the effects of aging. And, in the process, they'll create the biggest market the health and fitness industry has ever known.

What products and services will be most popular among baby boomers and other members of the mature market as the new century begins? Here's a list of some of them:

- exercise, fitness, and weight-reducing centers
- exercise and athletic equipment
- cosmetic surgery
- wellness-oriented publications and software packages
- exercise videotapes
- rehabilitation services (such as sports medicine)
- vitamins
- fitness and "rebirthing" vacations and camps (that is, where one's psyche is uplifted or rejuvenated)
- "anti-aging" personal care products (such as sunscreens, "anti-wrinkle" creams, skin moisturizers, and hair colorings)

- healthful foods such as fruits, vegetables, whole-grain breads and cereals, fish, poultry, and the "low" products (low fat, low calorie, low salt, low sugar, low cholesterol, and so forth)
- sports participation
- self-testing programs and products (such as health screenings and kits/equipment that check blood-sugar levels, blood pressure, or cholesterol)
- drugs and devices that combat or mask declines in health (cholesterol or sugar-lowering drugs, bifocal contact lenses, "invisible" hearing aids, and so forth)
- healthful food stores and restaurants

Several factors will combine to make some products and services especially "hot." For example:

1. A growth in the popularity of weekend vacations along with the rise in interest in fitness activities will create a huge market for "wellness weekends."
2. The quest for social fulfillment in the later years along with the fitness movement will create a boom in 50+ sports leagues and group activities in bowling, volleyball, golf, tennis for "doubles", bicycling, and so forth.
3. The popularity of walking among 50+ers in general, and older women, in particular, will give walking-oriented products and services the broadest market appeal of all "Fountain of Youth" opportunities. (Note: *Walking* magazine's rapidly growing circulation, particularly among older readers, is one early indication of this.)

Tip: The mature market's desire to look and feel young will also result in exceptional business opportunities for those in the fashion industry. Undoubtedly, tomorrow's 50+ers will line up for stylish-looking clothing that comfortably adorns their fuller figures. Thus, for market leaders and innovators like Levi Strauss & Co., the best may be yet to come!

Marketing Checklist: Seven Outstanding Mature Market Businesses in the Early Twenty-First Century

1. Those that provide products or services which can be used in or around the home.
2. Those that help pay for, treat, or manage problems associated with chronic health conditions.
3. Those that help mature adults enjoy their leisure time.

4. Those that provide counseling services to 50+ers, or counsel employers and marketers on the 50+ population.

5. Those that keep the mature market informed and/or increase their knowledge.

6. Those that help 50+ers accumulate, save, or manage their money.

7. Those that help the mature market look and feel young.

Another Opportunity: Serving a Graying World

The potential to serve older adults in the coming years isn't limited to our own shores. That's because the aging of America isn't a world aberration. As Figure 13-2 illustrates, many nations are witnessing the steady graying of their populaces. Further, as Figure 13-3 shows, numerous countries have more than 2 million people over 65. Many others will join that group in 2025. This growth is attributed to a number of factors:

- reductions in infectious and parasitic diseases
- improved nutrition
- declines in infant and maternal mortality
- relatively high birth rates in the 1920s
- improvements in public and private health services, education, and income

Although more than half of the 50+ population lives in the less developed countries, many of the grayest nations are located in Europe. In Sweden, for example, more than 20 percent of the population is over 60. By the turn of the century, Sweden is expected to be joined in the "20 Percent Plus" club by Italy, West Germany, and the United Kingdom.[11]

No country is aging more quickly than Japan. In a nation with the highest life expectancy among the world's major countries (77), the Japanese are experiencing stunning growth in the size of their aging population. Between 1970 and 1996, the percentage of Japanese citizens 65 and over will double, jumping from 7 to 14 percent of the population.[12] Already, this has contributed to the overcrowding of Japanese society. As a way of dealing with this growth, the Japanese government has proposed an "Extended Leisure Stays Abroad" plan. The plan, still very much in its infancy, would encourage older Japanese citizens to retire overseas, particularly in European resort areas that would be further developed by the program.

What opportunities does an aging world offer to America's marketers? Perhaps the best will be health-related. As in the United States, older populations in other developed countries require more medical care than younger groups. Similarly, they are substantially more likely to suffer from chronic,

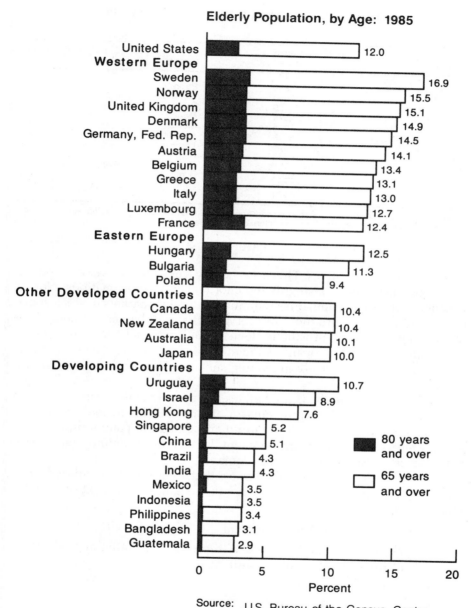

Elderly Population, by Age: 1985

Source: U.S. Bureau of the Census, Center for International Research, International Data Base on Aging; and appendix A, table 1.

FIGURE 13–2

Countries With More Than 2 Million Elderly in 1985

(Numbers in thousands)

Country	Population aged 65 and over	Country	Population aged 65 and over
China	52,889	Poland	3,484
India	32,698	Bangladesh	3,119
United States	28,609	Pakistan	2,818
Soviet Union	25,974	Mexico	2,797
Japan	12,125	Canada	2,651
Germany (Fed. Rep.)	8,812	Argentina	2,610
United Kingdom	8,466	Vietnam	2,393
Italy	7,443	Nigeria	2,307
France	6,748	Germany (Dem. Rep.)	2,217
Indonesia	5,901	Romania	2,155
Brazil	5,828	Turkey	2,093
Spain	4,274		

Source: United Nations, 1986, unpublished data from the 1984 Assessment of World Population Prospects; and U.S. Bureau of the Census, Center for International Research.

FIGURE 13–3

long-term health problems. This is especially true of those over 85, a population segment which is also growing enormously in those nations. Not surprisingly, American companies will find the foreign markets in greatest need of some of the same products and services that will be needed here: drugs, home health services, prosthetic devices, and personal care products.

Note: Some American companies—for example, pharmaceutical manufacturers—are already marketing such products and services in other countries.

Key Point: As in the United States, the cost of medical care for an aging population will drive governments in other countries to look for ways to keep people independent and within their homes and communities as long as possible. Amid such an environment, home and community-based products and services will be most in demand.

Aside from products and services that treat the ill or injured, many other opportunities will exist to serve the expanding international mature market. These include:

- Fitness and athletic equipment
- Special magazines and books (those that are tailored to the needs and interests of an older audience)
- Retirement housing
- Adaptive products
- Special foods (low-calorie, low-salt, and so forth)
- Vacation travel (such as tours to the United States)

Businesses looking to serve successfully the age 50 + population of other countries will face many challenges: social, cultural, economic, and political. Among these will be the need to develop a good understanding of other nations' demographic and psychographic makeup. For example, attitudes held by older adults or about aging are likely to vary greatly from one society to another.

Warning: Such differences could significantly alter the design of a marketing campaign. *Example:* In the United States, the word "silver" has positive connotations. In Japan, silver is a euphemism for "helpless" or "feeble."[12]

Warning: As in marketing to America's older consumers, businesses who use boilerplate strategies to serve 50+ers in other nations will significantly limit their mature market success.

Marketers will have to know as much as possible about other aspects of the countries whose older consumers they seek to serve. This includes having a firm grasp of their business practices. In many countries, for example, the path to the older consumer will be found only through engaging in cooperative relationships with foreign companies or governments.

Five Suggestions to Help You Anticipate the Best Mature Market Opportunities of the Future

No one knows exactly what products and services the older consumer of tomorrow will need, want, or buy. But there are a number of ways to improve your ability to forecast this. Here are five suggestions to help you more accurately anticipate where the best mature market opportunities will be in the early twenty-first century.

Suggestion 1: Track the Bellwether State

If there's one state whose older population already mirrors what the rest of the United States will look like in the early years of the twenty-first century, it's Florida. That's because Florida is the grayest state in America. Already, more than one-third of its residents are over 50, including 17 percent who are age 65+.[13] This compares with national figures of 26 percent and 12 percent respectively. Indeed, the rest of the United States will not match Florida's older demographic profile until around 2020.[14]

Florida's advanced state of maturity has placed it in the position of being the bellwether state for mature market activity. The Florida Chamber of Commerce, for example, has established a "Committee on the Fifty-Five-and-Over Age Group." It has also co-sponsored one of the two "aging and business" conferences held thus far in the state. In addition, a number of locally based businesses have been very active in promoting events and programs for older adults. These include Florida Power & Light, Publix Supermarkets, Sea World®, and Barnett Banks of Florida. Furthermore, several national companies, including Campbell's, Aetna Life and Casualty, and Kellogg Company, have used Florida as a test market for new products they've developed for the older consumer.

Many "Mom and Pop" businesses have also emerged within Florida to fill the largely unmet needs of its older residents. Family Partner Inc., for instance, monitors the well-being of older Floridians by doing such things as visiting their homes, arranging for necessary services, and taking care of emergencies. These services are paid for by middle-aged children, many of whom live outside the state. Drymon-Stumbo Management, on the other hand, settles estates, pays bills, and acts as a guardian for those who are primarily middle-class women over 70.

Tip: Pay particular attention to Florida's entrepreneurial ventures. They're likely to give you an excellent clue as to the best mature market opportunities of the future.

The aging of Florida has also prompted the state government to engage in several special projects and initiatives. In 1984, for example, then Governor Bob Graham established a Florida Committee on Aging to study aging issues and develop a plan for Florida's future. Thereafter, the Committee produced three reports, including its final one, "Pathways to the Future, Volume III," which was submitted to the governor in December 1986. This final report emphasized three major state objectives:

1. To maintain self-sufficiency among older Floridians
2. To restore self-sufficiency among older Floridians
3. To assist Florida's dependent older persons[15]

Within this framework, numerous strategies were suggested to help the state reach these objectives. These included the establishment and/or expansion of programs designed to

- Promote preventive medicine and wellness
- Encourage employment
- Stimulate alternative housing arrangements
- Improve access to transportation
- Provide long-term health care and social services[16]

Note: As you'll see, these strategies reflect some of the business opportunities discussed earlier in this chapter.

Tip: Marketers should read the "Pathways to the Future, Volume III" report; it provides a detailed picture of which products and services are likely to be among the most in demand in an aging America.

Because Florida's demographic profile is so much like the America of the future, marketers should track this state's mature market activity closely. This includes obtaining meaningful publications and reports, such as those provided by the state government, local newspapers and magazines, and various trade associations. It also includes attending relevant aging/business conferences whenever possible.

Caution: Florida's older population is, in some respects, different from the rest of the nation's. Unlike 50 + ers in other states, a sizable percentage of Florida's older residents are not native-born, but are retirees from other areas. This group tends to be healthier and more affluent than the overall retiree population. Because of this, businesses should look to Florida to obtain ideas, feedback, trends, and strategies—not necessarily to find the perfect blueprint for a long-range mature market strategic plan.

Suggestion 2: Monitor Activities in Other "Gray" Areas

While Florida may be the mature market bellwether state, it isn't the only one with lots of people over 50. Indeed, there are several other "gray" states, that is, those with either large numbers of 50 + ers and/or a large percentage of older residents. These include Pennsylvania, California, New Jersey, Massachusetts, Rhode Island, and Arkansas. There are also numerous counties and cities that fall into these two categories. While many of these cities are in Florida or in major urban settings (such as New York City and Philadelphia), others like Scranton, Pennsylvania; Wheeling, West Virginia; and Chico, California are not.

As in Florida, the aging of these areas is creating the need for both private and public sector responses. In some locales, new businesses are emerging which offer products and services to meet the needs of older residents and their families; legislators and government policymakers are devising special programs and initiatives to respond to this phenomenon. In California, for example, the Department of Aging has been given funding for a wide range of long-term care services including adult day health care and programs for victims of Alzheimer's disease. In Pennsylvania, government-sponsored and private programs are now assisting some of that state's family caregivers.

Tip: Businesses planning for the twenty-first century's mature market should keep an eye on developments in America's grayest areas. This could include:

- Identifying and monitoring the most "mature" locations through the assistance of the Census Bureau, state data centers, planning departments, and other public/private resources
- Staying in touch with key representatives of area agencies on aging and Chambers of Commerce

- Reading state Department of Aging newsletters and "seniors" newspapers
- Tracking relevant legislative bills and proposals

Marketers may also wish to consider the gray areas for market research studies or demonstration programs.

Tip: Businesses should also consider tracking developments in other graying areas of the world (for example, Sweden and Japan).

Suggestion 3: Know the Baby Boomers' and Women's Markets

No single force will have a greater impact on our political, social, cultural, and business environment in the early twenty-first century than will the aging of the baby boomers. As one writer said of the group, "In middle and old age, their continuing influence on the nature of American life could make their earlier years seem literally like child's play. What they become, the country will become—for the rest of their lives."[17]

Marketers who hope to thrive in the mature market of the future will have to know as much as possible about the baby-boom generation: its demographic makeup, lifestyles, attitudes, and consumer behavior. In addition, they'll need to know how this group perceives aging as well as how it wishes others to portray its aging. To some extent, imagining a society of older boomers isn't too difficult. For like the generations before them, the boomers of tomorrow will be greatly influenced by the events and experiences of their youth.

Warning: Like today's mature market, the baby boomers are also a heterogeneous group made up of many subsegments.

Along with the baby boomers, businesses will need to know as much as they can about the women's market of the future. Early in the twenty-first century, the mature market will include two especially large, sometimes overlapping groups of women: baby boomer females and older women living alone. Both of these groups are likely to have a profound impact on what products and services are needed by the 50+ population and which are successful.

A growing body of knowledge is being accumulated about today's baby boomer and women's markets. Much less information is available about such things as what these groups might look like, believe, or need 10 to 15 years from now.

Tip: Forward-thinking marketers will seek out whatever future-oriented information is in print. Furthermore, these marketers will also engage in primary research to obtain more of this kind of information.

Suggestion 4: Learn All You Can About the Future

There has been a growing interest in the future. Some have attributed this to the nearness of the year 2000; others, to the desire to gain control over the unknown amidst the rapid pace of social and technological change. Whatever the reason, there are more resources available than ever before which provide information about what the future may hold.

Key Point: To maximize your ability to succeed in tomorrow's aging world, you need to absorb this information today.

Where can you turn to learn about the future? Here are just a few possibilities.

1. *Futurist groups.* Some nonprofit organizations devote all of their energy to looking at the future. These include the World Future Society (WFS) and the federal government's Office of Technology Assessment. WFS is an international association that acts as a clearinghouse for forecasts about the future. By joining the group, members gain access to conferences, futuristic books, tapes, special reports, and an excellent bimonthly magazine, *The Futurist.* WFS also has local chapters.

2. *Publications.* In addition to *The Futurist,* there is also plenty of other good reading material of a futuristic nature. Several books and reports not only deal with the future, but with the aging phenomenon as well. These include Cheryl Russell's book on the baby boomers; *Aging 2000: A Challenge for Society,* by Phillip Selby and Mal Schechter; *Our Aging Society: Paradox and Promise,* edited by Alan Pifer and Lydia Bronte; *Age Wave: The Challenges and Opportunities of An Aging America* by Ken Dychtwald, Ph.D. and Joe Flower;[18] and reports on aging issued by the Census Bureau.

There are other useful print resources. *American Demographics* is full of ideas and information with a futurist-bent. The Naisbitt Group's "Trend Letter" and Kiplinger's newsletters are also good resources as are business publications like *The Wall Street Journal, Inc.,* and the advisory newsletters/reports put out by various investment firms.

Tip: Kiplinger's Florida, California, and Texas newsletters can be particularly helpful because they cover activities in three states with large 50 + populations.

Remember: Some publications and studies that are *not* future-oriented may also prove helpful to you in planning for the twenty-first century. For example, information about the purchases of today's 50 + market (obtained through resources like the Department of Labor's annual Consumer Expenditure Survey) may also give you clues as to what tomorrow's mature consumers will need or buy.

3. *"Think tank" organizations.* A number of individuals and businesses around the country help others better understand the world of tomor-

row. Many companies have called upon these futurists to help them develop competitive strategies for the years ahead.

4. *Professional speakers and seminar leaders.* Several speakers present keynote speeches and seminars about the future. Some specialize in a particular topic (such as demographics, trends, implications, opportunities, and strategies in an aging America). Others are futurists in a broader sense and discuss a wide range of issues. Both the National Speakers Association directory and the World Future Society are good places to check for competent professional speakers, trainers, and seminar leaders.

5. *Educational courses.* The interest in futurism has resulted in an increase in the number of courses and programs that cover the subject. Topics range from forecasting techniques to the study of the sociology of the future. Many colleges and universities including Drexel University, the University of Houston, and the University of Hawaii present such courses and some offer programs with degrees. Organizations with foresight will:

- encourage (or require) selected employees to attend one or more of these courses
- utilize these academic institutions as resources for information, training, consulting, and employee recruitment

Suggestion 5: Monitor Developments in Aging Research

Medical research involving both the older population and the aging process can provide some important clues about where the best mature market opportunities will be in the future. It suggests the need for certain products and services (such as specific foods, drugs, and fitness programs) and their potential market demand.

Research into the social and psychological aspects of aging can also be useful.

Keep in Mind: It isn't only knowing the results of this research that can be helpful. It's equally important to know what is being researched. That's because research projects are often the first means of addressing upcoming nationwide concerns. Thus, the problems tackled in aging-related studies are likely to represent some of the most pressing needs of future older adults.

To improve your fortune-telling marketing skills, your organization should be aware of the major studies and projects taking place in aging research. The best sources for this information will be government agencies, private and community foundations (such as the Andrus Foundation, the Robert Wood Johnson Foundation, and the Retirement Research Foundation), directories of foundations, and geriatric and gerontogical associations.

Marketing Checklist:
Five Ways to See Aging America's Future More Clearly

1. Track mature activity in Florida.
2. Be aware of developments in other "gray" states, counties, and cities.
3. Know as much as possible about the baby boomers' and women's markets of today—and tomorrow.
4. Open your mind to futuristic information.
5. Monitor developments in aging research.

Chapter Wrap-up

In an increasingly competitive national and international marketplace, long-range thinking and planning have become crucial. They will spell the difference between success and failure, survival and oblivion.

Despite the shroud of mystery that hangs over the twenty-first century, there is enough information available to make some reasonable projections—as they concern the mature market.

Keep these four thoughts in mind:

1. The graying of America will be a major factor in this nation's rapid transition to a twenty-first century economy that is primarily information and service-based.

2. As we enter the twenty-first century, the six key trends mentioned in Chapter 2 will be joined by four other trends:

   — Convenience—the desire to maximize one's leisure time and/or minimize the problems/responsibilities associated with everyday life

   — Continuum of care—the need to provide a wide range of social, medical, psychological, and financial products and services in a "one-stop shop"/packaged format to older adults, especially those with chronic health problems

   — Cyclical lifestyle—the pursuit of various activities in the middle and later years of life (education, volunteerism, work, travel, grandparenting, relaxation, and so forth)

   — Celebration of maturity—the widespread belief among older adults that, at ages 50+, almost anything is still possible, and the reflection of that attitude by the mass media

Key Point: Each of these trends will reflect major preferences or needs of the mature market. The products and services that address these preferences and needs will be the most in demand—and the most successful.

All of the trends, especially the continuum of care, will result in a variety of industry-integrated mature market products and services (such as ones that combine health care services with those in housing, travel, education, or banking).

3. Astute businesses will realize it is not just America that is aging . . . it is the world. In a global economy, they'll look for opportunities to meet the needs of other aging nations, not just our own.

4. Those who most accurately forecast the future will probably not be lucky; rather, they'll look for—and find—guideposts. Keep these words in mind: "By studying clues that are all around you in the present, you can learn to predict the future yourself. All you need to know is where to look and what to look for."[19]

America's graying population in the twenty-first century will present both opportunities and challenges for government agencies, businesses, and employers. Marketers who reap the most from this phenomenon will be those who are forward-thinking and action-oriented. They'll plan for the future and follow through with the programs, the products, and the services that are most needed and demanded by older consumers and those who assist them. And for that, their businesses will be justly rewarded!

---

1. U.S. Bureau of the Census, "Projections of the Population of the United States, by Age, Sex and Race: 1983-2080," *Current Population Reports*, Series P-25, No. 952, Washington, D.C.: U.S. Government Printing Office, 1984.

2. Ibid.

3. Ibid.

4. Ibid.

5. Russell, Cheryl. *100 Predictions for the Baby Boom*. New York and London: Plenum Press, 1987.

6. "Housing for Singles," *American Demographics*, February 1987, p. 62.

7. Dychtwald, Ken and Mark Zitter. *The Role of the Hospital in an Aging Society*. Emeryville, CA: Age Wave, Inc. 1986.

8. U.S. Bureau of the Census, "Demographic and Socioeconomic Aspects of Aging in the United States," p. 90.

9. Personal telephone conversation with David Pearce Snyder, June 1987.

10. Russell, Cheryl. op. cit., p. 47.

11. U.S. Bureau of the Census, "An Aging World," International Population Reports Series P-95, No. 78, p. 5.

12. Darlin, Damon, "Japanese Government Scales Back Plan to Export Some of Nation's Elderly," *Wall Street Journal*, October 14, 1987, p. 30.

13. Resener, Madlyn, with Linda R. Prout, "Targeting the Old Folks," *Newsweek*, January 6, 1986, p. 54.

14. Edmondson, Brad, "Is Florida Our Future," *American Demographics*, June 1987, pp. 38-39.

15. Florida Committee on Aging/Philip D. Lewis, Chairman, "Pathways to the Future III: Toward the Year 2000," December 1986.

16. Ibid.

17. Blonston, Gary, "An Aging Population Will Alter the Future," *Knight-Ridder News Service*, reprinted in *The Philadelphia Inquirer*, September 6, 1987, p. 1-H.

18. Russell, Cheryl. op. cit. Selby, Philip and Mal Schechter. *Aging 2000: A Challenge for Society*. Hingham, MA: MTP Press Limited, 1982. Pifer, Alan and Lydia Bronte. Our Aging Society: *Paradox and Promise*. New York: W.W. Norton & Company, 1986. Dychtwald, Ken, and Joe Flower. Age Wave: *The Challenges and Opportunities of An Aging America*. Los Angeles: Jeremy P. Tarcher, Inc., 1988.

19. Teague, Juanell, and Eileen Vennum, "Forecast your own business and career future," *Speak Out*, October 1987, p. 9.

Afterword

Will your business be among those to achieve lasting prosperity in an aging America? Even the best of marketers will be confronted with obstacles and challenges that cannot be anticipated, circumvented, or controlled. Nevertheless, there are a number of things you *can* and *should* do to maximize your potential for mature market success:

- understand as much as you can about the 50+ population as individuals, as a group, and as a customer segment
- track and capitalize on relevant trends
- learn how to reach and communicate effectively with older consumers
- utilize the many aging/futuristic resources available to you

Perhaps most important, your marketing and customer service efforts should be guided by the "eight keys" of Part II. While the mature market itself is a moving target, these eight strategies should remain firmly rooted over the next several decades.

In a few years, the first baby boomers will reach 50; in little more than two decades, they'll turn 65. While the mature market is already being recognized as a pivotal consumer segment, it will certainly be seen in that light in the future. For this reason, your organization must also understand and track the baby boom generation. Not only will this help you successfully serve today's older customers (such as in developing marketing programs that link the baby boomers and their parents), but it will also have a major impact on your ability to serve the multitude of gray-haired baby boomers who will soon permeate our landscape.

A few words of caution, however. If your business intends to prosper in an aging America, you'd better not stand idly on the sidelines waiting for the boomers to turn gray. Among the list of tomorrow's dinosaurs will be many businesses—large and small—who failed to build their mature market bridges *today*. In fact, by consciously building relationships with older consumers *now*, you'll be making a major investment in your company's long-term prosperity. You may also be building a better future for yourself: for many of us are—or someday will be—members of the 50+ population.

Remember, too, that our country has no monopoly on aging, or for that matter, on older customers. Indeed, many of the tourists who visit the United States and shop in our stores are also members of the mature market as are a growing number of consumers who buy products and services overseas. Aging is a world phenomenon. In the global marketplace we live in, it may offer your company enormous business potential if you can see beyond our own borders.

Prospering in an aging America won't be easy. For many organizations, it will represent a formidable, inescapable, "dog-eat-dog" challenge. But as with all challenges, this one holds a carrot along with the stick: The need to serve successfully the over-50 consumer will offer marketers an outstanding opportunity . . . the possibility of flourishing long into the next century.

Perhaps it's only fitting, then, to close this book with the prophetic words of the great American poet, Henry Wadsworth Longfellow. Said Mr. Longfellow more than 100 years ago:

"For age is opportunity no less
Than youth itself, though in another dress. . . ."

I submit to you that age is not only an opportunity for those who are aging, but for those who seek to serve them. Good luck!

Appendixes

Appendix **A**

Characteristics of the Mature Market

To help give you a composite picture of the 50 + population, this appendix provides you with information about the following characteristics of the mature market:*

- Size and growth
- Age distribution
- Life expectancy
- Race and ethnicity
- Sex ratios
- Marital status and living arrangements
- Housing
- Geographic distribution and migration patterns
- Education
- Employment
- Health
- Economic status (income, net worth, and purchasing power)
- Consumer expenditures

---

*Unless noted otherwise, the information presented in this appendix was obtained from *Aging America: Trends and Projections, 1987-88 Edition*, prepared by the U.S. Senate Special Committee on Aging in conjunction with the American Association of Retired Persons, the Federal Council on Aging, and the U.S. Administration on Aging.

Size and Growth

As Figure A-1 illustrates, America's older population has risen steadily since the turn of the century. In 1900, only 13 percent of our population—about 10 million people—was age 50 +. Only 1 in 25 Americans (4 percent) was age 65 and over. Today there are over 62 million persons age 50 + and more than 29 million who are at least age 65. Thus, more than 1 in 4 Americans today is age 50 +; and 1 in eight is age 65 and over. Indeed, the number of people over 65 exceeds the entire population of Canada.

The graying of America is expected to continue unabated well into the twenty-first century. By 2020, it is estimated that about 110 million Americans—a stunning 37 percent of our population—may be age 50 +. It is also projected that between 1985 and 2050 the total United States population will increase by a third; on the other hand, the 50-plus group is expected

Population 50 Years and Over, by Age: 1900-2050

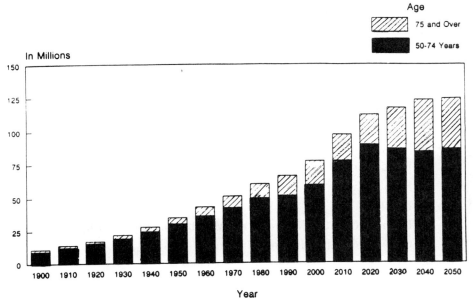

Source: U.S. Bureau of the Census. 1980 Census of Population, PC80-B1, *General Population Characteristics,* Tables 42 and 45; and *Projections of the Population of the United States, by Age, Sex, and Race: 1983–2080, Current Population Reports,* Series p-25, no. 952, Washington D.C.: U.S. Government Printing Office, 1984

FIGURE A–1

to more than double. The *major* force behind these phenomena will be the aging of our nation's 76 million baby boomers.

Age Distribution

Figure A-2 shows the number of 50+ers within the various age cohorts and the projected growth in these groups between 1985 and 2000. The majority of those within the mature market are—and will remain—between the ages of 50 and 64. Of all groups, the age 50-55 segment is expected to grow the most through 2000. It's important to bear in mind, however, that the aging of the baby boomers will cause the pendulum to swing in the twenty-first century. By 2030, the number of persons 65+ is projected to *exceed* those in the 50-64 segment.

Figures A-3 illustrates how the 75+ population represents a steadily growing percentage of the mature market. At the turn of the next century, *half* of those age 65+ will be age 75 or older. Fueling this rise is the tremendous growth in the number of persons over 85. According to the Census Bureau, by the middle of the twenty-first century, the 85+ population is expected to be seven times as large as it was in 1980.

Population: Present and Projected
Persons millions

Age	Population 1985	Growth 1985-2000
Total US	238.6	12.3%
under 50	177.0	8.5
50 & over	61.6	23.4
50-55	10.8	60.5
55-60	11.3	18.1
60-65	10.9	−4.2
65-70	9.2	−1.3
70-75	7.6	12.3
75 & over	11.8	46.7

Source: Linden, Fabian, *Midlife and Beyond: The $800 Billion Over-Fifty Market.* New York: Consumer Research Center, The Conference Board, Inc., 1985

FIGURE A–2

POPULATION 55 YEARS AND OVER BY AGE: 1900-2050

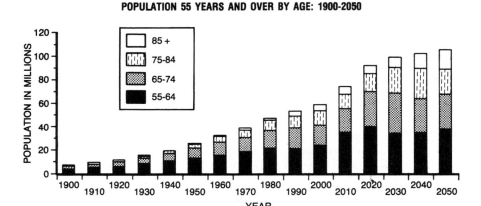

SOURCE: Taueber, Cynthia M., U.S. Bureau of the Census. "America in Transition: An Aging Society." *Current Population Reports* Series P-23, No. 128 (September 1983) (for years 1900–1980).
Spencer, Gregory, U.S. Bureau of the Census. "Projections of the Population of the United States, by Age, Sex, and Race: 1983 to 2080." *Current Population Reports* Series P-25, No. 952 (May 1984) (for years 1990-2050).

FIGURE A–3

Life Expectancy

Life expectancy in the United States has risen steadily for all groups since the turn of the century. In 1900, life expectancy for a newborn baby was 47 years. In 1986, average life expectancy at birth had increased to nearly 75 years.[1] While females have a longer life expectancy than males (about seven more years), the difference between the two sexes has declined somewhat over the past two decades.

The most dramatic changes in life expectancy came about during the first half of this century due to decreased infant and child mortality. Since 1970, smaller increases in life expectancy have occurred as a result of reductions in death rates among the middle-aged and older population groups. *One important byproduct of this for marketers is that life expectancy at age 65 has grown substantially in recent years and is now, on average, almost 17 years!* This trend is expected to continue long into the twenty-first century.

Although longevity has played a role in creating today's aging marketplace, the primary cause is the high birth rates which occurred before 1920 and after World War II. The precipitous drop in birth rates after the mid-1960s (the "baby bust") has also contributed to the graying of America.

Race and Ethnicity

The nonwhite and Hispanic populations have a smaller proportion of persons age 55 + within their ranks than the white population. While 22 percent of the white population is 55 and over, only 15 percent of blacks and 11 percent of Hispanics fall into that age segment. All three groups will see these percentages grow significantly over the next several decades as America turns grayer. Nevertheless, the population of white non-Hispanics will continue to have the highest proportion of 55 + ers within its overall group. In 1986, 89 percent of the age 55 + population was white, only 9 percent black and just 4 percent Hispanic.* But the mature adult black and Hispanic populations are growing very rapidly, much more so than the older white group. As a result, the percentage of older adults who are blacks and Hispanics will climb. For example, the proportion of age 65 + ers who are members of minority groups will grow from 13 percent in 1985, to 21 percent in 2020, to 30 percent in 2050.

Sex Ratios

Between the ages of 50 and 54, the number of older men is nearly the same as that of older women. In 1985, for instance, women ages 50-54 made up about 52 percent of that specific age group.[2] The difference in representation between the two sexes becomes substantially greater, however, with each age cohort thereafter.

Figure A-4 illustrates the great disparity between the numbers of men and women at age 65 and beyond. By age 85, women outnumber men by 2½ to 1!

Marital Status and Living Arrangements

Overall, most older men either live with spouses or in some other family setting. Conversely, most older women spend much of their later years as widows living alone. There are at least three reasons for this:

1. Men have a shorter life expectancy than women and so they tend to die before their wives.

---

*Percentages exceed 100% because Hispanic Americans may be of any race.

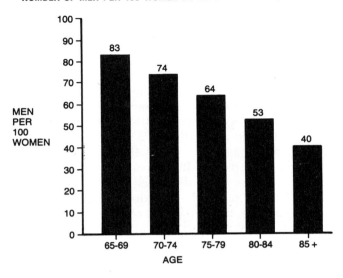

NUMBER OF MEN PER 100 WOMEN BY ELDERLY AGE GROUP: 1986

SOURCE: U.S. Bureau of the Census. "Estimates of the Population of the United States, by Age, Sex, and Race: 1980 to 1986."
Current Population Reports Series P-25, No. 1000 (February 1987).

FIGURE A–4

2. Men tend to marry women who are younger than they are.
3. Men who lose a spouse through divorce or death are much more likely to remarry than women facing the same circumstances.

The great disparity in the marital status and living arrangements of older men and women begins to evidence itself in mid-life and becomes wider and wider after age 65. Between the ages of 50 and 64, an estimated 75 percent of mature adults are married and living together. The rest of that group is divided between those living by themselves and those heading households that have another family member.[3] Included among those living alone is a sizable group of widows. More than 17 percent of women ages 55-64 were widowed in 1985. In contrast, less than 4 percent of the men in that age group were widowers.[4]

After age 65, the large majority of men (75 percent) are married and living with their spouse. Conversely, only about half as many women (38 percent) are married with a husband present. Less than 15 percent of the men over 65 live alone in comparison to over 41 percent of the women. The much higher proportion of widowed women (51 percent versus 14 percent for men) is a major factor in creating this discrepancy.

Housing

Single-family home ownership is most heavily concentrated among those over 50. More than 77 percent of those age 50 + own their own homes. This compares with less than two-thirds of all householders nationally. Older homeowners include 79 percent of those 50 to 65, 77 percent of those 65 to 75, and 72 percent of those age 75 + .[5] Among the older population, women, persons living alone, and those age 75 or older are more likely to rent rather than own homes.

Those over 65—whether homeowners or renters—tend to live in older homes. In 1983, nearly half of the 65 + population's homeowners lived in houses that were at least 34 years old. On the other hand, less than 30% of those under 65 lived in such housing. Close to half of *both* older and younger renters, however, lived in homes at least 34 years old.

Geographic Distribution and Migration Patterns

Most adults over 50 live within several states. In 1986, 49 percent of those 65 + lived in just eight states, each of which had over a million persons 65 and over. Ranked in order of the *size* of their age 65 + populations, these eight states are as follows:

- California
- New York
- Florida
- Pennsylvania
- Texas
- Illinois
- Ohio
- Michigan

However, the states with the largest *number* of mature adults are not necessarily those with the highest *concentration* of 50 + ers. For example, of the states shown in the "top eight" list, only Florida and Pennsylvania rank among the "grayest"; that is, those having the largest percentage of 50 + ers and the highest median ages. Ranked in order, the top five states in this category are

- Florida
- Rhode Island
- Pennsylvania

- Arkansas
- Massachusetts[6]

As Figure A-5 shows, the same holds true when looking at the percentage of 65 + ers within a state. Among the states having the largest number of persons over 65, only Florida and Pennsylvania also fall in the top eight "gray" category. The states with the highest percentage of age 65 + adults are primarily located in either the midwest farm belt area or the agricultural and heavily industrialized regions of the northeast.

Within the United States, there are also large "pockets" of gray: cities, suburban neighborhoods, towns, and counties where a significant percentage of the residents are age 50 +. For example, there are 178 counties in which the 65 + population comprises over 20 percent of the population. Many of these are located in rural areas where older persons have remained while their children have moved.

Many "gray metros" are also in Sun Belt communities. It is the relocation of retirees to the Sun Belt states which has caused many of those areas to experience a large increase in their older populations. Indeed, states in the south and west are experiencing the largest percentage increases in their 65 + populations. Not surprisingly, then, of the five states with the highest percentage increase in persons over 65 between 1980 and 1986, four of them—Nevada, Hawaii, Arizona, and New Mexico—were in the south and west. (Alaska was the other state.)

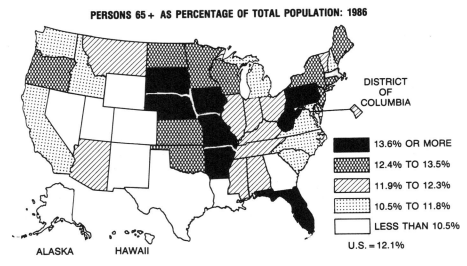

PERSONS 65 + AS PERCENTAGE OF TOTAL POPULATION: 1986

DISTRICT
OF
COLUMBIA

■	13.6% OR MORE
▨	12.4% TO 13.5%
▨	11.9% TO 12.3%
▨	10.5% TO 11.8%
□	LESS THAN 10.5%

U.S. = 12.1%

ALASKA   HAWAII

SOURCE: U.S. Bureau of the Census. "State Population and Household Estimates With Age, Sex, and Components of Change: 1981 to 1986." *Current Population Reports* Series P-25, No. 1010 (September 1987).

FIGURE A–5

The migration of older adults has been increasing over the past two decades. This is primarily due to increases in the income, education, and activity levels of the mature market. Higher income, education, and activity levels are all factors that tend to differentiate older movers from those who don't relocate. Persons who move are also more likely to have a spouse to accompany them.[7]

Overall, however, older adults are much less likely to move than are younger persons. Between March 1984 and March 1985, less than 10 percent of the 50 + population moved including only 6 percent of those 65 + .[8] Thus, while some older persons may *temporarily* relocate to other areas during specific times of the year (such as Florida in the winter), they and most members of the mature market tend to stay where they've spent the bulk of their adult lives. For more and more older persons, this is in the suburbs rather than the cities. In 1980, the number of older persons living in the suburbs *exceeded* those living in central cities for the first time.

Also note that some older adults return north after having moved to the Sun Belt states. Often, they move back to their home states (or to non-Sun Belt areas) to be near their children. These individuals are more likely to have low incomes and/or to be in poor health. This phenomenon, known as "countermigration" or "reverse migration," generally occurs among those over 65.[9]

Education

The younger segments of the mature market have completed more years of formal schooling than the older groups. For example, a little more than 40 percent of those age 75 + have finished high school and/or attended college versus more than two-thirds of those 55-64. Similarly, more than 40 percent of those of 75 + have had fewer than 9 years of formal education as compared with less than 20 percent of those 55-64. Nevertheless, the education gap between young and old has been closing over the last few decades as more educated adults move into the 50 + population.

While educational levels among the 65 + population do not vary much by sex, they do vary significantly by race and ethnic background. As a group, older blacks and Hispanics have had much less formal schooling than older whites.

Employment

As Figure A-6 illustrates, employment among the mature market is at its highest levels for *all* groups—whites, blacks, males, and females—between

LABOR FORCE PARTICIPATION RATES BY AGE, SEX, AND RACE: 1986
(annual averages in percent)

Sex and race	50-54 years	55-59 years	60-64 years	65-69 years	70 + years
Total male	88.9	79.0	54.9	25.0	10.4
Total female	62.0	51.3	33.2	14.3	4.1
White male	89.8	79.8	55.7	25.3	10.7
White female	62.0	51.0	33.1	14.3	4.1
Black male	81.1	70.8	45.9	21.0	7.2
Black female	62.1	52.9	33.3	13.9	4.6

SOURCE: U.S. Department of Labor, Bureau of Labor Statistics. *Employment and Earnings* Vol. 34, No. 1 (January 1987).

FIGURE A–6

the ages of 50 and 54. Thereafter, it begins a steady, downward spiral plummeting to less than 11 percent for all groups at age 70 +.

Since 1950 there has been a dramatic decline in the labor force participation of older men. In 1950, nearly 90 percent of men ages 55-64—and close to 50 percent of those 65 and over—were working. By 1986, those figures had dropped under 70 percent and 20 percent respectively. The real plunge occurred between ages 60 and 64. In 1986, for example, 79 percent of males ages 55-59 were working versus just 55 percent of those 60-64. Early retirement programs and increased Social Security, pension, and health benefits have all contributed to this phenomenon.

Employment among older women ages 55-64 is actually much *higher* than in 1950. Only 27 percent of women in this age group worked in 1950 as compared with 42 percent in 1986. Among women ages 65 +, however, work force participation has decreased—albeit only slightly—from about 10 percent in 1950 to just over 7 percent in 1986.

While most workers under 65—male or female—are in full-time positions, the situation changes significantly after age 65. In 1986, nearly half of the men working after 65 were in part-time positions along with over 60 percent of the women. Today a much higher percentage of men who work past age 65 are part-timers than were in 1950.

Our society's transformation from an agricultural and manufacturing-based economy to one that is information and service-oriented has also had an impact on the occupations of older persons. More than two-thirds of the jobs held in 1986 by workers ages 55-64 were of a *white-collar or service nature*. In addition, nearly three-fourths of those age 65 + occupied such positions. The latter statistic indicates that, when older persons do work, it is often their accumulated skills and knowledge which are being tapped.

Health

Self-Assessment of Health

According to results of the 1986 Health Interview Survey conducted by the National Center for Health Statistics, more than 8 of 10 persons ages 45-64 who live within the community describe their health as "excellent," "very good," or "good." Contrary to what some might believe, 7 in 10 of the noninstitutionalized 65 + population describe themselves in the same way. Among both age groups, a slightly higher percentage of women than men consider their health either "fair" or "poor." However, a much higher percentage of blacks than whites ages 45 + feel their health is no better than poor or fair.[10]

There is a clear relationship between one's self-assessment of health and his or her income. For example, among those over 65, the more income a person has, the more likely he or she feels in "excellent" health.

Medical Problems

In the earlier years of life, most people tend to suffer from acute medical problems like colds and the flu. As people enter their middle and later years, however, acute conditions become less frequent and chronic ones more prevalent. By age 65, more than 4 out of 5 persons age 65 + have a chronic problem and about one-third have three or more. The oldest members of this group are more likely to suffer from several chronic conditions.

As Figure A-7 illustrates, arthritis and hypertension (high blood pressure) are the most common chronic conditions among both the 45-64 and 65 + groups. Other prevalent conditions are hearing impairment, musculoskeletal problems (such as neck, back, knee, and leg conditions), sinusitis, and heart disease.

There are noticeable differences in the incidence of chronic medical problems between the sexes and races. For example, more men ages 45-64 have hearing problems, heart disease, and orthopedic impairment than women in that group. Conversely, women ages 45-64 are more likely to suffer from arthritis, high blood pressure, and sinusitis. These disparities hold true for the 65 + population except for orthopedic problems which occur more frequently among older women than men. For many women in this group, osteoporosis is a particularly troublesome disease. Older blacks of any age are more apt to be troubled by arthritis, diabetes, and hypertension.[11]

Although more members of the mature market suffer from chronic medical problems than do younger persons, the frequency with which they

Chart 4-2
MORBIDITY FROM TOP TEN CHRONIC CONDITIONS: 1986

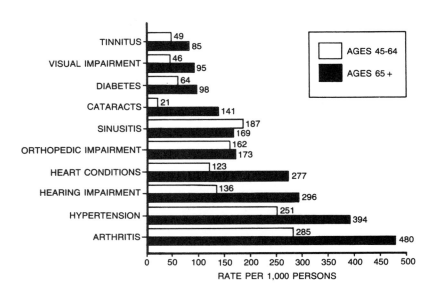

SOURCE: National Center for Health Statistics. "Current Estimates from the National Health Interview Survey, United States, 1986." *Vital and Health Statistics* Series 10, No. 164 (October 1987).

FIGURE A–7

report daily health problems is no higher than those ages 18-44.[12] Furthermore, even with their chronic problems, the majority of those older adults who live in the community are relatively healthy and mobile. In fact, nearly two-thirds of the noninstitutionalized 65+ population spent *no days* confined to bed in 1984.

The percentage of persons who report difficulty with one or more activities of daily living (such as bathing, dressing, eating, and walking) *does* increase with age. Between the ages of 65-69, 15 percent of the population indicate having such problems as compared with nearly half of those 85 and over. In both cases, older women report having these difficulties more than older men.

Causes of Death

Heart disease and cancer are the leading causes of death for those over 50.[13] For those under 65, cancer is the greater killer. The older one gets, however, the greater the likelihood that it will be heart disease from which people will die. Among the 65 + group, strokes are also a major cause of death. In fact, 75 percent of all persons age 65 + will die from heart disease, cancer, or stroke.

Use of Medical Services

A person's use of medical services increases with age. Thus, the 50 + population has a higher health care utilization rate than other age groups and the 85 + group has the highest utilization rates of all.

The older one gets, the more likely it is that he or she will be hospitalized. In 1986, persons over 65 accounted for 31 percent of all hospital discharges and 42 percent of all short-stay hospital days of care.

Not surprisingly, the likelihood of a nursing home stay also rises with age. For example, according to the 1985 National Nursing Home Survey, less than .1 percent of those under 65 are nursing home residents versus about 5 percent of those 65 +. Furthermore, approximately 90 percent of the nursing home population is made up of persons age 65 +; only about 8 percent are between 45 and 64 years of age.

While most nursing home residents are over 65, a disproportionate share of this group—84 percent—are over 75. Only 1 percent of those 65-74 are in nursing homes versus about 22 percent of the 85 + group. Nursing home residents tend to be older white women who have no spouse. These women are also less likely to have children than noninstitutionalized persons of the same age.

Economic Status

Income

In 1985, households headed by persons age 50 + possessed more than $950 billion in total income. This represented a higher amount than any other group of householders and 40 percent of all aggregrate household income.[14]

The under-65 age group. Among the mature market, it is those under 65 who hold the most income. The major reason for this is that, unlike those over 65, most members of the prime life group are still working. Those in the 55-64-year-old segment derive a substantial percentage of their income from earnings. For this group, Social Security, assets, and pensions collectively account for less income than what is received from work-related activity.[15] The youngest 50 + ers (those 50-54) earn the most income. Not surprisingly, then, households headed by those 50-54 have the highest after-tax median incomes of all household groups over age 50 and the third highest after-tax incomes of all household age groups.[16]

The 65+ age group. Households headed by persons over 65 have the lowest median household income among the mature market.[17] Retirement is a key reason for this. Other factors, such as death of a spouse and declining health, also help to account for this segment's lower income. Nevertheless, households headed by those over 65 have a higher average *per capita* after-tax income than all household groups under age 50.[18]

Retirement's impact on a person's sources of income is profound. Those over 65 derive just 17 percent of their income from earnings, as compared with those ages 55-61, 79 percent of whose income is employment-related. Social Security, pensions, and assets account for 80 percent of the 65+ group's income.

During the past two decades, age 65+ families have seen their income grow significantly. According to the Congressional Budget Office, the median income of such families grew over 50 percent between 1970 and 1986.[19] This increase was much higher than the 20 percent increase recorded by all families. Private pension plans, higher educational levels, and increased Social Security payments have helped cause the poverty rate among those 65+ to drop from more than 35 percent in 1959 to less than 12.5 percent in 1986. Other factors—such as special income tax/"in-kind" benefits (Medicare, Medicaid, and energy assistance)—have also contributed to this group's raised economic status.

Income Distribution

Like the heterogeneity of the entire mature market, there is a great diversity in income levels among members of the 50+ population. For example, middle-aged and older white males earn the most of all persons over 50. Women, especially those of minority groups, earn the least. In addition, while 12 percent of mature households have annual incomes in excess of $50,000, the remainder are divided about equally between those with incomes under $15,000 and those with incomes between $15,000 and $50,000.[20] (By the year 2000, an even greater percentage of 50+ers—21 percent—are projected to have incomes greater than $50,000, while a smaller portion are expected to earn less than $15,000.)[21]

Differences in income also surface both above and below age 65. In 1986, for instance, more than half of the families headed by persons 55-64 had incomes in excess of $30,000 and about 25 percent had incomes greater than $50,000. However, nearly 14 percent of those 55-64 had incomes near or below the poverty level.[22]

Similar disparities exist among the 65+ population. For example, while about 30 percent of the 65+ group's family-based households had incomes greater than $30,000, more than one-third had incomes below $15,000.[23] Those families ages 65-74 have much higher median incomes than the 85+ ones do, while the income of families of over age 85 far surpasses that of persons 65 + who do not live in family settings. For the latter group, there has been very little economic gain over the past few decades.

Among the 65 + group, more than 20 percent had incomes below or near the poverty level in 1986. Poverty is much more likely to be a problem for those over 75.

A number of factors may create impoverishment for members of the mature market, including loss of a job or spouse, divorce, and deterioration of health. Women, minorities, and those living alone characterize most of poverty's victims. Many of these individuals are "displaced homemakers," women who've lost the economic support of a spouse or the government program.

Net Worth

Members of the mature market possess the highest net worth of all age groups, nearly $7 trillion.[24] This amounts to 70 percent of the total net worth of all U.S. households.[25] Overall, persons age 50 + hold 77 percent of this nation's financial assets.[26] They own 80 percent of the money in savings and loans and hold more than two-thirds of all money market accounts.[27] And, they make about 40 percent of all stock and bond purchases.[28]

The major reason for these substantial holdings is that 50 + ers have had more years to accumulate savings, home equity, and personal property than have other groups. Another factor is that mature adults are America's foremost savers. As an example, householders over 65 have nearly triple the savings rate of 25-to-34-year olds.[29] As Figure A-8 shows, the older a mature market householder is, the more likely it is that his money will be in savings/checking accounts rather than in a business, a profession, or real estate investments. Among persons over 50:

- more than four in five have checking accounts
- about two-thirds have savings accounts
- about one-third have money market accounts
- about one-fourth own corporate stocks and bonds
- more than one-third own Certificates of Deposit[30,31]

Figure A-9 compares the mature market's net worth with other age cohorts. It is the 55-64 age that has the highest net worth. Many members of this group continue to work. As a result, they're still *accumulating* assets rather than having to *spend* them on retirement. Nevertheless, households headed by those over 65 have a median net worth nearly twice the national average.

As with income levels, the distribution of net worth among members of the mature market presents some striking contrasts. (See Figure A-10.) For example, while 24 percent of those households headed by persons 55-64 had

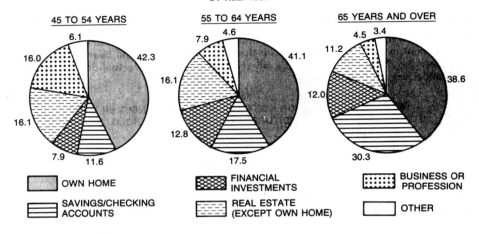

DISTRIBUTION OF TOTAL NET WORTH BY ASSET TYPE,
FOR HOUSEHOLDS 45 YEARS OF AGE AND OVER,
BY AGE: 1984

SOURCE: U.S. Bureau of the Census. "Household Wealth and Asset Ownership: 1984." *Current Population Reports* Series P-70, No. 7 (July 1986).

FIGURE A–8

less than $25,000 in net worth, more than 37 percent had net worths in excess of $100,000. While more than 30 percent of the age 75 + households had net worths under $25,000, an almost equal percentage had net worths above $100,000.

As Figure A-9 illustrates, home equity represents a significant portion of a householder's equity. This is particularly true for households headed by persons over 65. Indeed, almost 40 percent of the total net worth of this group comes from the home. A significant number of 65 +ers are "house rich" and "cash poor." For example, in 1984 more than 40 percent of age 65 + households had a net worth *excluding* home equity of less than $10,000.

Purchasing Power

The 50 + population holds about half of all discretionary spending power in America.[32] Discretionary income represents the money available for purchasing such nonessentials as fur coats, jewelry, luxury vacations, and whirlpools. While it is estimated that close to a third of all U.S. households have discretionary income, 38 percent of those households ages 50-64 and 27 percent of those 65 + possess such spending power.[33]

One factor that contributes to the mature market's purchasing power is that the group has little or no expenses for children or for mortgages. By age

MEDIAN NET WORTH BY AGE GROUP: 1984

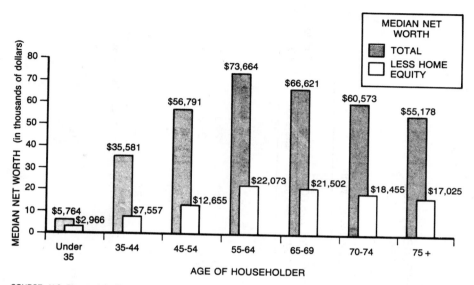

SOURCE: U.S. Bureau of the Census. "Household Wealth and Asset Ownership: 1984." *Current Population Reports* Series P-70, No. 7 (July 1986).

FIGURE A–9

55, many persons are empty nesters whose mortgages have already been paid off. At the same time, they're still earning good incomes. All of these factors help explain why households headed by those ages 55 to 64 have the *highest* average per capita after-tax incomes ... in excess of $10,200 in 1985.[34] Smaller households and little or no expenses for children or mortgage payments also help account for the 65+ group's surprising degree of discretionary spending power and its respectable per capita income of $9,152.[35]

Consumer Expenditures

The mature consumer plays a much bigger role in the American marketplace than many might believe. For example, according to the 1985 Consumer Expenditure Survey, households headed by those 55+—roughly one-third of all households—account for almost 30 percent of all monies spent on products and services. Moreover, when one includes those 50-54, the mature consumer represents more than one-third of the purchasing pie.

**DISTRIBUTION OF HOUSEHOLDS BY AGE
AND NET WORTH: 1984
(Excludes group quarters)**

Age of householder	All households	Percent distribution by net worth							
		Zero or negative	$1 to $4,999	$5,000 to $9,999	$10,000 to $24,999	$25,000 to $49,999	$50,000 to $99,999	$100,000 to $249,999	$250,000 or more
45-54	100.0	8.2	8.5	4.1	10.6	14.1	24.9	21.0	8.7
55-64	100.0	5.3	7.7	3.3	7.8	13.3	25.3	25.7	11.6
65 and over	100.0	6.7	8.7	4.0	9.1	15.5	24.7	23.1	8.2
65-69	100.0	6.8	6.8	2.9	8.2	15.1	25.7	24.9	9.6
70-74	100.0	7.2	9.8	3.4	9.4	14.5	25.0	21.9	8.7
75 and over	100.0	6.4	9.4	5.1	9.5	16.6	23.8	22.5	6.8

FIGURE A–10

SOURCE: U.S. Bureau of the Census. "Household Wealth and Asset Ownership: 1984." *Current Population Reports* Series P-70, No. 7 (July 1986).

The Aggregate Mature Market

Households headed by those over 55 spend about 17 percent less *per household* than the average household unit. Older households also spend less than average on all major expenditure categories except health care, personal care, and cash contributions. Among these categories, the 55 + households accounted for:

- nearly half of all health care expenses and contributions (gifts, donations, and so forth)
- more than one-third of all personal care expenses

These percentages—especially those concerning health care—tend to distort the older household's overall purchasing behavior. Of the $588 billion spent by age 55 + households in 1985, only about 7.5 percent was health care-related. Like all household units, the mature market's top three expenses were for housing, transportation, and food.

A closer look at consumption patterns reveals that age 55 + households are responsible for a significant percentage of the goods and services purchased in a wide range of expenditure categories. Moreover, the expenses that older households incur for many of these items actually *exceed* the national average. Figure A-11, which lists just a few products and services, illustrates how vital the mature market is to the success of many businesses and industries . . . including, of course, those that offer discretionary items.

As a group, members of older households spend less than the average household for such necessities as food, clothing, and shelter. There are several reasons for this. For one thing, they already own more than most younger households. And, the overwhelming majority have minimal—if any—mortgage payments to make. But most important, age 55 + households are smaller and have fewer people to support.

Because older households are smaller, it may be more meaningful to compare the *per capita* spending of mature households with persons in all households. When this is done, those in age 55 + households actually spend almost 3.5 percent *more* than the national average. They also exceed the national average for food and housing expenditures along with those for health care, reading, personal care, and contributions. Per capita spending among the individual mature market segments also compares favorably with that of the average household.

Paying the Bills

Members of older households are less likely to borrow money when making consumer purchases than are other persons. As Figure A-12 illustrates, an individual's willingness to take on installment debt decreases with age. When making their purchases, the oldest of these householders (those 75 +) are more likely to use cash or their checkbooks than credit cards. Fewer than 40 percent of the households headed by persons over 75

**PERCENTAGE OF THE OVERALL DOLLARS SPENT FOR
SPECIFIC PRODUCTS/SERVICES BY MATURE (AGE 55+)
HOUSEHOLDS**

• groceries	32 percent
• home repairs/remodeling	44 percent
• vacation homes	38 percent
• gardening/lawn care services	54 percent
• curtains and drapes	36 percent
• floor coverings	38 percent
• ranges	44 percent
• silver serving pieces	54 percent
• women's suits	40 percent
• new cars	30 percent
• airfares	34 percent
• beauty parlor services	41 percent
• newspaper subscriptions	42 percent
• out-of-town lodging	41 percent
• living room chairs	33 percent
• campers	36 percent
• away-from-home meals	38 percent
• life insurance	32 percent

Source: Bureau of Labor Statistics 1985 Consumer Expenditure Survey

FIGURE A–11

own credit cards. Nevertheless, 70 percent of those households in the age
50-64 group and 60 percent of those in the age 65-74 segment have credit
cards. Since 1970, the sharpest increases in credit card ownership have been
among households headed by people 55 and older.[36]

While persons in the age 75 + households may display a preference for
making their payments in cash, they are less likely to obtain that money from
an automated teller machine (ATM). Only 21 percent of those households
headed by someone over 65 have an ATM card. However, 34 percent of those
in households ages 55-64 and 40 percent of those in households ages 50-54
hold ATMS. As with the willingness to borrow money and use credit cards,
ATM ownership is higher for younger mature market households and those
with more income and a higher educational level.[37]

Spending by Segments

Figure A-13 shows how the expenses for age 55 + households stack up
against all households.* To differentiate the three groups of mature
housholds, I've given them the following designations:

---

*Information about those 45-54 is also provided since this group includes some age
50 + households.

WILLING TO BORROW

Americans are most willing to borrow for cars, for medical bills, or for educational expenses. Younger households and those with higher incomes are more willing to borrow, no matter what the reason.

(percent of householders who feel it is all right to use installment debt for different types of purchases, 1983)

	boats and hobby purchases	auto purchases	expenses due to illness	educational expenses	furniture purchases	vacation expenses	living expenses when income is cut	consoli- dation of bills	fur coat or jewelry
All households	19%	82%	82%	79%	49%	13%	46%	48%	5%
HOUSEHOLD INCOME									
Under $10,000	10%	63%	77%	65%	39%	11%	54%	53%	3%
$10,000–19,999	14	86	81	81	49	13	46	52	4
$20,000–29,999	24	91	84	87	55	15	49	50	5
$30,000–39,999	32	93	84	88	58	15	41	48	6
$40,000–49,999	25	91	84	85	55	15	40	44	5
$50,000 and over	37	90	89	90	59	17	45	47	10
AGE OF HOUSEHOLDER									
< 25	27%	88%	91%	89%	56%	18%	68%	66%	8%
25–34	28	90	84	88	57	17	52	55	6
35–44	26	90	83	87	52	15	46	48	5
45–54	17	84	82	82	50	12	42	50	5
55–64	14	82	80	76	47	10	45	44	4
65+	5	61	74	58	33	9	37	35	2

Source: 1983 Survey of Consumer Finances, Federal Reserve Board

FIGURE A–12

Reprinted from *American Demographics*, October, 1987.

**AVERAGE ANNUAL EXPENDITURES OF HOUSEHOLDS (HH)
IN 1985 DOLLARS***

	All HH	45–54	55–64	65–74	75+
Total expenditures	$22217	$29146	$23390	$17000	$12347
Food	3394	4435	3652	2922	2027
Housing	6687	8119	6259	5202	4157
Apparel	1161	1607	1173	747	364
Transportation	4555	5739	4820	3218	1776
Health care	1037	1178	1289	1539	1509
Personal care	198	263	235	198	149
Entertainment	1085	1409	1025	661	317
Reading	141	177	153	140	97
Education	304	690	209	78	27
Alcoholic beverages	283	334	248	185	84
Tobacco/smoking supplies	215	288	241	163	72
Miscellaneous	367	519	414	281	191
Contributions	805	1268	1192	841	1317
Personal insurance	2016	3121	2479	825	259

*Figures are rounded to the nearest dollar.
Source: Bureau of Labor Statistics 1985 Consumer Expenditure Survey

FIGURE A–13

- Age 55-64 segment—the "pre-retiree" households
- Age 65-74 segment—the "newly retired" households
- Age 75+ segment—the "long-since retired" households

The Age 55-64 Segment

Among mature market households, it is this group which, by far, spends the most money. Households in the age 55-64 segment spend 5 percent more than the national average. Moreover, they have the highest per capita spending of any household unit ($9,746)—a full 14 percent above the national average ($8,545).

There is very little difference between "pre-retiree" households and the average household unit when it comes to the proportion of money allocated to various major expenditure categories. Households headed by those age 55-64 spend at least as much as if not more of their income for every major expenditure category as does the average household . . . except when it comes to housing, entertainment, education, and alcoholic beverages.

Even more revealing is information on specific products and services which persons in these households buy. Despite their overall lower expenditures in the housing and entertainment categories, pre-retiree households spend more than the national average for such things as:

- wall-to-wall carpeting
- major appliances (including microwave ovens and dishwashers)
- housewares
- power tools
- fees and admissions
- videocassette tapes
- cable TV
- musical instruments
- photographic equipment

In addition, these households spend more than the national average on an array of other products and services shown in Figure A-14.

The consumer behavior of pre-retiree households reflects a number of demographic, socioeconomic, and lifestyle factors. For example, the departure of children from the "nest"—along with income from employment—provide many of these households with the time and money to go on cruises,

EXAMPLES OF PRODUCTS/SERVICES WHERE PRE-RETIREE HOUSEHOLD (AGE 55–64) SPENDING EXCEEDS THAT OF THE AVERAGE HOUSEHOLD

- away-from-home meals
- catered affairs
- utility bills
- men's suits, sportcoats, and shoes
- women's blouses and dresses
- infant clothing (such as pajamas)
- jewelry
- new trucks
- used cars
- gas/motor oil and auto maintenance/repairs
- reading materials
- life insurance, endowments, and annuities
- retirement and pension contributions
- numerous health care products and services

Source: Bureau of Labor Statistics 1985 Consumer
Expenditure Survey

FIGURE A–14

buy expensive jewelry and cars, dine out, attend concerts, refurnish the home, and garden. At the same time, many persons in this segment become grandparents, thereby explaining the appearance of infant wear in Figure A-14. This may also explain why households in this age group spend a surprisingly large amount (though less than the national average) on children's toys.

Along with empty nesthood and the joys of grandparenting, members of pre-retiree households may also experience serious health problems. This explains why the group's spending for medical services and products is almost 25 percent higher than that of the average household.

The Age 65-74 Segment

Households headed by those age 65-74 spend about 25 percent less overall than the national average. However, these households are nearly 25 percent smaller in size. Thus, when per capita spending is considered, the expenditures of this "newly retired" group are virtually the same as those of the average household (that is, $8,500 versus $8,545). Moreover, per capita expenses for this group are *higher* than those for any household unit under age 45.

Figure A-13 provides information on the expenses of the age 65-74 household unit. Some differences emerge between this group and the others shown. For example, while newly retired households apportion more of their income to food, housing, and health care than either the average household or pre-retiree households, they spend a smaller share on clothing, transportation, education, entertainment, and personal insurance. Even during this period, though health care costs still equal only 9 percent of all household expenses.

Food and housing expenditures become more significant for the age 65-74 household group for two main reasons. First, these expenses represent necessities whose costs vary little with household size. Second, due to retirement, many of these households have less income available to pay for their expenses. As a result, utility bills of the newly retired amount to nearly 10 percent of their household expenses.

Despite their reduced income and size, households headed by those 65-74 represent an important consumer group for a number of industries. This is particularly true when you compare their per capita spending to other household groups. For example, members of newly retired households exhibit the highest per capita spending for food and such items and services as

- color TV consoles
- curtains and draperies
- magazines

- cruises
- moving, storage, and freight expenses
- kitchen/dining room linens
- women's suits
- mattresses and springs
- vacation-related lodging and meals
- car tune-ups
- dental care
- window air conditioners
- church and other religious contributions

After reviewing the consumption patterns of newly retired households, it becomes clear that their purchasing behavior more closely resembles the pre-retiree households than those of the next group, the "long-since" retireds.

The Age 75+ Group

Households headed by those age 75 and over spend the least of all household units, about 56 percent of the national average. Furthermore, their per capita spending ($7,717) is the lowest of all household units age 25+ and is about 10 percent less than the average household. Still, this group's expenditures have become more closely aligned with those of the average household. In 1984, for example, household spending of the long-since retired was only 51 percent of the national average and per capita spending was 17 percent less.[38]

Figures A-13 shows how the age 75+ household's expenses are distributed across various expenditure categories. Several distinct spending patterns are visible. For one thing, long-since retired households spend more of their income on housing, health care, and contributions than any other group. Conversely, these households spend less of their income than the other groups for clothing, education, transportation, entertainment, personal insurance, alcoholic beverages, and tobacco.

The allocation of expenses among age 75+ households reflects what impact the final years of life have on consumer behavior. During this period, household size is the smallest of all groups and income is lower than all households except for those headed by persons under 25. Expenses for utilities, property insurance, and home maintenance take a bigger bite out of the pocketbook. Contributing to this is the fact that many of this group live in very old homes.

On the other hand, declines in health increase the age 75+ household's medical expenses dramatically. They also limit the ability to drive, thereby restricting mobility and the opportunity to enjoy out-of-home entertainment. Perhaps because of this, age 75 + households spend much less of their money on building personal estates . . . and a great deal more on giving what they have accumulated to others.

Typically, the consumer behavior of those over 65 has been lumped together. The Consumer Expenditure Survey, however, reveals how *different* the newly retired are from those in the oldest households. For example, age 65-74 households are 25 percent bigger and have about 50 percent more income than do those of the long-since retired. They also spend much more of their income for transportation, entertainment, and personal insurance. Conversely, the latter group spends much more of its money for housing, health care, and contributions.

Long-since retired households also spend about 30 percent less overall than newly retired ones do. And, they spend substantially less on such things as . . .

- away-from-home meals (46 percent less)
- furniture (68 percent less)
- major appliances (37 percent less)
- new cars (29 percent less)
- admission to movies, plays, and so forth (58 percent less)
- magazines (35 percent less)

Despite these facts and figures, age 75 + households —especially those with greater resources—represent an important consumer market for several specific products and services. This includes health insurance, inpatient and outpatient medical care, prescription drugs, and medical supplies. It also includes other items where—on a household or per capita basis—this group's spending compares very favorably with that of other age groups. Among such products and services are

- food
- home maintenance and repairs
- domestic services (such as housekeeping and lawn care)
- airline, bus, and train travel
- beauty parlor services
- newspapers
- refrigerators/freezers
- mass transit
- cruises

Furthermore, because of their inclination toward philanthropy, age 75 + households comprise a vital source of funding for those affiliated with religious, educational, medical, social service, or political organizations.

The Age 45-54 Households

Since more than half of these households are not a part of the 50+ market, a detailed accounting of their spending patterns is not provided. Nevertheless, Figure A-13 indicates that households headed by those 45-54 spend more than *any other household group.* They also spend more than the average household in each of the major expenditure categories except health care and contributions.

As they get older, consumers within today's age 45-54 households will no doubt have expenditures that more closely resemble those of today's age 55+ households. Nevertheless, some differences between the consumer purchases of these younger individuals—many who are already over 50—and those of the 55+ group are likely to remain. For example, even as they age, consumers within the age 45-54 households will probably continue to spend more money on such products and services as HMOs, personal computers, convenience store goods, and videocassette recorders than do today's older households. In addition, they'll be more likely to pay for these purchases with credit cards than are persons now within age 55+ households.

---

1. "Life expectancy in the U.S. hits record high 75 in 1986," *The Philadelphia Inquirer,* June 26, 1987, p. 10-A.

2. U.S. Bureau of the Census, *Statistical Abstract of the United States: 1987* (107th edition.) Washington, D.C., 1986, Table No. 20, p. 18.

3. Linden, Fabian. *Midlife and Beyond: The $800 Billion Over-Fifty Market.* New York: Consumer Research Center, The Conference Board, 1985.

4. U.S. Bureau of the Census, *Statistical Abstract of the United States: 1987* (107th edition.) Washington, D.C., 1986, Table No. 46, p. 39.

5. Linden, Fabian, op. cit.

6. "Old, older, oldest: The maturity market," *Sales and Marketing Management,* July 22, 1985, p. A-62.

7. Edmondson, Brad, "Inside the Empty Nest," *American Demographics,* November 1987, p. 26.

8. Robey, Bryant, "Altered States of America," *Adweek's Marketing Week,* February 1, 1988, p. 17.

9. The Retirement Migration Project, The Center for Social Research in Aging, The University of Miami, September 1984.

10. National Center for Health Statistics, "Current Estimates from the National Health Interview Survey, United States, 1986." *Vital and Health Statistics* Series 10, No. 164, October 1987.

11. Ibid.

12. Verbrugge, Lois M., "From Sneezes to Adieux," *American Demographics,* May 1986, p. 38.

13. National Center for Health Statistics, "Advance Report of Final Mortality Statistics, 1985," *Monthly Vital Statistics Report,* Volume 36, No.5, Supplement, August 28, 1987.

14. Linden, Fabian, "Middle-Aged Muscle," *American Demographics*, October 1987, p. 4.

15. Grad, Susan. *Income of the Population 55 or Over, 1986*. Publication No. 13-11871, Washington, D.C.: U.S. Social Security Administration.

16. U.S. Bureau of the Census. "Household After-Tax Income: 1985." *Current Population Reports* Series P-23, No. 151.

17. Ibid.

18. Ibid.

19. Pear, Robert, "U.S. Family Income Up But Not Uniformly," *New York Times*, February 26, 1988, p. D19.

20. Linden, Fabian, "Middle-Aged Muscle," op. cit.

21. Ibid.

22. U.S. Bureau of the Census. "Money Income and Poverty Status of Families and Persons in the United States, 1986." *Current Population Reports* Series P-60, No. 157, (July 1987).

23. Ibid.

24. Skenazy, Lenore, "These days, it's hip to be old," *Advertising Age*, February 15, 1988, p. 81.

25. Linden, Fabian. *Midlife and Beyond: The $800 Billion Over-Fifty Market*, op. cit.

26. Ibid.

27. Kramer, Allyn, "Welcome to the Mature Market Report," *Mature Market Report*, May 1987, p. 8.

28. King, Charles C., III, "Sheer Power," reprinted from *Texas Bankers Record* in *Maturity Market Update*, Volume 2, No. 3, November/December 1984, p. 6.

29. Sternlieb, George, and James W. Hughes, "The New Mortgage Market," *American Demographics*, April 1987, p. 28.

30. Costa, Kenneth J. *RAB Instant Background: Profiles of 50 Businesses*. New York: Radio Advertising Bureau, Fall 1987.

31. Avery, Robert B., Gregory E. Elliehausen, Glenn B. Canner, and Thomas A. Gustafson, "Survey of Consumer Finances, 1983," *Federal Reserve Bulletin*, September 1984, p. 687.

32. Linden, Fabian. Midlife and Beyond: *The $800 Billion Over-Fifty Market*, op. cit.

33. Ibid.

34. U.S. Bureau of the Census. "Household After-Tax Income: 1985." *Current Population Reports* Series P-23, No. 151.

35. Ibid.

36. Bloom, David E., and Todd P. Steen, "Living on Credit," *American Demographics*, October 1987, p. 24.

37. Riche, Martha Farnsworth, "How Americans Pay," *American Demographics*, July 1986, p. 46.

38. Lazer, William, "How Older Americans Spend Their Money," *American Demographics*, September 1987, p. 38.

Appendix **B**

Mature Market Resources

This appendix focuses on a number of different organizations, publications, and other references. You'll find a listing, and, in some cases, a comment or two, about many aging-related resources. The resources are grouped into five categories:

1. Agencies, Societies, and Associations
2. Periodicals
3. Books
4. Data and Information Suppliers
5. Miscellaneous (special reports, directories, and so forth)

Please keep the following important point in mind while reviewing this section. There is an abundant and ever-increasing supply of information about the 50 + population. It's extremely important for you to know where it is and to obtain it whenever appropriate. Of even greater significance, your ability to prosper in an aging America may very well depend on whether or not you *utilize* this external pool of knowledge and expertise to its fullest capacity.

1. Agencies, Societies, and Associations

Numerous public and private groups engage in activities which, in one way or another, concern the mature market. Here is a listing of many of these organizations.

Public Organizations

*ACTION**
806 Connecticut Ave., N.W.
Washington, D.C. 20525
(800) 424-8867

Comments: ACTION coordinates and administers several volunteer programs that utilize older adults (such as the Retired Senior Volunteer Program). This may make this agency a good source for ideas on recruiting 50+ers.

*Administration on Aging (AOA)**
330 Independence Ave., S.W.
Washington, D.C. 20201
(202) 245-0724

Comments: As the hub for all aging activity involving the various state and area agencies on aging, AOA can be an invaluable resource, especially for those seeking to serve the senior population.

*Area Agency on Aging (AAA)**

Comments: AAA is an agency that coordinates services for older adults in a specific geographic area. While most AAAs are public agencies, there are a good number that operate as private, nonprofit organizations. In either case, *AAAs are excellent resources to learn about the needs of, and programs for, age 65+ adults within specific locales.* AAAs may be found by checking the "Blue Pages" of the telephone directory (if this section is contained in your directory). You can also contact either the State Office on Aging (see listing under "Public Organizations") or the National Association of Area Agencies on Aging (see listing under "Private Organizations").

Federal Council on Aging
330 Independence Ave., S.W., Room 4545
Washington, D.C. 20201
(202) 245-2451

*Health Care Financing Administration (HCFA)**
200 Independence Ave., S.W.
Washington, D.C. 20201
(202) 245-6145

---

*This organization has either regional and/or local offices around the United States.

Comments: HCFA is responsible for funding and administering the Medicare program. It also assists the states in fulfilling this responsibility for the various Medicaid programs. The agency is an excellent resource for learning about the age 65 + population's health care expenses, use of medical services, and insurance coverage.

> *National Institute on Aging*
> 9000 Rockville Pike, Building 31C
> Bethesda, MD 20892
> (301) 496-1752

> *Office of Technology Assessment* (OTA)
> Congress of the United States
> Washington, D.C. 20510-8025
> (202) 228-6204

Comments: OTA's futuristic perspective along with its reports on the impact of an aging America make it an organization about which businesses need to be aware.

> *Service Corps of Retired Executives* (SCORE)*
> Small Business Administration
> 1129 20th St., N.W.
> Washington, D.C. 20036
> (202) 653-6279

Comments: SCORE utilizes retired and semi-retired businessmen to counsel new and existing small businesses.

> *Social Security Administration* (SSA)*
> 6401 Security Blvd.
> Baltimore, MD 21235
> (301) 965-3120

Comments: The local Social Security offices can be especially good sources of information about older adults in the community and local seniors programs/groups.

> *U.S. House Select Committee on Aging*
> 300 New Jersey Ave., S.E.
> Room 712, Annex #1
> Washington, D.C. 20515
> (202) 226-3375

Comments: Both the House Select Committee on Aging and its counterpart in the Senate (see below) are great places to find out about existing, pending, or anticipated legislation involving older adults.

U.S. Senate Special Committee on Aging
Dirksen Office Building
Washington, D.C. 20510
(202) 224-5364

State Office on Aging

Comments: This public organization, also referred to as a "State Unit on Aging," serves as the focal point for all matters relating to the needs of older persons within a given state. Each state has an office on aging as do the District of Columbia and the United States Territories. To obtain the address and telephone number of the state office on aging you may be interested in, you can contact:

- one of the state's area agencies on aging
- the Administration on Aging
- the National Association of State Units on Aging (referred to later in this appendix)

Private Organizations

1. Membership organizations with a significant age 50+ representation

    American Association of Retired Persons**
    1909 K St., N.W.
    Washington, D.C. 20049
    (202) 872-4700

    American Legion National Organization**
    1608 K St., N.W.
    Washington, D.C. 20006
    (202) 861-2711

Comments: While the American Legion isn't made up solely of those age 50+, it does include a *large* group of older veterans. *American Legion Magazine*, for example, has a circulation of more than 2.5 million whose average reader is 60 years old.

Note: Various service organizations such as the Rotary, Lions, Kiwanis, and Elks also have large age 50+ constituencies. These groups also have both local and regional clubs.

**This organization has local and/or regional chapters.

Catholic Golden Age**
P.O. Box 3658
Scranton, PA 18505-0658
(800) 982-4367 (PA), (800) 233-4697 (rest of the
United States)

Gray Panthers**
311 S. Juniper St.
Philadelphia, PA 19107
(215) 545-6555

Comments: The Gray Panthers is a coalition of persons of all age groups actively involved in supporting a number of social causes. The organization works particularly hard to fight ageism and to promote intergenerational relationships, shared housing, and healthcare consumerism.

National Alliance of Senior Citizens**
2525 Wilson Blvd.
Arlington, VA 22201
(703) 528-4380

National Association for Retired Credit Union People
P.O. Box 391
Madison, WI 53701
(608) 238-4286

National Association of Retired Federal Employees**
1533 New Hampshire Ave., N.W.
Washington, D.C. 20036
(202) 234-0832

National Caucus and Center on the Black Aged**
1424 K St., N.W., Suite 500
Washington, D.C. 20005
(202) 637-8400

*National Committee to Preserve Social Security
  and Medicare* (NCPSSM)
2000 K St., N.W., Suite 800
Washington, D.C. 20006
(202) 822-9459

Comments: NCPSSM is a highly vocal organization and one of the largest lobbying groups in America.

National Council of Senior Citizens**
925 15th St., N.W.
Washington, D.C. 20005
(202) 347-8800

National Gardening Association (NGA)
180 Flynn Ave.
Burlington, VT 05401
(802) 863-1308

Comments: About 75 percent of NGA's members are age 50 +.

National Hispanic Council on Aging**
2713 Ontario Rd., N.W.
Washington, D.C. 20009
(202) 745-2521

National Senior Sports Association (NSSA)
317 Cameron St.
Alexandria, VA 22314
(703) 549-6711

Comments: NSSA's members are sports-minded men and women age 50 +. In addition to receiving a publication, they receive discounts on sports activities (such as golf, tennis, and bowling), clothing and equipment.

Older Women's League (OWL)**
730 11th St., N.W., Suite 300
Washington, D.C. 20001
(202) 783-6686

Comments: The importance of understanding and marketing to mid-life and older women makes OWL a particularly important organization and information resource.

People's Medical Society**
14 East Minor St.
Emmaus, PA 18049
(215) 967-2136

Sears Mature Outlook**
P.O. Box 3096
Arlington Heights, IL 60006
(800) 336-6330

2. Organizations whose primary or sole activities concern the older population and/or aging-related issues

> *American Association for International Aging*
> 1511 K St., N.W., Suite 443
> Washington, D.C. 20005
> (202) 638-6815

> *American Federation of Labor-Congress of Industrial Organizations* (AFL-CIO)
> Social Security Department
> 815 16th St., N.W., Room 306
> Washington, D.C. 20006
> (202) 637-5200

> *American Society on Aging* (ASA)
> 833 Market St., Suite 512
> San Francisco, CA 94103
> (415) 543-2617

Comments: ASA is a very proactive organization comprised of educators, service providers, researchers, administrators, policy makers, businesspersons, advocates, and older adults. In addition to serving as an advocate for the older population, ASA provides it members with publications, educational kits, and training programs. Its Business Forum on Aging offers conferences of interest to those who employ or market to the mature adult.

> *Americans for Generational Equity* (AGE)
> 608 Massachusetts Ave., N.E.
> Washington, D.C. 20002
> (202) 546-3131

Comments: Marketers may find AGE is a useful resource for information about what challenges and problems our society may face in a graying America—especially as they concern the aging of the baby boomers.

> *The Association for Gerontology in Higher Education*
> 600 Maryland Ave., S.W., West Wing 204
> Washington, D.C. 20024
> (202) 484-7505

> *Children of Aging Parents, Inc.* (CAPS)**
> 2761 Trenton Rd.
> Levittown, PA 19056
> (215) 945-6900

Comments: Marketers may find CAPS literature helpful in tracking and understanding caregiver concerns. They may also want to learn about the local meetings and workshops of CAPS chapters around the country.

Generations United
c/o Child Welfare League of America
440 First St., N.W., Suite 310
Washington, D.C. 20001-2085
(202) 638-2952

Comments: Generations United is a coalition of more than 70 national, nonprofit organizations. Its major purpose is to promote intergenerational understanding, programs, and projects.

Gerontological Society of America (GSA)
1411 K St., N.W., Suite 300
Washington, D.C. 20005
(202) 393-1411

Comments: Marketers may find GSA a valuable resource in gaining an accurate understanding of aging and its effects on older adults. They may also benefit from GSA's information services. (See DATA AND INFORMATION SUPPLIERS.)
Note: There are various state and regional gerontological societies. Many of the organizations listed in this appendix, including GSA, can help you identify them.

International Society of Preretirement Planners (ISPP)**
11312 Old Club Rd.
Rockville, MD 20852
(800)-327-ISPP

Comments: Marketers may find ISPP a good resource to learn about older worker/retiree issues, needs, clubs, and programs. They may also learn about employer and union involvement in these matters.

Mature Market Institute
20 Chevy Chase Circle, NW
Washington, D.C. 20015
(202) 363-9644

Comments: The Mature Market Institute is a nonprofit membership organization that researches, gathers, coordinates, and disseminates useful information about consumers age 50 and over.

National Association for Senior Living Industries**
(NASLI)
125 Cathedral St.
Annapolis, MD 21401
(301) 263-0991

Comments: NASLI is a particularly good resource for those having an interest in the development and marketing of retirement housing.

National Association of Area Agencies on Aging (NAAAA)
600 Maryland Ave., S.W., Suite 208
West Wing
Washington, D.C. 20024
(202) 484-7520

Comments: Marketers may find NAAAA very helpful in enhancing their knowledge of—and relationships with—the aging network's Area Agencies on Aging.

National Association of Senior Travel Planners
44 Cushing St.
Hingham, MA 02043
(617) 740-1185

National Association of State Units on Aging (NASUA)
2033 K St., N.W., Suite 304
Washington, D.C. 20006
(202) 785-0707

Comments: NASUA is a national organization that provides information, technical assistance, and support to its members —the state units on aging. (See "State Offices on Aging" under "Public Organization" heading). Marketers may find NASUA a useful source of information about state aging activities. This includes its "National Aging Data Base" on services for older persons (see DATA AND INFORMATION SUPPLIERS).

National Council on the Aging, Inc. (NCOA)
600 Maryland Ave., S.W., West Wing 100
Washington, D.C. 20024
(800) 424-9046, (202) 479-1200

Comments: NCOA is a central clearinghouse for information, publications, and programs about older adults. Some marketers will find its membership units especially good resources. They include The National Institute

of Senior Centers, The National Institute on Adult Daycare, the National
Center on Rural Aging, and the National Institute of Senior Housing.

> National Interfaith Coalition on Aging
> P.O. Box 1924
> Athens, GA 30603
> (404) 353-1331

3. Health, fitness, and social service organizations whose activities
   concern older adults

> Alzheimer's Disease and Related Disorders Association
> (ADRDA)**
> 70 East Lake St., Suite 600
> Chicago, IL 60601
> (312) 853-3060

Comments: ADRDA may also be a good organization to work with on
educational or cause-related marketing programs. In addition, the group's
members and chapters include many family caregivers.

> American Aging Association
> c/o Dr. Denham Harman
> 42nd and Dewey Ave.
> Omaha, NE 68105
> (402) 559-4416

> American Association of Homes for the Aging (AAHA)**
> 1129 20th St., N.W., Suite 400
> Washington, D.C. 20036
> (202) 296-5960

> American Geriatrics Society
> 10 Columbus Circle, Suite 1470
> New York, NY 10019
> (212) 582-1333

> American Health Care Association (AHCA)**
> 1200 15th St., N.W.
> Washington, D.C. 20005
> (202) 833-2050

Comments: AHCA is the largest organization representing long-term
health care facilities. It is an especially good resource to learn about what's
happening in the nursing home industry.

American Hospital Association (AHA)**
840 N. Lake Shore Dr.
Chicago, IL 60611
(312) 280-6000

Comments: AHA produces seminars and booklets specifically about marketing to older adults. It also has a section devoted solely to aging and long-term care services.

American Red Cross**
431 18th St., N.W.
Washington, D.C. 20006
(202) 737-8300

Comments: Marketers should note that the American Red Cross and its chapters have been involved in joint ventures with several private corporations. In addition, more than 60 percent of Red Cross' donors are older than 50, and they have better than average education and income levels.

National Association for Home Care (NAHC)**
519 C St., N.E.
Washington, D.C. 20002
(202) 547-7424

Comments: Many marketers may find NAHC to be an important resource since the "home-based" market for older consumers will create numerous health care and nonhealth care opportunities in the years ahead.

National Geriatrics Society
212 W. Wisconsin Ave.
Milwaukee, WI 53203
(414) 272-4130

U.S. National Senior Olympics**
222 S. Central
Suite 505
St. Louis, MO 63105
(314) 726-4550

4. Academic institutions with major aging or gerontological activities

Many academic institutions have gerontology or aging studies departments. Some of these offer programs and services—such as courses, conferences, or reports—which are available to the outside business and professional community. Listed below are a few of the most prominent of these organizations.

Duke University
Center for the Study of Aging and Human Development
Box 3003
Duke University Medical Center
Durham, NC 27710
(919) 684-2248

Florida International University
The Southeast Florida Center on Aging
North Miami Campus TC320
North Miami, FL 33181
(305) 940-5550

Hunter College
Brookdale Center on Aging
425 E. 25th St.
New York, NY 10010
(212) 481-4426

Portland State University
Institute on Aging
P.O. Box 751
Portland, OR 97207
(503) 229-3952

University of Bridgeport
Center for the Study of Aging
Bridgeport, CT 06601
(203) 576-4358

University of Maryland
Center on Aging
PERH-2611
College Park, MD 20742
(301) 454-5856

University of Miami
Center for Social Research in Aging
P.O. Box 248092
Coral Gables, FL 33124
(305) 284-2701

University of Michigan
Institute of Gerontology
300 N. Ingalls
Ann Arbor, MI 48109-2007
(313) 764-3493

University of Southern California
Ethel Percy Andrus Gerontology Center
University Park, MC 0191
Los Angeles, CA 90089-0191
(213) 743-5156

5. Organizations that fund aging research and programs

Along with government agencies, numerous groups provide funding for programs that address the older population and its needs. Information about—and from—the projects undertaken by such organizations can be extremely helpful to those who want to better understand the mature market and anticipate/respond to its concerns. A few of these organizations are identified below. (See the other four resource categories to identify additional groups that support this activity.)

AARP Andrus Foundation
1909 K St., NW
Washington, D.C. 20049
(202) 872-4700

American Federation for Aging Research
725 Park Ave.
New York, NY 10021
(212) 570-2090

The Commonwealth Fund
One East 75th St.
New York, NY 10021
(212) 535-0400

The John A. Hartford Foundation, Inc.
55 E. 59th St., 23rd floor
New York, NY 10022
(212) 832-7788

Pew Charitable Trusts
3 Parkway
Suite 501
Philadelphia, PA 19102-1305
(215) 568-3330

The Retirement Research Foundation
1300 W. Higgins Rd., Suite 214
Park Ridge, IL 60068
(312) 823-4133

The Robert Wood Johnson Foundation
P.O. Box 2316
Princeton, NJ 08543-2316
(609) 452-8701

Sandoz Foundation for Gerontological Research
P.O. Box 10
East Hanover, NJ 07936
(201) 386-8519

The Travelers Foundation/Older Americans Program
One Tower Square-5SHS
Hartford, CT 06183-1060
(203) 277-9161

The Villers Foundation, Inc.
1334 G St., N.W., Suite 3
Washington, D.C. 20005
(202) 628-3030

6. Futurist organizations

World Future Society (WFS)**
4916 St. Elmo Ave.
Bethesda, MD 20814
(301) 656-8274

Comments: Marketers will find WFS a good resource to help them anticipate and respond to trends affecting the mature market and the world around them.

2. Periodicals

Numerous general interest, business, marketing, and human resource publications provide information which, in one way or another, is useful to those who market to the 50+ consumer. Generally speaking, their coverage of the mature market is sporadic or sketchy. Thus, businesses who want to keep in closer touch with mature market activity should utilize other periodicals to supplement these general reading materials. The following list identifies those that you may find particularly helpful.

Magazines/Newsletters for the Mature Market

Golden Years
233 E. New Haven Ave.
P.O. Box 537
Melbourne, FL 32902-0537
(407) 725-4888

Grandparents Today
249 W. 17th St.
New York, NY 10011
(212) 645-0067

Mature Outlook
One North Arlington
1500 W. Shure Dr.
Arlington Heights, IL 60004
(800) 336-6330

Modern Maturity
3200 E. Carson St.
Lakewood, CA 90712
(213) 496-2277

New Choices
28 W. 23rd St.
New York, NY 10010
(212) 633-4600

Renaissance
143 Newbury St.
Boston, MA 02116
(617) 262-4515

Magazines, Newsletters, and Journals Primarily for Those Who Employ, Serve, or Market to the Mature Adult

Aging
Office of Human Development Services
U.S. Department of Health and Human Services
200 Independence Ave., S.W.
Washington, D.C. 20201
(202) 245-0019

Aging Network News
P.O. Box 1223
McLean, VA 22101
(703) 734-3266

Contemporary Long-Term Care
P.O. Box 24649
Nashville, TN 37202-4649
(615) 329-1973

Generations
833 Market St., Room 512
San Francisco, CA 94103
(415) 543-2617

The Gerontologist
1411 K St., N.W., Suite 300
Washington, D.C. 20005
(202) 393-1411

Home Health Line
Port Republic, MD 20676
(301) 586-0100

Housing the Elderly Report
8555 16th St., Suite 100
Silver Spring, MD 20910
(301) 588-6380

Mature Market Report
801 E. Campbell, Suite 110
Richardson, TX 75081
(214) 669-0997

Newsletter of the Mature Market Institute
20 Chevy Chase Circle, NW
Washington, D.C. 20015
(202) 363-9644

Older American Reports
951 Pershing Dr.
Silver Spring, MD 20910
(301) 587-6300

The Older Worker
8555 16th St., Suite 100
Silver Spring, MD 20910
(301) 588-6380

Perspective on Aging
600 Maryland Ave., S.W., West Wing 100
Washington, D.C. 20024
(800) 424-9046

Retirement Planning
11312 Old Club Rd.
Rockville, MD 20852-4537
(800) 327-ISPP

Selling to Seniors
8555 16th St., Suite 100
Silver Spring, MD 20910
(301) 588-6380

Senior Market Report
244 W. 54th St.
Suite 706
New York, NY 10019
(212) 974-3285

Other Suggested Publications

American Demographics
108 N. Cayuga St.
Ithaca, NY 14850
(800) 828-1133

The Futurist
4916 St. Elmo Ave.
Bethesda, MD 20814
(301) 656-8274

Modern Healthcare
740 Rush St.
Chicago, IL 60611
(312) 649-5355

Note: Many of the groups referred to under AGENCIES, SOCIETIES, AND ASSOCIATIONS also produce magazines, newsletters, or journals which your organization may find helpful. Only a few of these have been referenced in the periodicals listed above.

3. Books

A number of books have been published in the past few years which provide information about the 50+ population. A few of these concern employing or marketing to the older adult. Others discuss the demographics, lifestyles, relationships, and needs of today's or tomorrow's older adults. There are also books covering topics like retirement or the aging process.

Listed below are several books. As you read this list, remember that prosperity in an aging America will come to those who understand, anticipate, and respond to the needs and concerns of the older consumer. For this reason, it may be as important to read publications written *for* mature adults as those written *about* this group.

Bell, Marilyn J. *Women as Elders*. New York: The Haworth Press, 1987.

Boston Women's Health Book Collective. *Ourselves, Growing Older*. New York: Simon & Schuster, 1987.

Bowman, Norman H., et al. *The Grandparenting Book: 101 Tips and Ideas on Enjoying Life with Your Grandchildren*. Mountain View, CA: Blossom Valley Press, 1982.

Brody, Stanley J. and Nancy Persily. *Hospitals and the Aged: The New Old Market*. Rockville, MD: Aspen Systems Corporation, 1984.

Butler, Robert N. *Why Survive? Being Old in America*. New York: Harper & Row, 1985.

Cadmus, Robert R. *Caring for Your Aging Parents*. Englewood Cliffs, NJ: Prentice-Hall, Inc., 1984.

Casale, Anthony. *Tracking Tomorrow's Trends*. Kansas City, MO: Andrews, McMeel & Parker, 1986.

Cherlin, Andrew and Frank Furstenberg. *The New American Grandparent: A Place in the Family, a Life Apart*. New York: Basic Books, 1986.

Crichton, Jean. *The Age Care Sourcebook: A Resource Guide for the Aging and Their Families*. New York: Simon & Schuster, 1987.

Davis, James A., and Richard H. Davis. *TV's Image of the Elderly*. Lexington, MA: Lexington Books, 1985.

Dennis, Helen. *Retirement Preparation*. Lexington, MA: D.C. Heath and Co., 1984.

Dickinson, Peter. *The Complete Retirement Planning Book: Your Guide to Health, Happiness and Financial Security*. New York: E.P. Dutton, 1984.

Dychtwald, Ken. *Wellness and Health Promotion for the Elderly*. Rockville, MD: Aspen Publishers, Inc., 1986.

Dychtwald, Ken, and Joe Flower. *Age Wave: The Challenges and Opportunities of An Aging America*. Los Angeles, CA: Jeremy P. Tarcher, Inc., 1988.

Ginsberg, Genevieve Davis. *To Live Again*. Los Angeles: Jeremy P. Tarcher, Inc., 1987.

Hayes, Helen with Marion Glasserow Gladney. *Our Best Years*. Garden City, NY: Doubleday, 1984.

Horne, Jo. *Caregiving: Helping an Aging Loved One*. Washington, D.C.: American Association of Retired Persons, 1986.

Jones, Landon Y. *Great Expectations: America & the Baby Boom Generation*. New York: Coward, McCann & Geoghegan, 1980.

Kingson, Eric, and Barbara Hirshorn. *Ties that Bind: The Interdependence of Generations*. Washington, D.C.: Gerontological Society of America, 1986.

Leutz, Walter N., et al. *Changing Health Care for an Aging Society*. Lexington, MA: Lexington Books, 1985.

Linkletter, Art. *Old Age is Not for Sissies*. New York: Viking Press, 1987.

Maddox, George L. *The Encyclopedia of Aging*. New York: Springer, 1986.

Massey, Morris. *The People Puzzle: Understanding Yourself and Others*. Reston, VA: Reston Publishing Co., Inc., 1979.

McConnell, Adeline, and Beverly Anderson. *Single After Fifty: How to Have the Time of Your Life*. New York: McGraw-Hill, 1980.

Miller, Sigmund, Jullian Miller, and Don E. Miller. *Lifespan Plus*. New York: The Macmillan Co., 1985.

Montana, Patrick. *Retirement Programs: How to Develop and Implement Them*. Englewood Cliffs, NJ: Prentice-Hall, Inc., 1985.

Moore, Pat with Charles Paul Conn. *Disguised: A True Story*. Waco, TX: Word Books, 1985.

Myers, Albert and Christopher Andersen. *Success After 60*. New York: Summit Books, 1986.

Naisbitt, John. *Megatrends: Ten New Directions Transforming Our Lives*. New York: Warner Books, Inc., 1982.

Parnes, Herbert S. *Retirement Among American Men*. Lexington, MA: Lexington Books, 1985.

Perelman, Michael and Carol Colman. *Late Bloomers: How to Achieve Your Potential At Any Age.* New York: Macmillan, 1985.

Pifer, Alan and Lydia Bronte. *Our Aging Society: Paradox and Promise.* New York: W.W. Norton & Company, 1986.

Rosen, Benson and Thomas Jerdee. *Older Employees: New Roles for Valued Resources.* Homewood, IL: Dow Jones-Irwin, 1985.

Russell, Cheryl. *100 Predictions for the Baby Boom: The Next Fifty Years.* New York: Plenum Publishing Corporation, 1987.

Schewe, Charles, *The Elderly Market: Selected Readings.* Chicago: American Marketing Association, 1985.

Selby, Philip and Mal Schechter. *Aging 2000: A Challenge for Society.* Hingham, MA: MTP Press Limited, 1982.

Seskin, Jane. *Alone—Not Lonely: Independent Living for Women Over 50.* American Association of Retired Persons, 1985.

Shahan, L. *Living Alone and Liking It.* New York: Harper & Row, 1981.

Silverstone, Barbara and Helen Hyman. *You and Your Aging Parent.* Pantheon Books: New York, 1982.

Slaybaugh, Charles S. *The Grandparents' Catalog.* Garden City, NY: Doubleday & Company, 1986.

Stokell, Marjorie, and Bonnie Kennedy. *The Senior Citizen Handbook: A Self-Help and Resource Guide.* Englewood Cliffs, NJ: Prentice-Hall, Inc., 1985.

Struntz, Karen A., and Shari Reville. *Growing Together: An Intergenerational Sourcebook.* Washington, D.C. and Palm Springs, CA: American Association of Retired Persons and Elvirita Lewis Foundation, 1985.

Weinstein, Art. *Market Segmentation.* Chicago: Probus Publishing Company, 1987.

Willing, Jules Z. *The Reality of Retirement.* New York: William Morrow & Co., 1981.

Winston, William J. *Marketing Long-Term and Senior Care Services.* New York: The Haworth Press, 1984.

4. Data and Information Suppliers

Many organizations, public and private, collect and disseminate information that concerns the mature market. Listed below are some of the major suppliers of such data.

Government Agencies

U.S. Department of Commerce
Bureau of the Census
Data User Services Division
Washington, D.C. 20233
(301) 763-4100

U.S. Department of Health and Human Services
National Center for Health Services Research and Health
  Care Technology Assessment
Parklawn Building, Room 18-12
5600 Fishers Lane
Rockville, MD 20857
(301) 443-4100

U.S. Department of Health and Human Services
National Center for Health Statistics
3700 East-West Highway
Hyattsville, MD 20782
(301) 436-8500

U.S. Department of Labor
Bureau of Labor Statistics (BLS)
441 G St., N.W.
Washington, D.C. 20212
(202) 523-1944, (202) 272-5156

Comments: BLS provides data on the older worker/retiree populations and their benefit programs. It also produces the annual Consumer Expenditure Survey, which includes information about the mature consumer's purchasing behavior. This survey can be extremely helpful not only in identifying how the 50+ group spends its money, but in spotting changes and trends in the mature market's purchasing behavior. (BLS has regional offices around the United States.)

Note: Many other government agencies, such as the Social Security Administration and Health Care Financing Administration, also collect data and produce reports that contain useful information about the older population. To learn about what each of these agencies offer, contact them directly by referring to the "Public Organizations" listings in the first resource category, AGENCIES, SOCIETIES AND ASSOCIATIONS. You can also utilize "The Federal Interagency Forum on Aging-Related Statistics" Telephone Contact List referred to in the fifth resource category, MISCELLANEOUS.

Private Organizations

Consumer Information

Many private organizations provide comprehensive data or special reports about the demographics, psychographics, purchasing behavior, or media preferences of the mature market. Some of these groups produce "off-the-shelf" industry studies which may include information about the mature consumer of today and of the future.

Listed below are several of these organizations. To learn specifically what each business does, contact it directly. To learn about other companies that offer similar services, you can refer to such directories as American Demographic's *The Insider's Guide to Marketing Know-How* and The American Marketing Association's *International Membership Directory and Marketing Services Guide.*

> *American Demographics Institute*
> c/o American Demographics, Inc.
> 108 N. Cayuga St.
> Ithaca, NY 14850
> (800) 828-1133
>
> *Business Trend Analysts*
> 2171 Jericho Turnpike
> Commack, NY 11725
> (516) 462-5454
>
> *CACI*
> 8260 Willow Oaks Corporate Drive
> Fairfax, VA 22031
> (800) 292-2224
>
> *Claritas*
> 260 Madison Ave., 17th floor
> New York, NY 10016
> (212) 532-8200
>
> *Consumer Research Center*
> The Conference Board
> 845 Third Ave.
> New York, NY 10022
> (212) 759-0900

The Data Group, Inc./PrimeLife Marketing
Meetinghouse Business Center
2260 Butler Pike, Suite 150
Plymouth Meeting, PA 19462
(215) 834-3003

FIND/SVP
625 Avenue of the Americas
New York, NY 10011
(800) 346-3787

Frost & Sullivan
106 Fulton St.
New York, NY 10038
(212) 233-1080

Goldring & Company, Inc.
737 North Michigan Ave.
Chicago, IL 60611-2697
(312) 440-5252

Information Resources, Inc.
150 N. Clinton St.
Chicago, IL 60606
(312) 726-1221

Langer Associates
19 West 44th St., Suite 1601
New York, NY 10036
(212) 391-0350

Mediamark Research, Inc.
341 Madison Ave.
New York, NY 10017
(212) 599-0444

National Decision Systems
539 Encinitas Blvd., Box 9007
Encinitas, CA 92024-9007
(619) 942-7000

National Planning Data Corporation
P.O. Box 610
Ithaca, NY 14851-0610
(607) 273-8208

A.C. Nielsen
Nielsen Plaza
Northbrook, IL 60062
(312) 498-6300

Simmons Market Research Bureau, Inc.
219 E. 42nd St.
New York, NY 10017
(212) 867-1414

SRI International
333 Ravenswood Ave.
Menlo Park, CA 94025
(415) 859-3835

Mature Market Lists and Co-op Programs

Donnelley Marketing Information Services
70 Seaview Ave.
P.O. Box 10250
Stamford, CT 06904
(203) 353-7439

Metro Mail Corporation
901 W. Bond St.
Lincoln, NE 68521-3694
(402) 475-4591

Senior Direct
9319 LBJ Highway, Suite 120
Dallas, TX 75243
(800) 222-5488

Senior Citizens Unlimited
711 Westchester Ave.
White Plains, NY 10604
(800) 431-1712

Survey Sampling, Inc.
One Post Rd.
Fairfield, CT 06430
(203) 255-4200

Larry Tucker, Inc.
607 Palisade Ave.
Englewood Cliffs, NJ 07632
(201) 569-8888

Special Data Bases

Age Base
The Brookdale Foundation
126 E. 56th St., Tenth Floor
New York, NY 10022
(212) 308-7355

AgeLine
c/o BRS
555 E. Lancaster Ave.
Wayne, PA 19087
(800) 468-0908

Comments: Produced by the AARP, AgeLine is an on-line bibliographic database focusing exclusively on middle age and aging.

Data Archive for Aging and Adult Development
Center for Study of Aging and Human Development
Box 3003
Duke University Medical Center
Durham, NC 27710
(919) 684-3204

National Archive of Computerized Data on Aging
P.O. Box 1248
Ann Arbor, MI 48106
(313) 763-5010

National Database on Aging
National Association of State Units on Aging
2033 K St., N.W., Suite 304
Washington, D.C. 20006
(202) 785-0707

Comments: A comprehensive information system with statistics about the older population and services provided by the aging network.

National Older Worker Information System (NOWIS)
American Association of Retired Persons
Worker Equity Department
1909 K St., N.W.
Washington, D.C. 20049
(202) 662-4959

Comments: Computerized information file of special corporate programs involving older workers.

State Data Center Programs

Comments: State Data Center Programs make census information available to the public through a network of public/private organizations including state agencies, universities, libraries, and regional and local governments. To reach the State Data Center you want, contact the appropriate Bureau of Census Regional Office or check *Data Resources in Gerontology.* (See "Reference Publications" in resource category 5, MISCELLANEOUS.)

Special Publishers

American Custom Publishing Corporation
121 West Park Ave.
Libertyville, IL 60048
(800) 828-8225

General Learning Corporation
P.O. Box 3060
Northbrook, IL 60065
(800) 323-5471

Helpful Publications, Inc.
P.O. Box 339
Glenside, PA 19038
(800) 666-5473

Other Data and Information Resources

American Enterprise Institute
1150 17th St., N.W.
Washington, D.C. 20036
(202) 862-5800

The Bureau of National Affairs, Inc.
2445 M St., N.W., Suite 275
Washington, D.C. 20037
(202) 452-4420

The Brookings Institution
1775 Massachusetts Ave., N.W., Suite 405
Washington, D.C. 20036
(202) 797-6266

The Conference Board
845 Third Ave.
New York, NY 10022
(212) 759-0900

Congressional Institute for the Future
218 D St., S.E.
Washington, D.C. 20003
(202) 544-7994

Employee Benefit Research Institute
2121 K St., N.W., Suite 600
Washington, D.C. 20037
(202) 659-0670

Institute on Aging, Work and Health
Washington Business Group on Health
229½ Pennsylvania Ave., S.E.
Washington, D.C. 20003
(202) 547-6644

National Gerontology Resource Center
American Association of Retired Persons
1909 K St., N.W.
Washington, D.C. 20049
(202) 872-4700

The National Real Estate Development Center (NRDC)
Triangle Towers Building
4853 Cordell Ave.
16th Floor, Suite 5
Bethesda, MD 20814
(301) 657-8068

Comments: NRDC frequently sponsors conferences on retirement housing.

Population Reference Bureau, Inc.
777 14th St., N.W., Room 800
Washington, D.C. 20005
(202) 639-8040

Shared Housing Resource Center
6344 Greene St.
Philadelphia, PA 19144
(215) 848-1220

The Urban Institute
2100 M St., N.W.
Washington, D.C. 20037
(202) 833-7200

5. Miscellaneous

Booklets and Pamphlets

American Association of Retired Persons. *Truth About Aging: Guidelines for Accurate Communications*. Washington, D.C.: AARP, 1984.

American Association of Retired Persons. *A Consumer Guide to Advertising: How to Understand the Ads You See and Hear*. Washington, D.C.: AARP, 1986.

Note: Along with the above two publications, the AARP offers numerous other booklets and pamphlets that can help you better understand and serve the mature market.

Careers for Later Years, Inc. *The Older Worker: A Silver Opportunity*. Cambridge, MA: CIS, Inc., 1986.

Rix, Sara E. *Older Women: The Economics of Aging*. Washington, D.C.: Women's Research and Education Institute, 1984.

Films, Videos and Cassettes

"Adult Children, Aging Parents: A Common Sense
  Approach" (4-cassette album)
Rita M. Smith and Associates
7101 E. Briarwood Drive
Englewood, CO 80112
(303) 773-1099

"Late Bloomer" (cassette & booklet)
Connie Goldman Productions
P.O. Box 7488
Fairfax Station, VA 22039
(703) 866-5993

My Mother, My Father
Terra Nova Films, Inc.
9848 Winchester Ave.
Chicago, IL 60643
(312) 881-8491

Staying Active: Wellness After Sixty
Spectrum Films, Inc.
2755 Jefferson St.
Carlsbad, CA 92008
(619) 434-6191

Note: A number of public and private organizations have produced films, videos, and/or cassettes about older adults. The groups and other reference sources mentioned in this appendix should be able to help you learn more about such media resources.

General Newsletters

Consumer Markets Abroad
American Demographics, Inc.
108 N. Cayuga St.
Ithaca, NY 14850
(800) 828-1133

John Naisbitt's Trend Letter
1101 30th St., N.W.
Washington, D.C. 20007
(800) 368-0115

Marketing to Women
Kurtz Company
210 Chestnut St.
P.O. Box 834
Oneonta, NY 13820
(607) 432-9066

The Numbers News
American Demographics, Inc.
108 N. Cayuga St.
Ithaca, NY 14850
(800) 828-1133

The Public Pulse
The Roper Organization, Inc.
205 E. 42nd St.
New York, NY 10017
(212) 599-0700

Research Alert
Alert Publishing, Inc.
30-87 37th St.
Long Island City, NY 11103
(718) 626-3356

Trends & Forecasts
Cambridge Reports, Inc.
675 Massachusetts Ave.
Cambridge, MA 02139
(617) 661-0110

Washington Letter/Florida Letter/California Letter
The Kiplinger Washington Editors
1729 H St., N.W.
Washington, D.C. 20006-3938
(202) 887-6400

Media Programs and News Services

"The Best Years" (TV)
c/o Rene Genereux
Canadian Broadcasting Company
700 Hamilton St.
Vancouver, B.C. V6B 2R5
(604) 662-6262

"Late Bloomer" and "I'm Too Busy to Talk Now:
Conversations with Creative People Over 70" (radio)
Connie Goldman Productions
8888 Appian Way
Los Angeles, CA, 90046
(213) 656-6113

Maturity News Service (print)
National Press Building
529 14th St., N.W., Suite 968
Washington, D.C. 20045
(202) 662-8895

Reference Publications

Directory of State and Area Agencies on Aging
National Association of Area Agencies on Aging
600 Maryland Ave., S.W., Suite 208
Washington, D.C. 20024
(202) 484-7520

Conference Calendar
Gerontological Society of America
1411 K St., N.W., Suite 300
Washington, D.C. 20005
(202) 393-1411

Current Literature on Aging
The National Council on Aging, Inc.
P.O. Box 7227
Ben Franklin Station
Washington, D.C. 20044
(800) 424-9046

Data Resources in Gerontology
Gerontological Society of America
1411 K St., N.W., Suite 300
Washington, D.C. 20005
(202) 393-1411

Directory of Experts, Authorities and Spokepersons
Broadcast Interview Source
2500 Wisconsin Ave., N.W.
Washington, D.C. 20007
(202) 333-4904

The Federal Interagency Forum on Aging-Related
Statistics (Telephone Contact List)
c/o Bureau of the Census
Special Population Staff
Washington, D.C. 20233
(301) 763-7883

The Insider's Guide to Demographic Know-How
American Demographics, Inc.
108 N. Cayuga St.
Ithaca, NY 14850
(800) 828-1133

International Directory of Organizations in Aging
American Association for International Aging
1511 K St., N.W., Suite 443
Washington, D.C. 20005
(202) 638-6815

The National Directory of Educational Programs in Gerontology
The Association for Gerontology in Higher Education
600 Maryland Ave., S.W., West Wing 204
Washington, D.C. 20024
(202) 484-7505

National Guide to Funding in Aging
The Foundation Center
79 Fifth Ave.
New York, NY 10003
(212) 620-4230

RAB Instant Background: Profiles of 50 Businesses
Radio Advertising Bureau, Inc.
304 Park Ave., South
New York, NY 10010
(212) 254-4800

*Sourcebook of Demographics and Buying Power for Every Zip
  Code in the U.S.A.*
CACI
1815 N. Fort Myer Drive
Arlington, VA 22209
(800) 292-2224

Statistical Abstract of the United States
U.S. Department of Commerce
c/o U.S. Government Printing Office
Washington, D.C. 20402
(202) 783-3238

Survey of Buying Power (2-part special issue)
Sales and Marketing Management magazine
633 Third Ave.
New York, NY 10017
(212) 986-4800

U.S. Directory and Sourcebook on Aging
American Association for International Aging
1511 K St., N.W., Suite 443
Washington, D.C. 20005
(202) 638-6815

U.S. Government Books
Superintendent of Documents
U.S. Government Printing Office
Washington, D.C. 20402
(202) 783-3238

Washington Information Directory
Congressional Quarterly, Inc.
1414 22nd St., N.W.
Washington, D.C. 20037
(202) 887-8500

Comments: Includes information about government agencies, congressional committees, and private associations with aging-related activities.

Special Mature Market Reports

U.S. Senate Special Committee on Aging, U.S. Administration on Aging, and
    American Association of Retired Persons. *Aging America: Trends and
    Projections, 1987-88 edition, 1988.*

American Council of Life Insurance, et al. *The Prime Life Generation.* Washington, D.C.: American Council of Life Insurance/Health Insurance Association of America, 1985.

The Bureau of National Affairs, Inc. *Older Americans in the Workforce: Challenges & Solutions*. Rockville, MD: The Bureau of National Affairs, Inc., 1987.

Center for Corporate Public Involvement, *1987 Social Report of the Life and Health Insurance Business*. Washington, D.C.: American Council of Life Insurance/Health Insurance Association of America, 1988.

Comments: This report provides information on community programs sponsored by companies in the life and health insurance industry. These include programs for older adults. The Center also publishes *Response*, a quarterly magazine discussing such activities.

The Conference Board, Consumer Research Center. *Midlife and Beyond: The $800 Billion Over Fifty-Market*. New York: The Conference Board, Inc., 1985.

The Conference Board, Consumer Research Center, *Baby Boomers in Mid-Passage*. New York: The Conference Board, Inc., 1987.

Cubillos, Herminia with Margarita M. Prieto. *The Hispanic Elderly: A Demographic Profile*. National Council of La Raza, October 1987.

Dychtwald, Ken and Mark Zitter. *The Role of the Hospital in an Aging Society: A Blueprint for Action*. Emeryville, CA: Age Wave, Inc., 1986.

FIND/SVP. *The Affluent Market*. New York: FIND/SVP, 1987.

FIND/SVP. *The Maturity Market: Americans 55 and Over*. New York: FIND/SVP, 1985.

Florida Committee on Aging. *Pathways to the Future III: Toward the Year 2000*. Tallahassee, FL: The Executive Office of the Governor, State of Florida, 1986.

Lidoff, Lorraine. *Supports for Family Caregivers of the Elderly: Highlights of a National Symposium*. Washington, D.C.: National Council on the Aging, 1985.

Longino, Charles. *The Oldest Americans: State Profiles for Data-Based Planning*. Coral Gables, FL: University of Miami, Center for Social Research in Aging, 1986.

Longino, Charles. *The Comfortably Retired and the Pension Elite*. Coral Gables, FL: University of Miami, Center for Social Research in Aging, 1986.

Marien, Michael. *Future Survey Annual*. Bethesda, MD: World Future Society, 1988.

Office of Technology Assessment. *Technology and Aging in America*. Washington, D.C.: U.S. Government Printing Office, 1985.

Schick, Frank, *Statistical Handbook on Aging Americans*. Phoenix, AZ: Oryx Press, 1986.

SRA Technologies, Inc. and Needham Porter Novelli. *Channels of Communication for Reaching Older Americans.* Washington, D.C.: The National Council on the Aging, 1985.

SRI International. *Privately Speaking: Corporate Community Involvement in Meeting the Needs of Older Americans.* National Association of Counties, U.S. Conference of Mayors, Administration on Aging, Chevron U.S.A., Inc., 1984.

Suzman, Richard and Matilda White Riley. *The Oldest Old.* New York: Cambridge University Press, Spring 1985 (special issue of Milbank Memorial Fund Quarterly/Health and Society).

Taeuber, Cynthia M., Kevin Kinsella, and Barbara Boyle Torrey. *An Aging World.* Washington, D.C.: U.S. Government Printing Office, 1987.

The Villers Foundation. *On the Other Side of Easy Street.* Washington, D.C.: The Villers Foundation, 1987.

Wolfe, David B. *Life Satisfaction: The Missing Focus in Marketing to Seniors.* Annapolis, MD: National Association for Senior Living Industries, 1987.

Zitter, Mark. *Marketing Healthcare to Older Adults.* Emeryville, CA: Age Wave, Inc., 1988.

Workbooks and Seminar Materials

American Bankers Association and American Association of Retired Persons. *Older Bank Customers: An Expanding Market.* Washington, D.C.: American Bankers Association, 1985.

Leavenworth, Elaine and Teri Louden. *The Older Adult Market: Designing Effective Strategies.* Chicago: Louden & Company, 1986.

National Association of State Units on Aging. *Marketing Strategies for Recruiting Older Individuals.* Washington, D.C.: National Association of State Units on Aging, 1985.

National Council on Aging, Inc. *Facing Our Future.* Washington, D.C.: National Council on Aging, 1985.

Comments: This program is directed to mid-life and older women.

Index